D1381195

Designers on Mac

Designers on Mac

Produced by
Takenobu Igarashi

Text by
Diane Burns

Published by
Graphic-sha

Designers on Mac

Produced by Takenobu Igarashi © 1992
Text by Diane Burns © 1992
Published by Graphic-sha Publishing Co., Ltd. © 1992

ISBN 4-7661-0660-1

Printed in Japan by Koyosha, Ltd.

First Edition 1992

Graphic-sha Publishing Co., Ltd.
1-9-12 Kudan-kita
Chiyoda-ku
Tokyo 102
Japan
Telephone 03-3263-4318
Facsimile 03-3263-5297

Contents

7 **The Muse in the Monitor**
by Junji Ito

8 **The Making of *Designers on Mac***

10 **The Evolving World of Macintosh Design**
by Takenobu Igarashi

11 **About this Book**
by Diane Burns

12 **Neville Brody**

36 **Emigre Graphics**

62 **Susumu Endo**

82 **April Greiman Inc.**

102 **Kazuo Kawasaki**

124 **Javier Mariscal**

146 **Yukimasa Okumura**

168 **Erik Spiekermann / MetaDesign**

192 **Why Not Associates**

The Muse in the Monitor

Today, across all cultural fields, there seem to be two basic and divergent trends, one hi-tech, the other low-tech. For instance, while it is possible in this day and age to see dozens of engineers stand up on stage and play mixing boards like an orchestra, there is also a worldwide boom in acoustic and traditional music.

Likewise, in visual arts, the hottest media art creations are being spawned through satellite communications, video and high definition technology – space-age concepts all – though at the same time, in the so-called conceptual art revival, one is seeing the beginning of an iconographic, strongly religious art movement.

In the midst of this polarization, one thing remains common to all forms and movements. This is the use of the diminutive Macintosh to produce "hi-tech" expressions, whatever the medium. A rock group in England has gone so far as to do a whole concert with the support of a single Mac. I myself use a Macintosh SE 30 and a IIcx, plus dozens of pieces of software, to write stories and create exhibit proposals.

In the field of graphic design, however, it is not going too far to say that the Macintosh is nearing deification. The Mac can be used throughout the entire process of design, possessing the software and fonts to produce almost anything. The fact that it is acknowledged as a state-of-the-art machine only further enhances its preeminence in the design world.

But is the Mac really omnipotent? My answer is a firm "no way." There has never been a more unreliable machine, in fact. I know I am not the only user who lives in fear of seeing the deadly system "bomb." I cannot count how many times I have lost stories in my machine. And my real opinion is that DTP, Paint and other software programs don't quite match up to the daily strains of CAD and other tasks. And I'm not asking this brilliant but feeble-bodied system to do high-end work, either. If anything, the opposite.

Why is it, then, that designers continue to use the Mac in spite of its known weaknesses? The answer is that its appeal has nothing to do with high performance, or the capacity to reliably process raw material. Rather, designers like the Mac because it acts as a partner in thought and imagination, a muse, so to speak. It is safe to say this is the the first time in history that humans have had anyone but God to accompany them in their creative work. Now they have the Macintosh, too.

In our interaction with the Mac we rediscover that "hi-tech" is not a product of machines, or advanced civilization, but instead of the "low-tech" world of our own imagination.

Junji Ito
Tokyo, Japan

Junji Ito received a M.A. in French Literature from Waseda University; studied at the University of Paris, the Sorbonne and Ecole d'Louvre under a French Government foreign study grant. Presently he is an art critic, a member of the board of the Saison Modern Art Foundation, a consultant to Pia Integrated Research Center, and a member of the Japan Cultural Design Forum Board. Known for introducing new art from abroad to Japan, and for organizing various art events. Author of *Contemporary Art* (Parco Publishing Co., Ltd.), *Art Runner – 9.79* (Tokyo Shoseki Publishing Co., Ltd.) and others.

The Making of *Designers on Mac*

This chart is meant to present only the most basic steps in the creation of this book. It does not take into account the two complete sets of proofs that were needed to insure the quality of the finished product, or the fact that the cover design was done by Igarashi Studio.

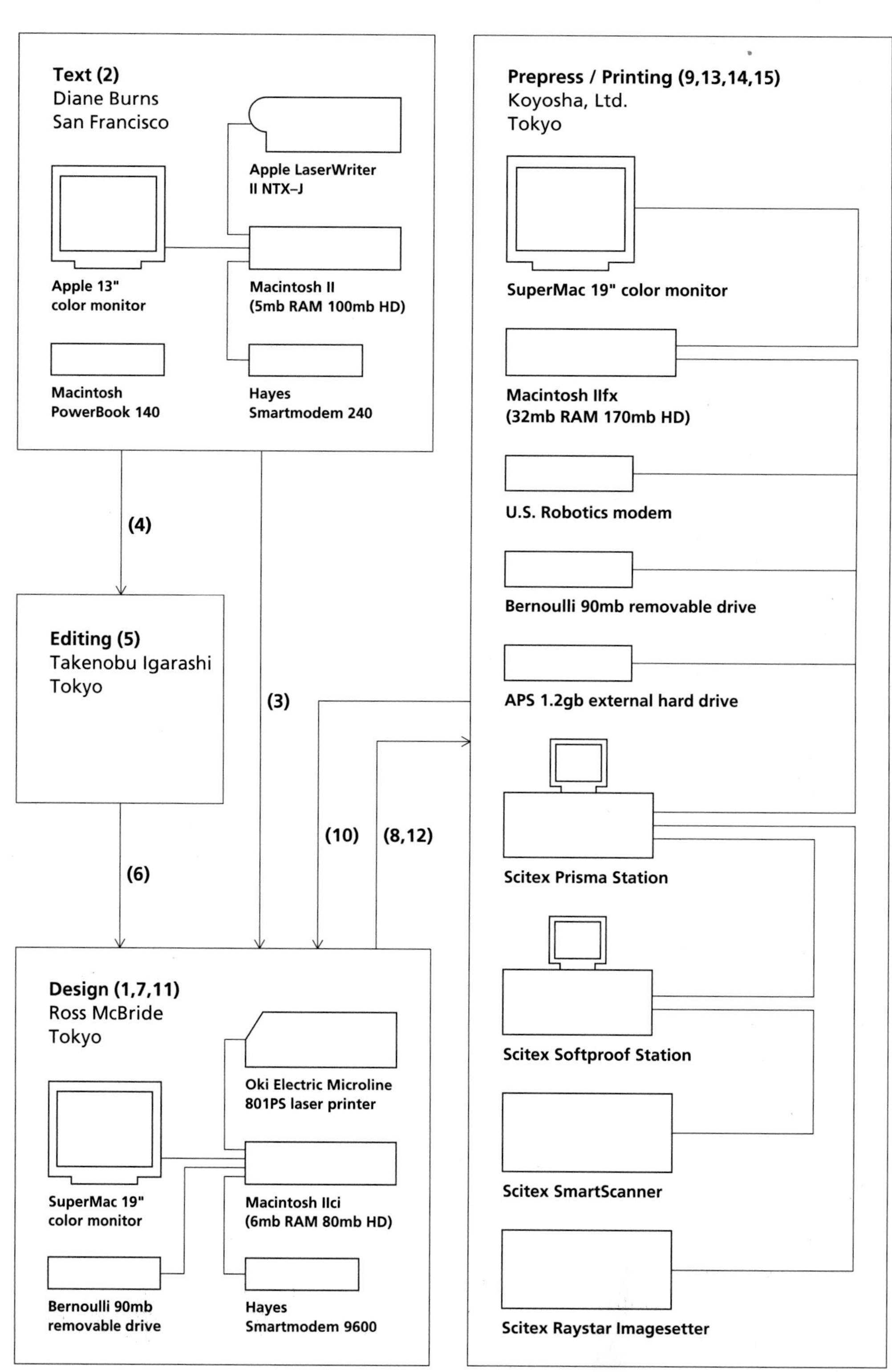

1 The basic format and layout for *Designers on Mac* is created.

2 Designers are interviewed worldwide. Text is edited and images are collected.

3 Text is sent by modem to the designer.

4 Images are shipped to Igarashi Studio.

5 Images are edited.

6 Transparencies of images are sent to the designer.

7 The designer places text in a QuarkXPress document and creates windows for images.

8 The designer sends laser copy of document without the images along with transparencies of the images to the printing company.

9 Images are scanned at high-resolution (365 dpi / 175 lpi), and all necessary retouching and color correcting is done. Low-resolution (72 dpi) versions of the images are then produced on the Macintosh.

10 Low-resolution images are sent to the designer.

11 Low-resolution images are placed in their appropriate windows in the document and final adjustments to layout are made.

12 Complete QuarkXPress file with all text and images in place is sent from the designer to the printer.

13 File is converted to Scitex format for film output. Low resolution images in the layout are automatically replaced by the high-resolution images stored on Scitex.

14 Film is output for printing.

15 *Designers on Mac* is printed and bound.

The Evolving World of Macintosh Design

The Macintosh has brought about dramatic changes in the field of graphic design. This tool has made it possible for non-professionals to achieve professional-like results. Professionals, meanwhile, are using the computer to reinvent the world of graphic design. The new technology itself does not deserve the credit for these developments; it simply evolves on a day to day basis, with no inherent purpose. For designers, not everything is made possible by this new technology, nor is it clear what its ultimate influence will be.

As a designer who uses the Macintosh on a daily basis, I am constantly aware of the problems it poses. Whether physically, mentally, creatively, or practically speaking, this tool is having a profound influence on our imaginations and in the work we produce.
This book, appearing in the midst of this evolutionary period, introduces the environment, ideas, and work of nine designers who are doing imaginative and creative work on the Macintosh. And, as shown in the chart on the previous page, this book was itself created by the process of electronic publishing.

The advantage of design by this process is that most of the entire process, from concept to final product, is controlled by the designer. No typesetters are needed; instead the size and spacing of type is done on the Macintosh screen. And although the images were displayed in low-resolution, the designer was able to position and trim the images, lay out the text, and to some degree, check the color balance. Changing the format was very easy, since every page could be changed automatically.

However, it took a large amount of time to treat the images on the screen, and to print them to a laser printer. It took more than 48 hours to output the 224 pages of this book to a laser printer. Improvements in the software are needed. For example, easily arranging signatures automatically for printing is not yet possible. Also, clients and printers alike need to understand that the responsibility and the workload of the designer has greatly increased with this technology.

For this book, Diane Burns interviewed each designer individually. Designer Ross McBride worked on his first electronic publishing project. Koyosha, Ltd. bravely attempted, for the first time, linking the Macintosh to a Scitex system. The nine designers herein helped smooth the process by using PressLink (a telecommunications program) and facsimile. This book was given birth by an international electronics network of designers, hardware and software companies and printing companies.

Takenobu Igarashi
Tokyo, Japan

About this Book

Over two years ago, Mr. Takenobu Igarashi approached me with the idea to create a book that would show the tremendous influence the Macintosh computer has on the world of design. As it turned out, the book you now hold in your hands does this, hopefully, and more. Designers on Mac is a kind of "time capsule," showing the relationship today between technology and design as we move toward the next millennia.

One of our most difficult tasks was the selection of designers to include in the book. So many talented and influential designers use the Macintosh that our task seemed, at times, impossible. We knew that we wanted to show how the world's top designers have been affected by this technology. We knew that we wanted a group of designers that represented different countries. And we knew we wanted to show substantively how designers are working on Macs. Over a period of months, our list grew only to grow smaller again in the interest of substance.

The designers finally chosen share many things in common. Each is greatly influential in his or her field, and most became so prior to using the Macintosh. All were educated in the traditional aspect of design, the "craft" of design, and all advocate that traditional education is essential to successful entry into the world of digital design.

Yet each designer is, of course, unique and each uses the Macintosh quite differently. Some of the designers still sketch out their ideas on paper, others begin their sketching on the Macintosh. For some the Macintosh is simply a new tool, for others, a new medium to explore.

Our initial plan was to present the text of the book in narrative form, but after the very first interview it became apparent that the best way to convey each designer's thoughts and feelings about the Macintosh was to present the designer's own words. Each interview was taped, and each tape transcribed. At times, words that had been heard and understood in person seemed hard to understand when written verbatim in the transcript; but while editing was required, hopefully the feeling and intention of each designer is still conveyed to the reader.

To supplement the designers' words, each has shared a specific project that was created on the Macintosh. The intention of showing projects step-by-step is to present ideas about the variety of ways in which the Macintosh is used.

Finally, a portfolio of each designer's finished works is shown, with credits that include the software and techniques used in creating each piece.

The Macintosh computer has truly a profound influence on so many designers, yet the key ingredient to design remains unchanged: the human creative spirit. It is this more than anything else we hope our book conveys.

Diane Burns
San Francisco, U.S.A.

To these and so many others I give my thanks:
Apple Japan, Inc.
David Park Brown
Lorene Burns
Albert Chu
The Designers
Fred Ebrahimi
Leigh Evans
Kaz Fukuda
Leticia Guevara Di Lallo
Yoshie Haggerty
Yuko Hayakawa
Hugh and Kathryn Harkins
Yuichi Inomata
Kay Kavanaugh
ico Komanoya
Denise Lever
Ross McBride
Kent McFall
Mary Moegenburg
Grace Moore
Noreen Morioka
Kim Nogay
Seiki Okuda
Alice Polesky
Susan Robinson-Equitz
Yurika Sasaki
David Smith
Sharyn Venit
and Takenobu Igarashi

Neville Brody

Neville Brody is perhaps the best known British graphic designer of his generation. His early work at the London College of Printing in the late 1970s was not well regarded; it was considered too experimental. After graduation, he became involved with creating designs for record album covers and in 1981, he joined the staff of a magazine called *The Face*. His shaping of *The Face*, with its hand-drawn typography and other graphic techniques, helped change the way designers view that medium. ¶ Brody was catapulted into the international limelight in 1988 with an exhibit and book, *The Graphic Language of Neville Brody*. Since that time, he has been the visual director of several magazines, developed corporate identities for clients worldwide and created numerous posters and book covers. He has also become a technical wizard on the Macintosh, which has come to play a key role in shaping his graphic language of today.

How did you first come to use the Macintosh in your work?

I knew about the Macintosh for a while before I started using it, but my attitude was that if you could do something by hand, you shouldn't use a machine. I always felt you would lose something in the translation from hand to machine. At *The Face*, we used to draw all the type by hand, even each headline for each feature, and the whole magazine was produced in the space of five days. I felt that if we could do that, what did we need this machine for, what's the point? Before I was hand-drawing type, I used rub-down lettering, like Letraset, and I would draw on it, manipulate it, cut it, play with the spacing and use it with other physical processes, like photocopying.

When I first saw the Macintosh, a Macintosh Plus, I was in a studio we were running in Central London. In the studio above was a photographer named Ian McKinnell, a Macintosh fanatic. He bought one of the first four in the country and so he had one in his studio where I often visited. I saw this strange machine and I hated it. Ian was then using the Macintosh to create illustrations for Macintosh magazines, which had not been on the market long, and had also become one of the main photographers for these magazines.

Finally, in 1987, I slowly forced my hand to hold this strange plastic object called a "mouse." We borrowed Ian's Macintosh one day and I played around with the bitmap technology. I still felt it couldn't do what I was doing by hand. In the beginning I just worked in SuperPaint. It was wonderful because you could wildly distort the bitmap type and objects.

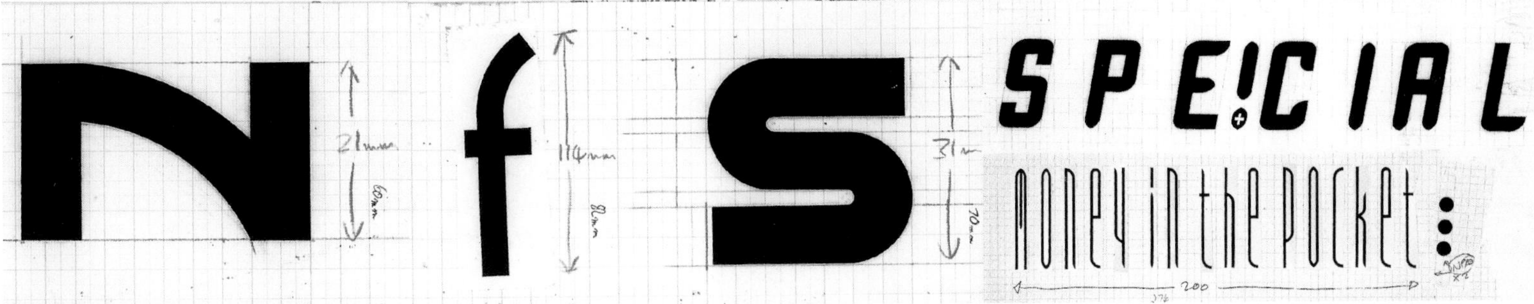

Some of Brody's hand-drawn headlines for *The Face* magazine.

Using the Macintosh seriously was, I think, a very slow process until we got our first game. At this point we realized we could become reliant on it. By now, I'd left *The Face*, and was working on *Arena*. We finally bought our own Macintosh, and really, the way I learned how to use the mouse was by playing Crystal Quest, a game. We learned how to use the mouse because you had to avoid rockets coming at you. Everyone in the studio learned a lot using this game. In fact, the long games took an hour and a half and we went through a period of low productivity.

Around this time, I had to produce an illustration using the Macintosh for graphic magazine called *Graphic World*. They asked me create a drawing to test two programs and I said: "Of course; I know everything about the Macintosh."

It was the biggest nightmare trying to do this, because I really didn't know what I was doing. But it was part of the learning process and during that project, I realized I was hooked.

There's a point when it clicks, when you see you're actually in control; the machine's not controlling you anymore. It's strange, I can even remember the moment it happened; I suddenly thought to myself: "I'm in control of this." Then I'd find myself working on it at 3 o'clock in the morning, not realizing the time had passed.

How do you use the Macintosh in your studio?

In the early days of working with the machine, we used to have ideas and make sketches, and then use the Macintosh as a production tool for the certain things we knew it could do. A while later, when we had all become very literate with the machine, I found I wasn't doing sketches anymore, but was going straight to the Macintosh and trying things on the screen, developing from developments and trying to create a series of options from this.

In the end, I wasn't using a pencil. I think I didn't use a pencil for over a year, and certainly never used one to make any work sketches. I didn't regret this because it was an opportunity to learn and challenge the machine. In fact, I still feel I haven't challenged the machine properly. It was an important period because I think in order to be really in control of the machine, you must enter into battle with it, otherwise you always end up with the default solutions.

The Macintosh doesn't have a "no" button, meaning you can create almost an infinite number of variations on one idea. What we need is a feature that will have the machine stop you after you've created ten different options for the same idea. Sometimes I'll be working on a logo project and see there's a file called "AG 100," indicating that I've done one hundred variations on that logo idea; I'll think, "What am I doing"?

I found that when I step away from the Macintosh with a pen and a pad, and just make a couple of sketches of the last idea I had, I'll be steps ahead already. So it's not that it's a faster process, it's just that your time is used differently.

Simon, who works here, pointed out the other day that working on the Macintosh can become like "the monkeys and typewriter." That is, if you have a thousand monkeys sit in front of a thousand typewriters for a thousand years, sooner or later one of them will write Shakespeare. That's what it's like with the Macintosh sometimes — if you sit there long enough and try enough different things, by accident one of them is going to be okay.

So now, just in the past few weeks, we've taken kind of a reverse approach, which means I force myself to pick up a pencil to create initial work sketches. It was shocking. I had to search all the cupboards to find one. When you find you can do everything on the screen, why move from your chair? Why shouldn't I tape this mouse to my hand?

The whole process we've been trying to work out with the Macintosh is to make it react in an organic manner. Because of the default settings, there are certain things built in. You're always dealing with lines of constant thickness; there's no program that will give you a Postscript line that you can vary the

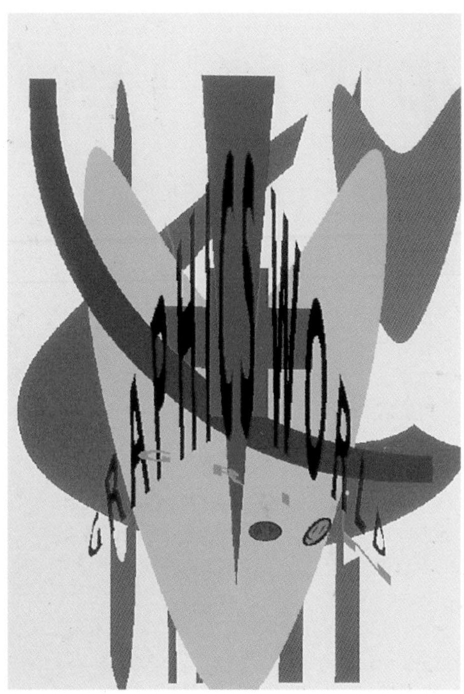

Brody's first piece of work done on the Macintosh for *Graphic World* magazine.

thickness on, for instance. Each program has an inherent grid, which is sometimes based on points, sometimes on other units, and which everything locks to. Even if you're working in, say, centimeter units, it still has a basic grid. The grid is generally a linear grid, and you can't, for example, place the grid at an angle or you can't have a soft grid. It is not organic; it's just a good emulator of organic processes. It's basically a mathematical system.

So all along, we've been challenging the machine. The feeling has been that the more times you could make the machine crash, the more successful you were. If the machine didn't crash for a week, we'd worry. We were trying to force it to do things it really wasn't supposed to do, things like opening 300 dpi images in MacPaint and trying to reduce the size. I like the idea of it being an open environment where you can move from one application to another, which Apple's System 7 is supposed to do. We've been trying to make it a single environment already, mixing Photoshop files with FreeHand, Illustrator with QuarkXPress, MacPaint with FontStudio. We try to mix all of these together and learn about every single program as deeply as possible. I think you have to, because if you just concentrate on one or two programs, you're limiting your vision and your choices drastically. I think all designers are morally obliged to learn as many programs as possible.

I've been feeling recently that a lot of the work I've been doing has come from trying to make the Macintosh respond as an emotional vehicle, trying to produce objects or visuals that communicate something on an emotional level. I've been trying to use the Macintosh language and make it never look like Macintosh. For example, manipulating type without it looking like it has been manipulated by the Macintosh, because when you expand type, bits go thick and when you see it you think "Macintosh"; that's the first thing that piece of work communicates. Some people think this should be the whole point of it, but I believe there are certain disciplines that can elevate themselves above that. For instance, take a pencil drawing. You look at a pencil drawing and you think somewhere in your mind that it's a drawing, but that's actually not the dominant thing.

We think the Macintosh effects are great, but we tend to use them once, then that's it. For example, the new version of FreeHand has some wonderful options, especially the ability to "paste inside." You can convert type outlines into artwork and paste objects inside, which up until now has been a bane for me. And so I'm sure we'll do two or three jobs that really utilize that process, and then never use it again, unless it's just part of something else.

In a way, the Macintosh is like the great leveler, because everyone can produce a clean line now, a square that is a square. At the moment, those Macintosh capabilities are hiding the real ability and creative force underneath. It's very easy on the Macintosh to produce a high, finished product that emulates something else.

We can't get lost in the capabilities of the Macintosh, yet at the same time, we need to know every detail of what it can do. Throughout my career, I've ensured that alongside the work, I've continued to explore and experiment. If you don't do that, there's no way to feed into the jobs you're doing, apart from reference to jobs that other people have done or your own other jobs.

So a great deal of my time is spent locked away, pushing the technology and trying things. Those experiments then get incorporated into my work. I've always done that. Somewhere there are just boxes and boxes of stuff that were produced using a photocopier or a photostat machine. Now, I have thousands of disks full of useless experiments, but all of which I learned from. I think it's absolutely essential to make time to experiment, and not use the Macintosh as a production tool only. It is a tool, yes, but it's so important to try and discover what it's capable of doing beyond production.

Has using the Macintosh in your studio changed the way you interact with your clients?

Well, it's interesting; when we first brought the Macintosh into the studio, there was a period in which a client might expect that since we were using the Macintosh, our services should be cheaper. But they don't think that today; people have realized that design is design. There's no substitute for a good idea, and the Macintosh doesn't cut down on the thinking time.

In fact, it sometimes takes longer, because there are more possibilities. What we're doing now, as part of a deliberate process, is to encourage as many of our clients as possible to become Macintosh-based themselves. In these cases, we don't make identity guide manuals, we make disk templates, which means the structure is just there, they don't have to read about it.

One of our clients is an art gallery; they produce lots of newsletters, and catalogs. Recently they've become

Brody hard at work in his London Studio.

Macintosh-based. We've given them templates in QuarkXPress, including style sheets, which let them format text correctly with a single keystroke. They're in control of the typesetting themselves now, and they know exactly how it's going to look, not from the design point of view, but they can see how the text will run and can check for things like widows and proper line breaks, before we get it to finish it off. It's working just great.

We're really working hard now to educate our clients. Another client is the French magazine *Actuel*. The magazine is created completely on the Macintosh, with a central file server, so that the editors, the subeditors and the design staff will have access to the central server. The editors write articles, or get articles from their authors, and put them on the fileserver; the subeditors retrieve it, edit it, put it back on the fileserver; it then goes to design and once it's designed, the subeditors make their final check. It's really efficient and centralized. The only problem for magazines that do this is that sometimes when they change from having production done outside to inhouse, they may not increase their staff, even though more tasks are actually being performed. A lot of companies do that; they miscalculate manpower needed to run a desktop system inhouse.

One thing companies using the Macintosh means is that more people have access to a means of printed communication and the standard is higher because of the defaults on the Macintosh. You can't paste type on an angle, for example, unless you specifically intend to, and it's easier to center things on a page. The distinction between amateur and professional design is becoming blurred because of the computer, which is a great. I'm all for that; I'm really in support of everyone having access to the technology and everyone becoming visually educated.

The mystique of design is broken down a bit, and the designer isn't in such a protected role anymore, which I think is the best thing that ever happened. Most people can write, yet you still have great writers. So why not have everyone become capable of visual communication, yet still have great visual communicators? I'm against the idea that design should still be a protected industry. If it's to be protected, it will only protect the people who have the most to lose, those people who are not very good at communicating. I'm all for those barriers of mysticism breaking down in every way, in every single case. If a client can learn how to do what we do on a technical basis, that's wonderful. Now, with a client in Berlin, for instance, we send him a disk of the work we're doing for him. He brings it up on the screen, has a look at it and phones us to say whether he likes it or not. He may not understand why we've made certain design decisions, but he'll understand the process.

What do you think about design education today, that may start young designers using computers right away?

I am really thankful for my traditional education and the years of experience I've had using traditional methods. If I hadn't known how to draw things by hand, I think I would have been very limited when it came to using the Macintosh. I think the problem for people starting out begins at school, where people are just being trained on computer. In a way, hands become redundant, which I think is a tragedy. My advice to people just starting out in their design education is that for every hour they put in on the Macintosh, they should put in an hour of hand craft.

People forget that one of the basic elements necessary to good design is the knowledge of drawing. With the Macintosh you don't need to draw; but you need to draw, really, in order to design, because you need to be able to understand things about harmony, weight, light and shade. Those things can only be learned by observation.

With the Macintosh it's easy to produce a great looking piece of work, which has all the right elements in it. A lot of people who use the Macintosh are potentially great artists or illustrators, but they've missed out on the process of traditional training, so they're relying intuitively on the ability of the machine. I think that is a real problem.

When we first had the Macintosh, I still had time to go to life-drawing classes. I was going once a week. Now I don't have time to take classes because I'm traveling so much. The other day, though, I actually got out both a pencil and a compass. I drew a circle by hand, which I then filled with a felt-tipped marker. It was exhilarating; you just get a different feeling from the way the arm moves when drawing than you do from your finger clicking a mouse button. The next day, however, I scanned the whole thing in and finished working on it using the Macintosh. Suddenly, it was easier.

Do you think the computer allows you new capabilities as a designer that you wouldn't otherwise have, or does it just make the production process easier?

Certainly it has opened up new possibilities. Take a program like Photoshop, which allows mixing of colors in a way that wasn't actually possible any other way, except maybe on a Scitex system. Photographically you couldn't possibly have seen all those variations with that kind of speed; nor could you control the degree of transparency, or paste an image over another, using just the light part of the image. These things were certainly not possible before, and I've really been exploring them. It's time-consuming, but absolutely necessary.

Programs such as FreeHand and Illustrator have allowed us to do things with type that were really not possible using physical means, like giving us the ability to distort the outline of the actual character. Programs like FontStudio, ATF, and Fontographer have allowed us to create typefaces.

I think these font creation programs really are the next creative step in digital technology. They give us the ability, for instance, to scan in an object, turn it into a PostScript outline, and turn that outline into an character of the alphabet that you can just type in from the keyboard.

Often I do entire projects using just FontStudio. Because it has drawing capabilities, I can create a different logo idea under each character, which I can then save as a font, open in FreeHand or Illustrator, and manipulate as a typeface. I can have up to 256 different shapes or ideas as one typeface. We're using FontStudio as a graphic tool, not just a type creation tool.

It also becomes a great archiving tool. Recently I was working on designing some postage stamps. These stamps had a floral motif, so I used FontStudio to create 50 different flower motifs. I was able to do it very quickly, and could play with them very easily. It's really exciting, because now I have that set of flowers archived as a typeface. We're currently scanning in different objects using FontStudio to archive them. Each object will be assigned to a letter on the keyboard. It's a much easier way then using a normal clip art system.

We have a new project we're doing for FontShop International. It's a quarterly magazine that will include four typefaces by selected designers; the magazine comes with four posters, each showing use of the typeface, as well as the typeface itself on disk. The designers who participated in it were encouraged to be as experimental as possible, without necessarily making the typefaces easy to read; the people who buy them are encouraged to open the typefaces in FreeHand or Illustrator and manipulate them further. The next issue won't have type characters at all, but each key pressed will yield shapes that interlock, or produce a block of a particular color, for example. We're trying to move forward, taking the next step in thinking digitally.

Of course, there are some things the Macintosh doesn't let you do, and probably never will. It doesn't have the speed, really, of just getting a crayon out and drawing; you can't take a paintbrush and paint a really huge figure, nor can you rub a pencil over textured material underneath. The Macintosh doesn't have a pair of scissors that you can just cut things with. What I really want on the Macintosh is a virtual reality interface — armholes in either side of the box so you can reach in and move logos around; a real paintbrush so that you can feel the texture of the surface underneath.

Step by Step

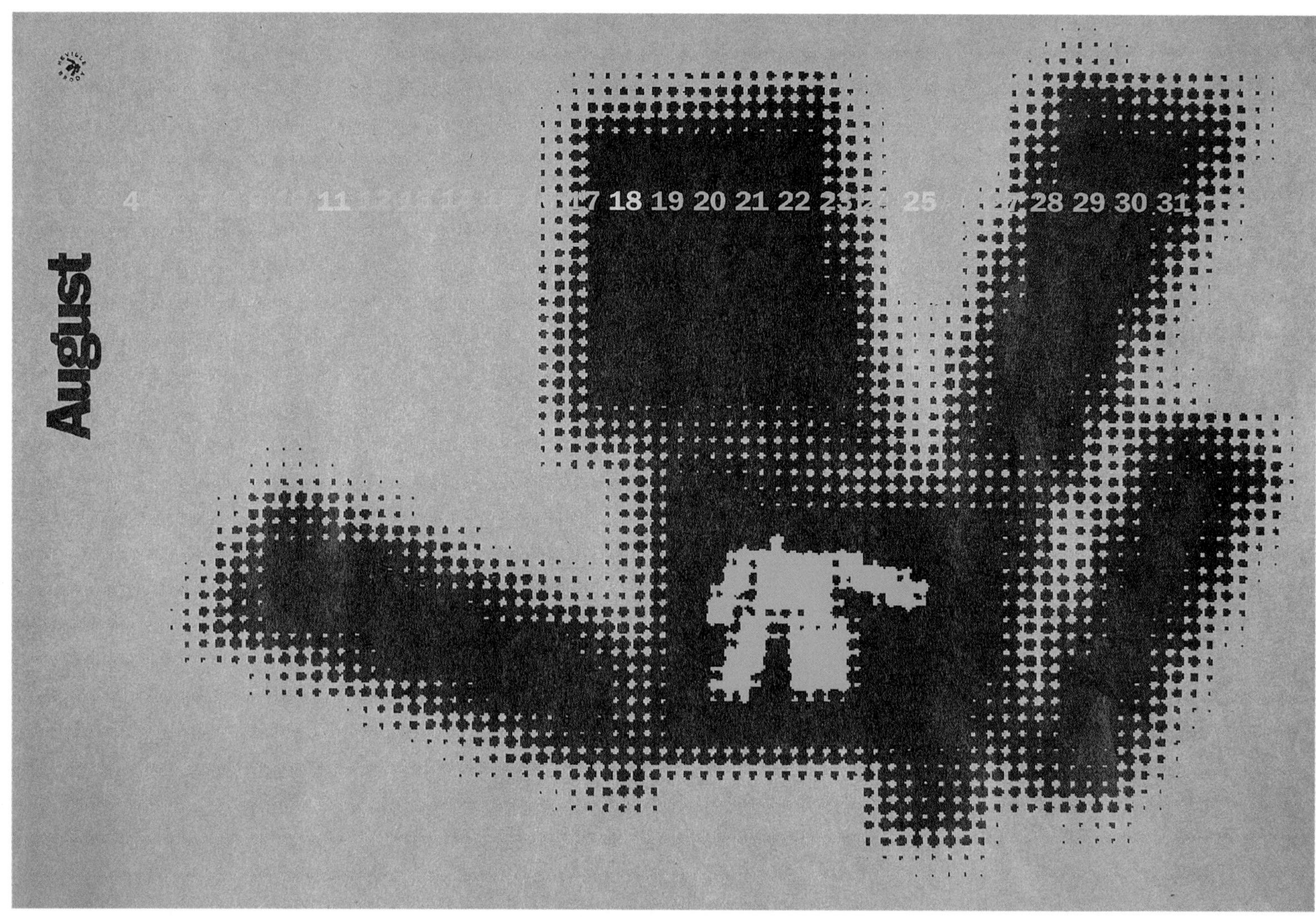

Parco Department Store, one of the largest and most prestigious in Japan, invited Brody to have an exhibition of his work in their Shibuya gallery. One of the several promotional items created for this event was a calendar. The page for August, like that for other months, was created by using several different programs to form the look Brody required.

The production cycle for the August page was a circular one, in a sense. The primary image for the page was first drawn in Aldus FreeHand, opened in MacPaint, manipulated in ImageStudio, then again in MacPaint, and finally brought back into FreeHand to create the final page layout.

The primary image for the calendar page was an abstraction of a man. The simple figure, composed essentially of blocks, was quickly drawn in FreeHand.

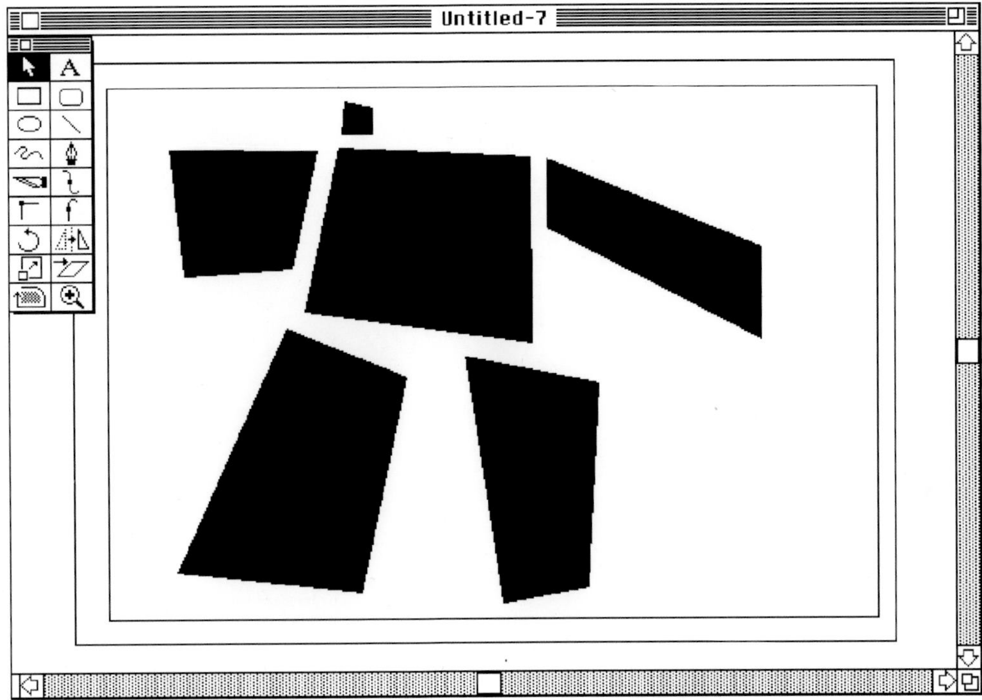

Using Option-Copy, Brody pasted the screen PICT of the PostScript drawing from FreeHand into MacPaint, where he experimented with several different arrangements of the image, until he found the one that he felt was right.

The MacPaint file was opened in ImageStudio. Special filters, such as "blurring" and "soften" were used to further change the image until the desired effect was achieved.

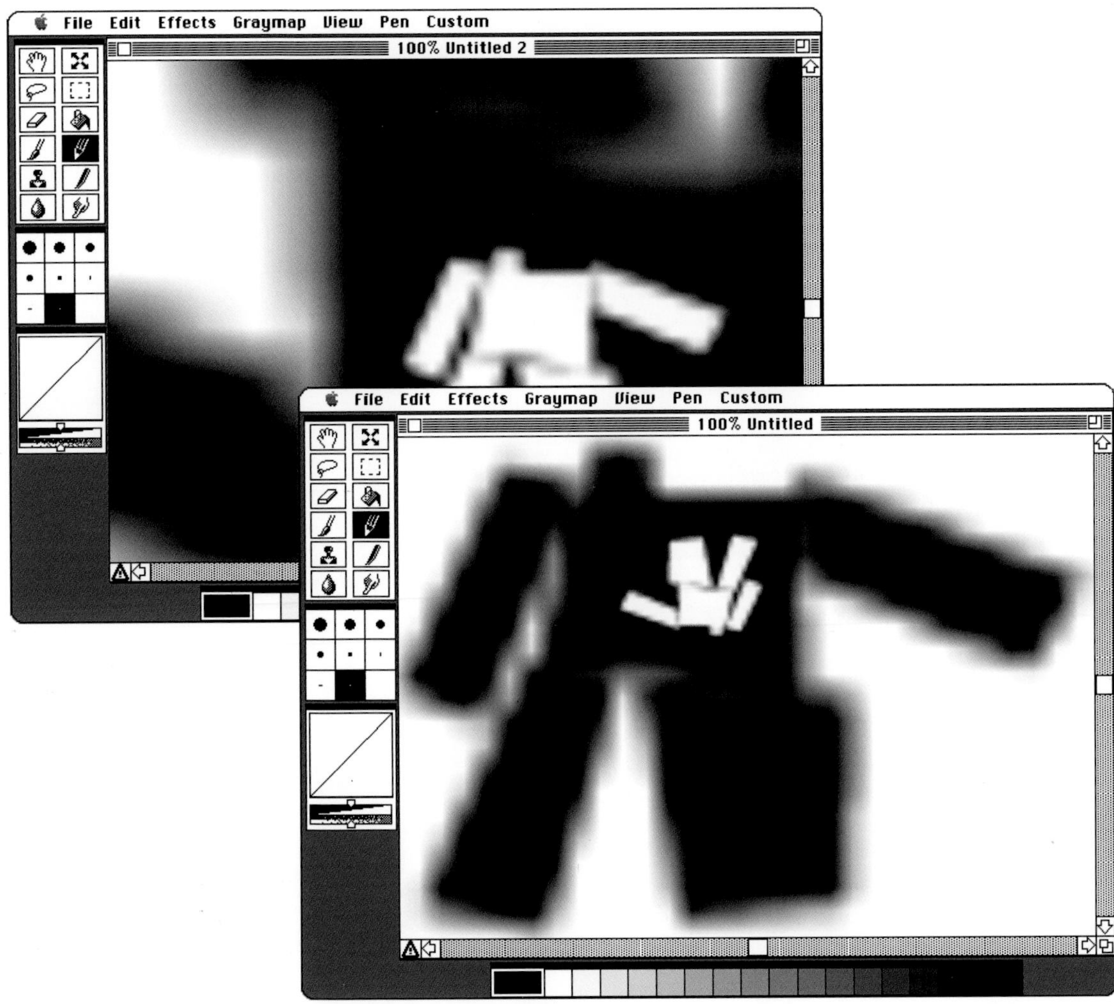

The ImageStudio file was then saved as a MacPaint file, with the option for Special Dither Patterns selected.

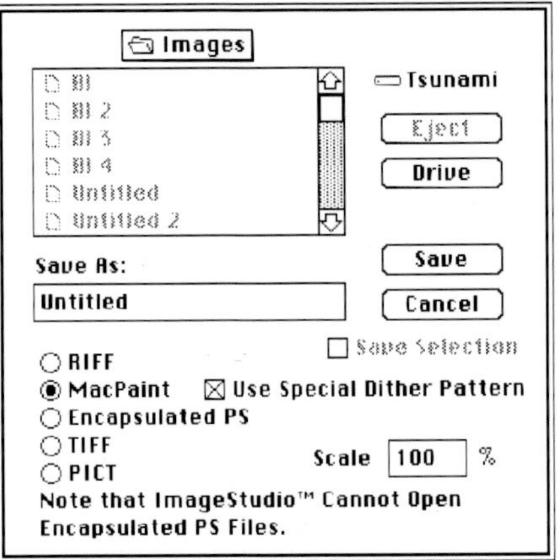

Each dither pattern yielded a different result.

The different images were placed back into FreeHand, and many variations of the calendar page were created.

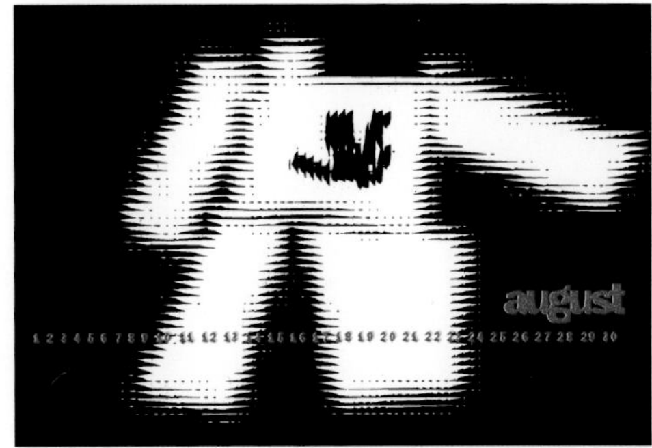

Each calendar page had a small logomark, incorporating the primary image from that month's page. The logos were all contained in one FreeHand file and copied onto the appropriate pages as needed.

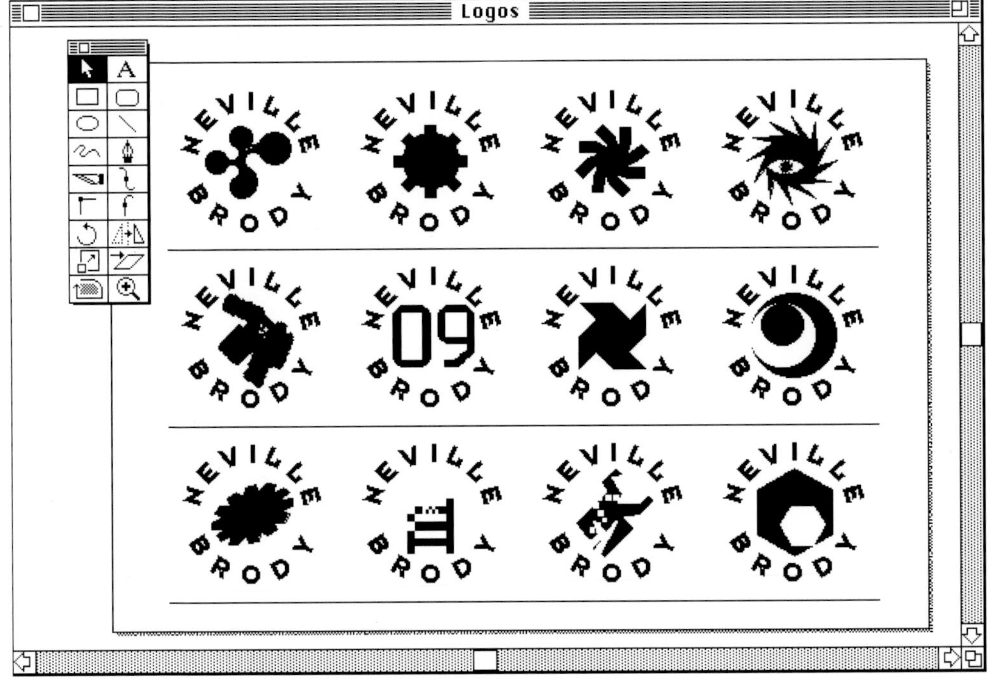

The final image and type were composed in FreeHand. Film was generated directly from the FreeHand file. A service bureau in London output the film, which was then shipped to Tokyo for printing.

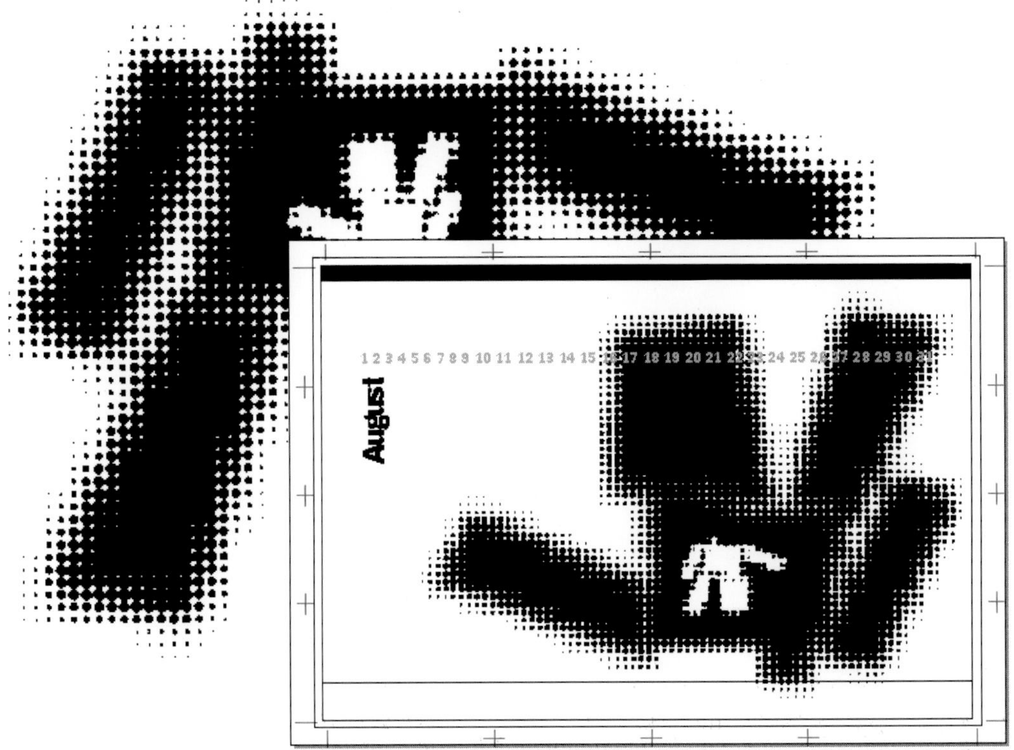

Portfolio

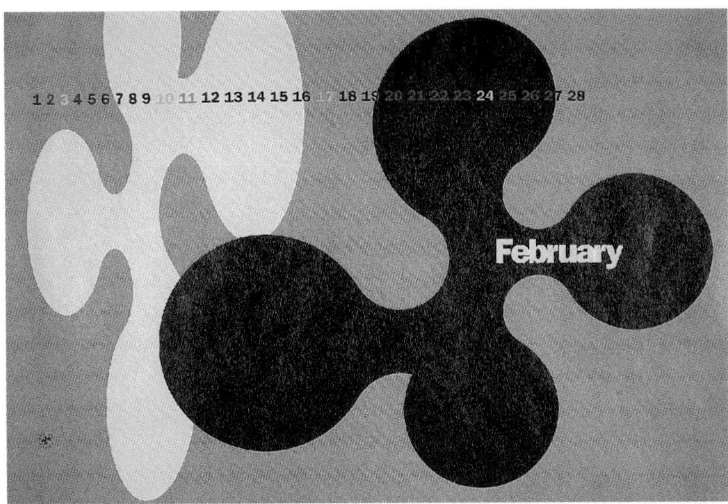

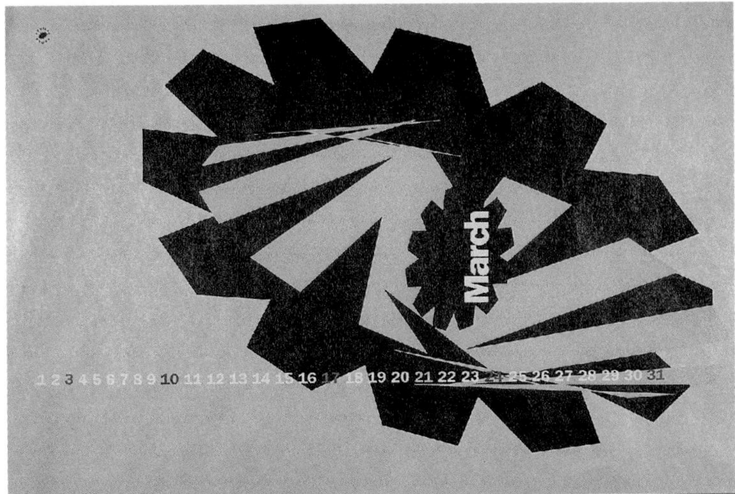

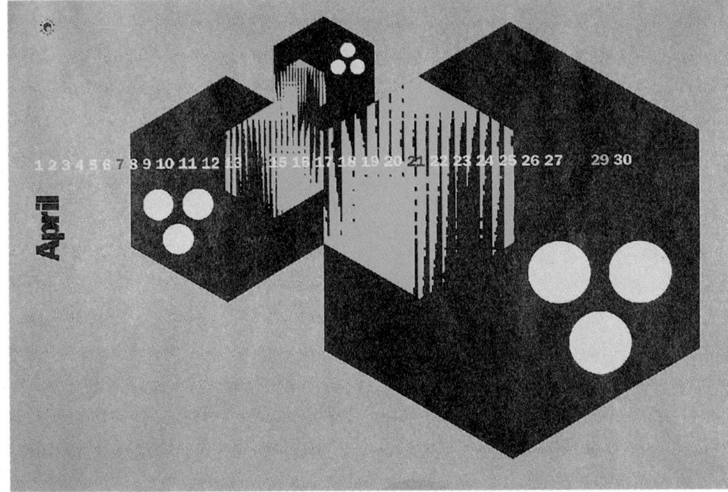

Calendar, 1990
1991 Calendar for Neville Brody exhibition, Parco Space Part 3
Aldus FreeHand, Adobe Illustrator, MacPaint, ImageStudio, Studio 8

Watch, 1990
Commemorative watch for The Graphic Language of Neville Brody exhibition, Parco Department Store
Aldus FreeHand

Following page:

Poster, 1991
Promotion for State font, created for FontShop
Adobe Illustrator

FUSE A LINE THROUGH THE CHAOS OF COMMUNICATION

POSTER DESIGN **NEVILLE BRODY** TYPEFACE **F STATE** POSTER ©1991 FONTSHOP INTERNATIONAL ©1991 NEVILLE BRODY

Arcadia[1]

ABCDEFGHIJKLMNOPQRSTUVWXYZ
abcdefghijklmnopqrstuvwxyz 1234567890 (',/.;:")

Industria[2]

ABCDEFGHIJKLMNOPQRSTUVWXYZ
abcdefghijklmnopqrstuvwxyz 1234567890 [,/.;:]

Industria Inline[3]

ABCDEFGHIJKLMNOPQRSTUVWXYZ
abcdefghijklmnopqrstuvwxyz 1234567890 [,/.;:]

1-4 Typefaces, 1990
Linotype Ltd.
Hand-drawn, Fontographer,
FontStudio, ATF

5 Typeface, 1991
Fuse, published by
FontShop International
Fontographer, FontStudio, ATF

6-7 Typefaces, 1991
FontFont, a division of
FontShop International
Fontographer, FontStudio, ATF

Insignia[4]

ABCDEFGHIJKLMNOPQRSTUVWXYZ
abcdefghijklmnopqrstuvwxyz
1234567890 (',/.;:")

STATE[5]

ABCDEFGHIJKLMNOPQRSTUVWXYZ
ABCDEFGHIJKLMNOPQRSTUVWXYZ
1234567890

TYPEFACE SIX[6]

ABCDEFGHIJKLMNOPQRSTUVWXYZ
ABCDEFGHIJKLMNOPQRSTUVWXYZ
1234567890 (',/.;:")

TYPEFACE SEVEN[7]

ABCDEFGHIJKLMNOPQRSTUVWXYZ
ABCDEFGHIJKLMNOPQRSTUVWXYZ
1234567890 (',/.;:")

POSTER DESIGN NEVILLE BRODY ©1991 FSI GMBH

FUSE 1

FUSE IS A NEW VENTURE IN TYPE DESIGN, CONTAINING FOUR EXPERIMENTAL FONTS DIGITISED FOR MACINTOSH. THE FUSE DISC IS ACCOMPANIED BY FOUR A2 POSTERS SHOWING EACH TYPEFACE IN CREATIVE APPLICATION.

ISSUE ONE FEATURES FOUR BRITISH DESIGNERS :

PHIL BAINES
NEVILLE BRODY
MALCOLM GARRETT
IAN SWIFT

PRODUCED BY FONTSHOP INTERNATIONAL
AND DISTRIBUTED EXCLUSIVELY
THROUGH THE FONTSHOP NETWORK

FONTSHOP BELGIUM
MAALTECENTER BLOK C
DERBYSTRAAT 247
9051 ST. DENIJS-WESTREM
(091) 20 65 98
FAX (091) 20 34 45

FONTSHOP CANADA
401 WELLINGTON ST. WEST
TORONTO, ONTARIO M5V 1E8
1-800-36-FONTS
LOCAL CALLS (416) 348-9837
FAX (416) 593-4318

FONTSHOP GERMANY
BERGMANNSTRASSE 102
1000 BERLIN 61
(0 30) 69 00 62 62
FAX (0 30) 69 00 62 77

FONTSHOP HOLLAND
LAAN VAN BEEK & ROYEN 1B
3701 AH ZEIST
(034 04) 323 66
FAX (034 04) 249 52

FONTSHOP SWEDEN
TEGNÉRGATAN 37
111 61 STOCKHOLM
(08) 21 52 00
FAX (08) 21 28 80

FONTWORKS UK
65-69 EAST ROAD
LONDON N1 6AH
071-490-5390
FAX 071-490-5391

Previous page:

Poster, 1991
Promotion for Fuse fonts, created for FontShop
Adobe Photoshop, Adobe Illustrator

This page:

1 Frisbee, 1990
Promotional Frisbee for *Men's Bigi*
Aldus FreeHand

2 Carrier bag, 1989
Men's Bigi
Adobe Illustrator

Designed with Ian Swift

1

2

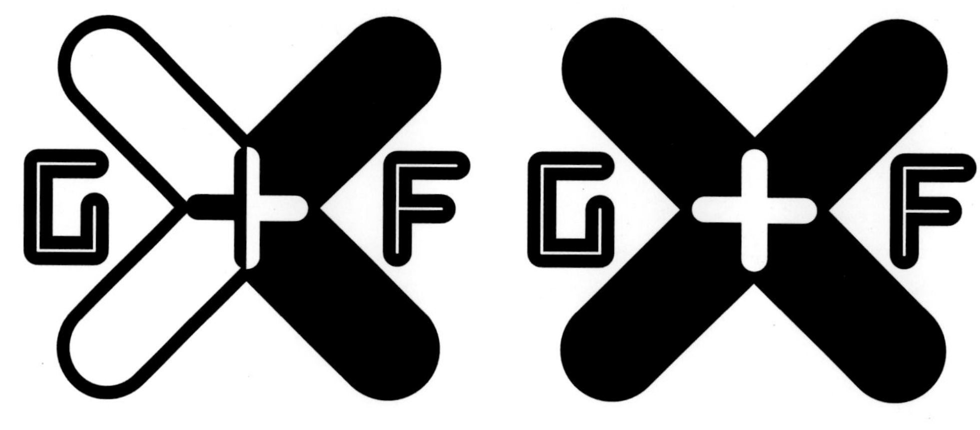

G GLOBAL FORCE F

G GLOBAL FORCE F

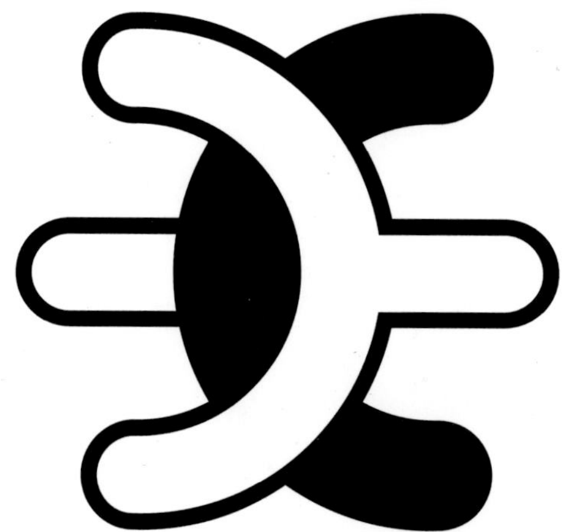

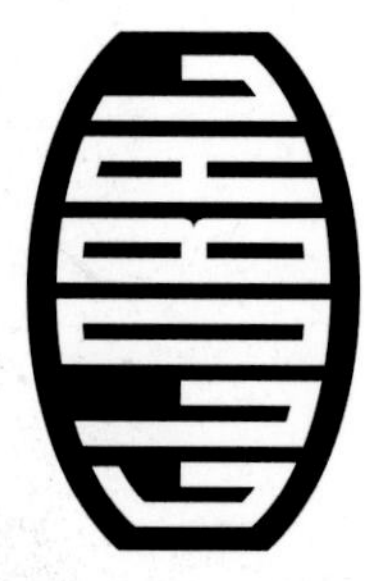

PROTECTOR

Previous page:

Logos, 1990-91
Joint U.K./Japan cultural project
Aldus FreeHand

This page:

Catalog section divider, 1990
FontShop Typeface Catalog
Aldus FreeHand, MacPaint,
QuarkXPress

Logo, 1991
Philips CD sponsorship logo
Aldus FreeHand

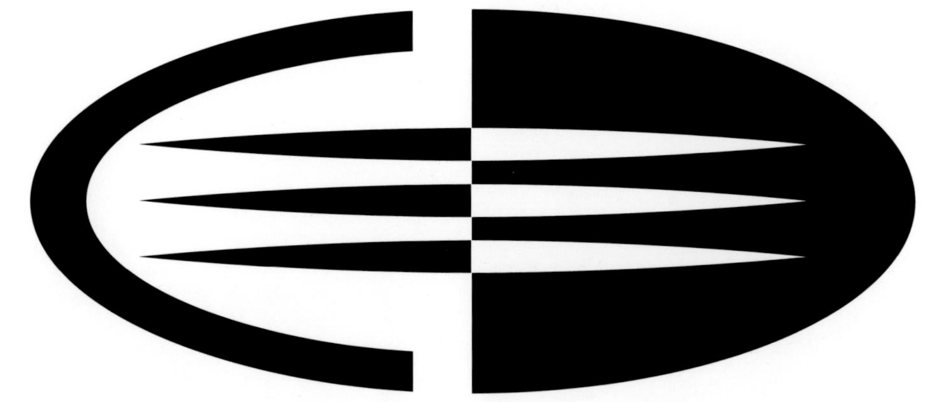

Logo, 1991
Logo for German television program
Aldus FreeHand
(Designed with Simon Staines)

Poster (front and back), 1990
Mute Records Manscape CD
Photocopies, Aldus FreeHand

Designed with Jon Wozencroft

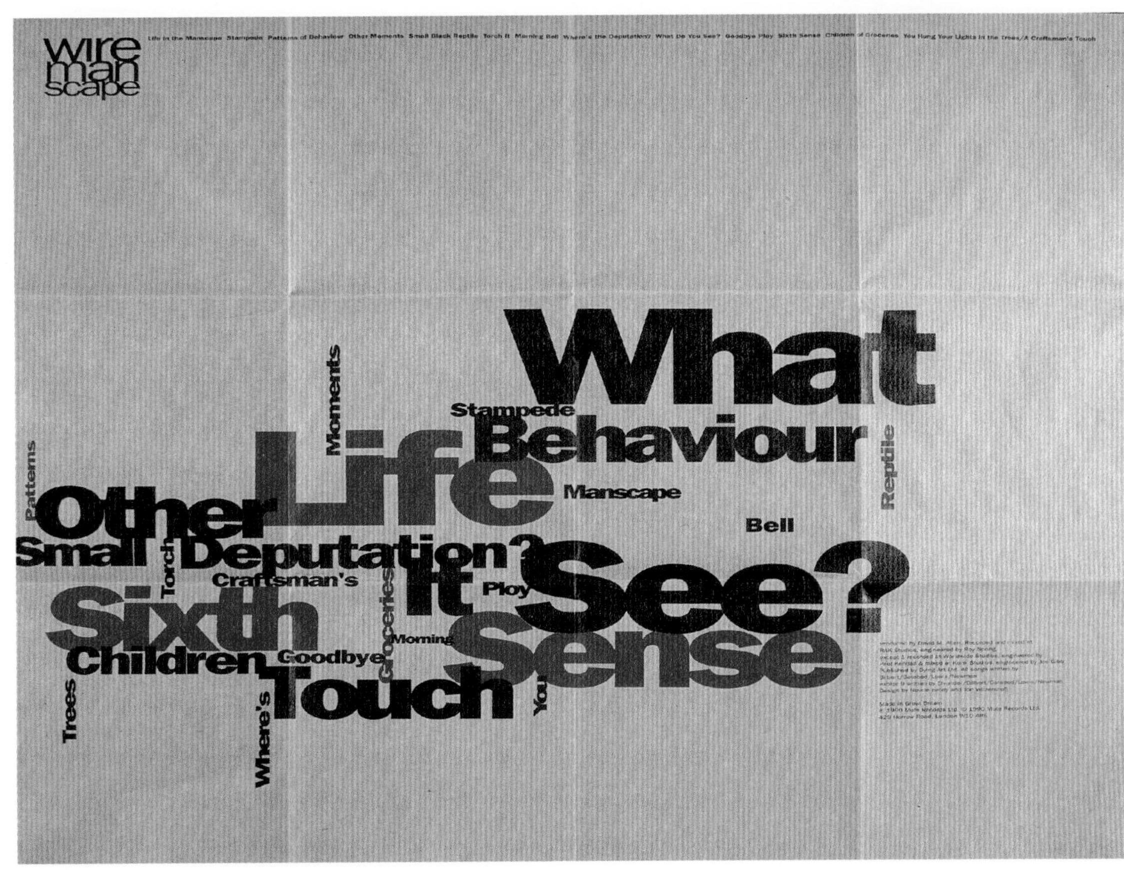

MIKE
TYSON
TONY
TUBBS
WORLD
HEAVYWEIGHT
CHAMPIONSHIP
FIGHT
TOKYO
DOME

Poster, 1988
Tyson vs.Tubbs Fight, Tokyo Dome
Original drawn by hand, reworked in Aldus FreeHand

Poster, 1989-90
Promotion for Neville Brody exhibition, sponsored by *Tempo* magazine, Germany
Clay, PixelPaint, ImageStudio, QuarkXPress

BRODY

Die Zeichensprache des Neville Brody

17. bis 29. Oktober 1989. Täglich außer Montag 11 bis 18 Uhr. Mittwoch bis 20 Uhr.
Refektorium des Karmeliterklosters,
Karmelitergasse 9, 6000 Frankfurt 1.
Veranstaltet von **TEMPO**

MONT BLANC
PHILIP MORRIS
LIGHT AMERICAN
ALDUS
swatch+

Emigre Graphics

Rudy Vanderlans is an émigré, in the strict definition of the word. After training in his native Holland at the Royal Academy of Art in The Hague, Vanderlans made his home Berkeley, California and today he designs and edits the highly experimental *Emigre*, the "magazine that ignores boundaries." The magazine is an exploration of innovative type design, of "organic" grid structures as opposed to the rigid composition espoused by his Dutch training. *Emigre* also showcases Emigre fonts, some of the most original fonts used by designers on the Macintosh today, most of which are designed by Vanderlans' wife and partner in Emigre Graphics, Zuzana Licko. ¶ The road from The Hague to Berkeley has been a circuitous one, with the Macintosh playing a large part in the evolution of Vanderlans' design.

Emigre's "non-stop" design seems somewhat anti-thematic to that represented by the Royal Academy of the Arts at the Hague. How did you get from there to here?

I grew up in Holland, and also went to design school there in the mid 1970s. The Academy's educational approach was based on the Swiss and International style. It was a hands-on, very pragmatic education based upon "purity," and "clarity" and "The Grid," and you could only use two typefaces, Univers and Baskerville. This is kind of an exaggerated view, but I think that's what it came down to. At that time, most design in Western Europe was still heavily influenced by the Bauhaus school, and The Royal Academy, too, was very rigid and very strict.

After graduation, I worked for three different design studios in Holland. However, I soon became quite disillusioned with graphic design because the graphic design studios I worked for were mostly involved in working for large corporations, designing corporate identities. It was graphic design as an organizational discipline, which was tremendously boring and disappointing for me because I had imagined design to be much more expressive and individualistic. After three years of working in Holland, I decided to stop. I traveled around the United States for six weeks and finally ended up at the University of California at Berkeley, where I thought it might be interesting to go back to school. I was admitted to study photography, and so, in 1981, I moved to the United States.

After two years of studying, and having met Zuzana, my wife, I quite by accident landed a job at the *San Francisco Chronicle* newspaper where I worked for three years as a designer and illustrator.

There were two things about working at the newspaper that were most educational for me. One was the whole involvement with content. Before then that's something I had never been too much involved in. I think that's actually one of the shortcomings of my graphic design education — they taught us to look at text as boxes or blocks of grey, and there is usually no real content to be read. At the newspaper, which was primarily put together by editors, graphic design was completely subservient to the contents.

The second most important thing I learned when working at the newspaper was timing. When I worked on a design project in Holland, everything always took months to finish, but at the *Chronicle*, everyday I'd work on two or three projects that I'd have to finish that same day. I planned a design one day and the next day I'd see it printed, and the day after that, I'd see it on the street on the ground, or on the bottom of a bird cage. In the end there was so little respect for design that it started to hurt. Eventually, I wanted do something that would last a little longer than one day.

Again, I was becoming restless, and Zuzana and I decided to start our own business. About that time, the Macintosh came along.

How did you first discover the Macintosh?

We were in the right place at the right time. At the newspaper, I had done so much illustration work and gotten so much exposure — they print 750,000 copies everyday, so you get tremendous exposure of your work — my illustration work was becoming well known, and at that time, I used a variety of traditional media.

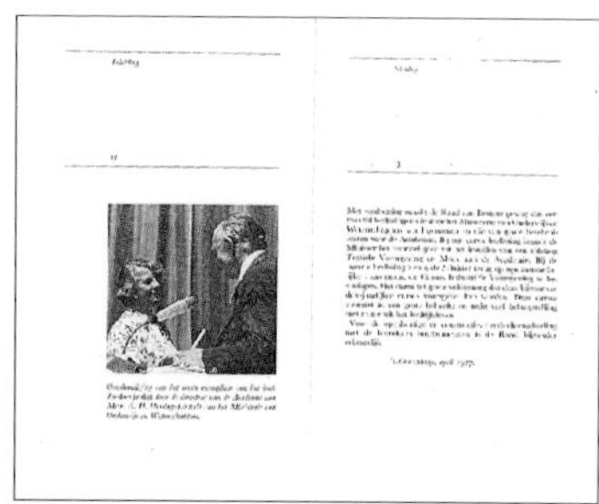

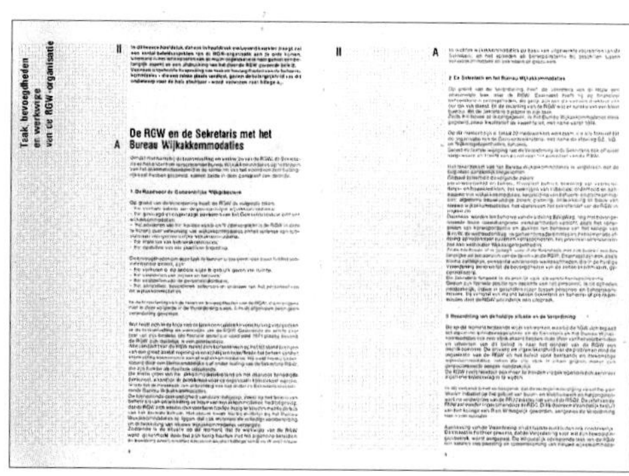

Taak, bevoegdheden en werkwijze van de RGW-organisatie

A De RGW en de Sekretaris met het Bureau Wijkakkommodaties

Two of Vandrerlans' earliest pieces including a spread from the 1977 catalog for the Royal Academy of Art in the Hague, done in collaboration with Vorm Vijf, and a spread from the annual for the city of Rotterdam done in collaboration with Reynoud Homan.

1,2 Some of Vanderlans' pre-Mac Illustrations for *TV Week* and the *San Francisco Chronicle* .

3 An early illustration for *Macworld* created with MacPaint, ThunderScan, and conventional paste-up.

Then one day I got a call from *Macworld* magazine, a new magazine that was to be devoted to the Macintosh computer. The magazine was desperately looking for people who were willing to do illustrations on the computer. I did not know anything about computers. But I thought since I was using so many different media already, I might as well add a computer to the list. So I went over to the magazine's offices with Zuzana, and there was a little Macintosh with its trash can and pencil. We worked there for over an hour in total amazement at what we saw.

We took it home for the weekend and the next Monday, we went to buy one. Unfortunately, they were on backorder. I remember that very well. It was 1985, and you could not get your hands on the Macintosh at that point because they were just selling like hotcakes. We had to wait for three weeks.

Finally, we brought one home. We opened it immediately and we sat behind it. Zuzana just locked herself up for about a month and I couldn't even talk to her. She started designing typefaces from the moment she turned it on.

How exactly did Emigre fonts and *Emigre* magazine come about?

In the early days, we used a public domain software package called Font Editor that allowed you to design your own pixelated fonts. There were, of course, standard fonts available for the Macintosh, such as Geneva and Chicago, which we thought were okay, but we thought it was very exciting that you could make your own fonts, and that you could store them in your computer and use them.

This was an incredible revelation. Of course, we've always been able to design our own fonts; in fact, in order to graduate from art school, we had to design two fonts, a serif and sans serif. I spent a year doing this and I ended up with 26 characters in each typeface, but they were pen drawings, so you couldn't do anything with them except look at them.

With the Macintosh, all of a sudden, you could create fonts, store them in the computer, and then you could actually use them freely. This was great because it coincided with the fact that I had already been publishing *Emigre* — we were then working on our second issue. The first issue was created entirely on a typewriter, and for the second issue we used this machine, the Macintosh. In a sense, it replaced the typewriter.

We printed all the type out on the ImageWriter, a low resolution dot-matrix printer, because there was no PostScript printer at that time. Apple's LaserWriter and PostScript were not yet released, so we used the ImageWriter and printed out the text as big as we could with a fresh, black printer ribbon. Then we reduced it with a stat camera and pasted down the galleys by hand. That's how we started using the Macintosh.

At the same time, *Macworld*, very eager to find illustrators, invited me to do many illustrations for them, and before I knew it, I was doing a great deal of illustration work for *Macworld*, Apple Computer, and others. I used mostly MacPaint at that time.

This was an entirely new market, and there was no competition. There were a lot of illustrators invited by *Macworld* to do illustrations on the Macintosh, but I'd say about 90% of them weren't interested in using the computer. Perhaps they had a problem with the "eye-hand coordination," because with the mouse here and the actual drawing there, the process of executing of the drawing is somewhat separated from the result.

Anyway, there was a great market and a lot of money to be made. However, the most exciting thing was that there were absolutely no standards and no examples of how to do this kind of work, which was very liberating.

For the first two or three years, we worked for a variety of clients, but at some point, about a year ago, the typefaces were doing so well and were taking up so much of our time that we decided to see what the real potential would be if we invested all our time and effort in producing the typefaces and the publishing the magazine. So we said good-bye to all of the people who had been our clients to devote all our time to Emigre.

At first, the computer helped us to develop our own design aesthetic. That was very important in the beginning, but later on, we realized how the computer really helped us become more than just designers. We could actually become manufacturers of typefaces. It was clear that we could design typefaces, which we could always do, but now we could also manufacture these typefaces, copy them from a master disk, and sell them. I think this has given us a lot of courage with other projects as well. We've learned a lot about manufacturing, distribution, and how to promote and sell our products. This knowledge can be applied to a lot of different areas, not just to magazine-making, or type, but also, for example, to music. I've always been interested in music, so we recently started releasing records under our own label, Emigre Music. It was a logical extension for us.

How exactly do you work with the Macintosh when creating *Emigre*?

In the beginning, I used it like a typesetting machine. Then you find yourself going between your drawing table and your computer, and you find out more and more about the computer. You see how straight everything is on the computer and that you can't match that in your paste-up, so you force yourself to use the computer for everything possible, because it can do the repetitive and precise work so perfectly and quickly.

By now we're at the stage where everything is printed out onto negatives and given to the printer, and all the printer does is shoot the halftones and drop them in. The most recent issue, though, ironically enough, has a letterpress-printed cover.

What I usually do while I'm working on the design of a magazine page, which measures 11 1/4" x 16 3/4", is print it out at a 60% reduction so each page fits on a letter size LaserWriter sheet. When I get to the point that it looks right, I print every page out at 100% in four parts, or tiles, which is a big hassle because it means I have to paste them all together. Those printouts end up functioning as the dummy for the printer.

I'm actually still working with Ready SetGo 4.5. I haven't moved on to the newer version, called DesignStudio, because I think that a lot of the new options can be distracting. For example, DesignStudio lets you rotate your type at every angle, and I think that is one of those options that is sometimes better not to have. It's so difficult to solve design problems in a simple way, and I think all these distractions are not so beneficial. Too often I find myself "doodling" with the software without having any creative thoughts going on through my mind, and that's wrong. So I tend to restrict myself and use simpler software.

Do you set up a grid structure to design *Emigre* magazine?

Emigre is spontaneously designed, and I purposely do not use a pre-set grid. Some sort of grid might develop, but only on hindsight. I want to give myself the flexibility to stray entirely from the grid and to just let my own intuition and my own sense of the page and what is on the page or what "needs" to be on the page take precedent over what the grid dictates.

I've started to develop an approach I refer to as "organic grids." Think about it: why would you want to set up a grid? It comes from the time when everybody was doing these things by hand. When you work on magazines or books, there's a repetitive element. You saved a lot of time and a lot of decision-making if you just designed a grid and preprinted it in light blue on boards. Your design was basically done, and it just made life very easy and made the whole process go very fast. You can easily do that on the computer, too, but the thing is, on a computer, you can design a book and draw a different size column for text on every page. And you can still do it in a matter of minutes.

I feel sorry that the designers of the Swiss and International schools didn't have this machine because it is the ideal machine for the International style. This was a group of people who came up with a "rational" way of designing, but they were 20 years too early; the Mac is the perfect machine to design rationally with. At the same time, I think it's also a great machine to do very intuitive work. I don't think people have quite seen that yet. I think designers like April Greiman and Jeffery Keedy know that, but a lot of people use it purely as a production tool, which is fine, too, because it's very good for that.

Emigre's Berkeley studio.

Where does Emigre Music fit into all of this?

Actually, releasing music is a rather natural outgrowth of our intentions with Emigre Graphics. The goal we have set with *Emigre* magazine, for instance, is to feature the work of graphic designers that we feel has been overlooked by the major design magazines and design competitions. Usually these are designers whose work does not conform to mainstream ideas or hasn't matured to the point of predictability; their work is still developing. By publishing their work, we intend to help exhibit and explain it, and ultimately provide the graphic design world with a more complete picture of the state of graphic design.

Our Emigre typefaces are released with similar intentions; to make available those typefaces that we believe will not be made by established type foundries. They are highly unusual typefaces that are nonetheless designed with a great deal of mastery and ones that could be useful to certain graphic designers.

With Emigre Music, we hope to contribute to the development of certain musical talents whom we greatly admire. We are also quite intrigued by and have an affinity with how some of these musicians work. Their methods of layering and composing are not much different from how we work in graphic design. Some actually do their final editing on the Macintosh; they cut and paste their music like we cut and paste text. It's really amazing, and kind of scary, too. So much is possible and it becomes more and more difficult to say this is the answer, or that is the final solution. I think one of the most difficult things about working on the computer is that so much is possible.

What's your advice to designers who are afraid of or opposed to computers?

I can understand why some designers may be intimidated by the computer, because I still am. It's a very intimidating field because you still have to go through a lot of technical stuff. But actually, there are other aspects of design that were also intimidating for me, such as printing. And printing is so closely related to design that you can't really view it separately from design. And, just like with the computer, I'm still learning about offset printing. Printing is another field that is difficult to understand if you are not a technical person.

The reason I think designers should use computers is because that's the direction in which the industry is moving. Before too long, offset printers will have computers sitting in their offices for one reason or another. There are still people who are doing letterpress, which I'm not opposed to at all, because I think you can do beautiful things with letterpress; look at the cover of *Emigre #16*, which was printed on letterpress by Bruce Licher. The only problem is that letterpress has become very expensive to do. And expense is one of the reasons why designers are going to have to use the computer, because, sure, you can do things by hand, and paste things up by hand, but in about 10 years, though you'll still be able to make beautiful things, they'll be very expensive. One thing I've always had trouble with about graphic design is that you can spend an enormous amount of money on a design without necessarily making it good, or better, and one of the things we've had to do to make it all possible is to look for the cheapest ways of doing it, to be resourceful. One of the reasons we've been able to publish the magazine is the Macintosh computer. It cut our typesetting bill from $5,000 to $300. At the same time, it gave us a tremendous power and control over typesetting, more than we've ever had.

So people may say that it is inhuman, a machine, but so is a pencil! It's piece of wood with lead in it. There always has to be a human being sitting behind it.

Step by Step

Emigre #17 includes an interview with the Dutch designer Piet Schreuders. Vanderlans conducted and wrote the interview, then used ReadySetGo 4.5 to design the article using a new Emigre font, Journal. The design challenge was to combine three distinctly different elements in one article: Vanderlans' interview, a lecture and slides presented by Schreuders at a recent conference, and an introduction written by Schreuders himself.

Vanderlans designed this piece as he does all others — spontaneously. He did not begin with a pre-set grid, though a grid structure eventually evolved on it's own. By using the features and commands of ReadySetGo, issues formerly addressed by a pre-set grid, such as alignment and symmetry, were managed automatically by the software.

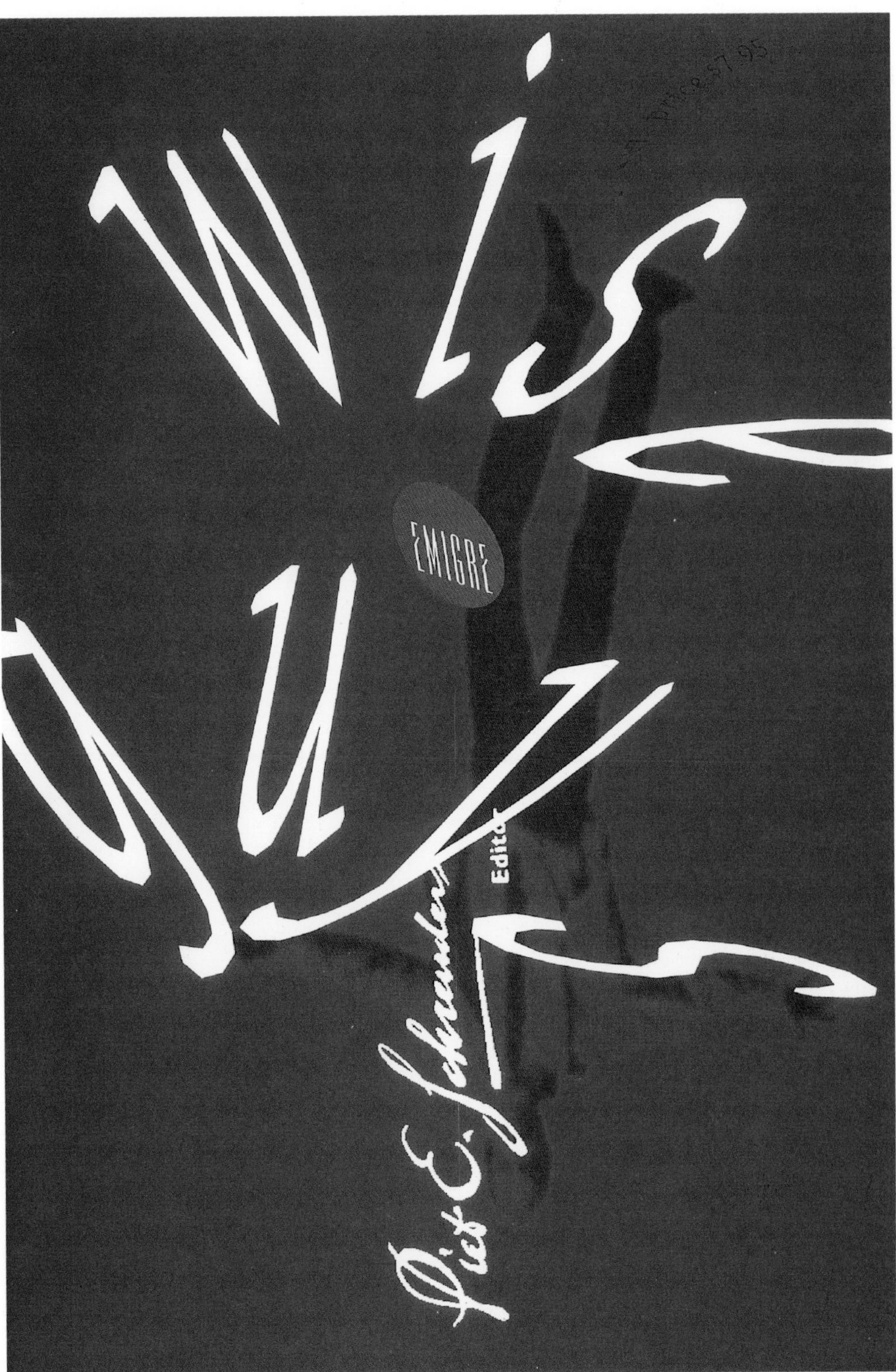

Vanderlans began with a facing page spread, set up to the page dimensions of the magazine, 11 1/4" x 16 3/4". Center crop marks were drawn manually; outside crops were automatically generated by ReadySetGo.

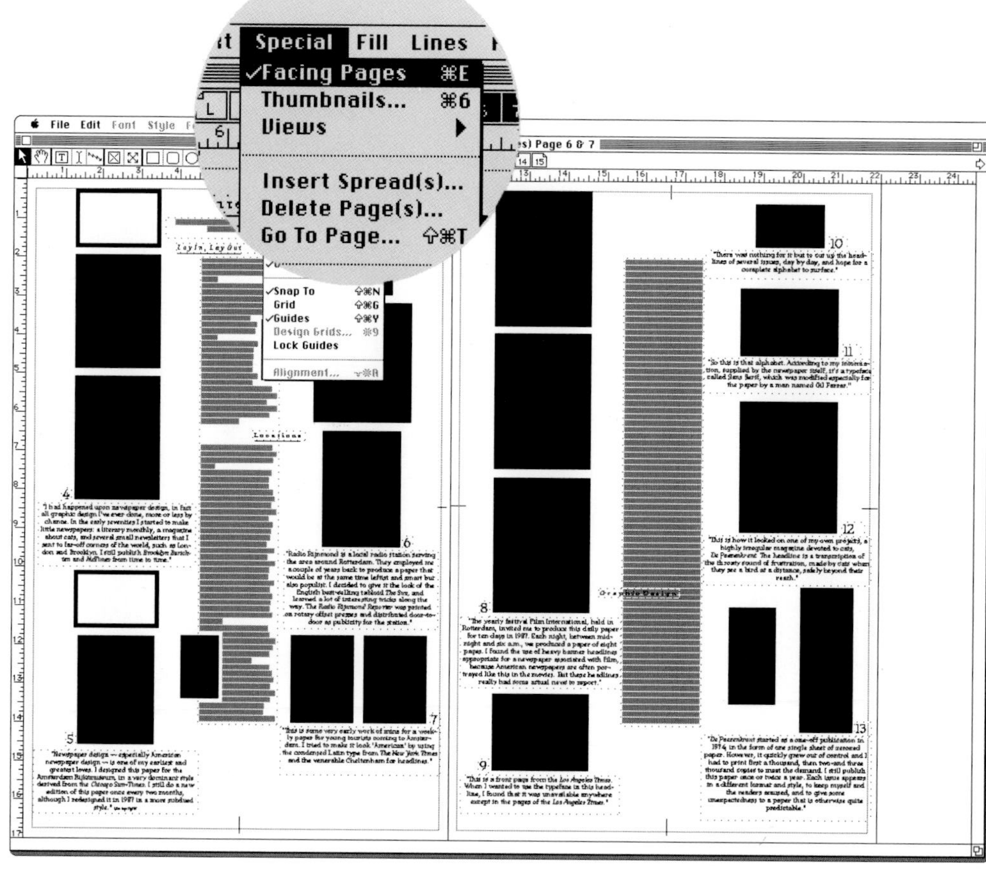

Next, one of the elements of the article, the introduction by Schreuders, was flowed onto the page. Other parts of the article were flowed in and positioned on the page.

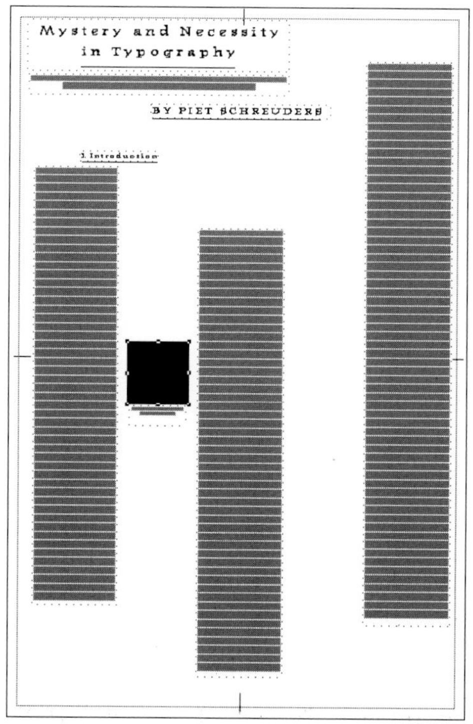

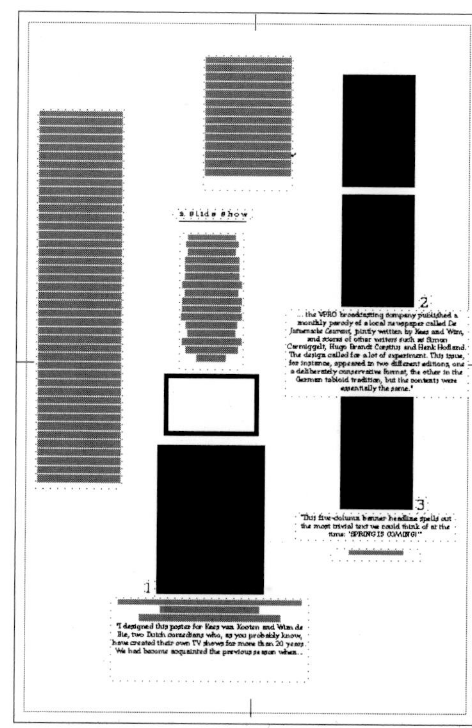

In this version of the design, text of the lecture appears on the outside of each page, and is interwoven between boxes drawn where the visuals would later be stripped in by the printer. The column of text and graphic boxes were easily aligned using ReadySetGo's Align Objects command.

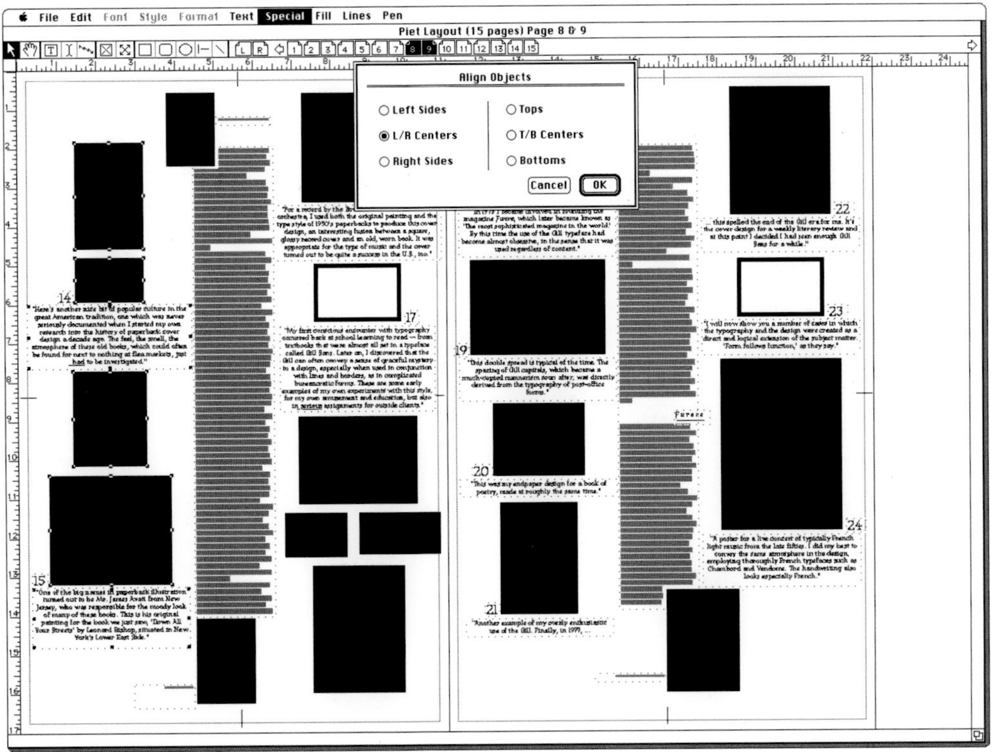

A new font, Journal, was featured for all elements of the article. Journal, and other Emigre fonts, are created using Altsys Fontographer.

"We have a new font called Journal, which is a traditional-looking font, but it actually doesn't have any curves in it; it's made out of little splines. The whole idea behind Journal is that we think phototypesetting has hurt type more than anything else, because phototype cleaned up fonts that were never meant to be so clean in the first place. The way typefaces were designed, like the original Times and Garamond, was for letterpress. They were designed with the thought that they were going to be pressed into paper, with a kind of gritty look, which you can see if you blow them up. Someone decided these fonts had to be entirely cleaned up and be very crisp, and there's a real division in the type community as to what was the real intention of the typeface. We think it was not to be so sterile and clean, and Journal reflects that."

Rudy Vanderlans

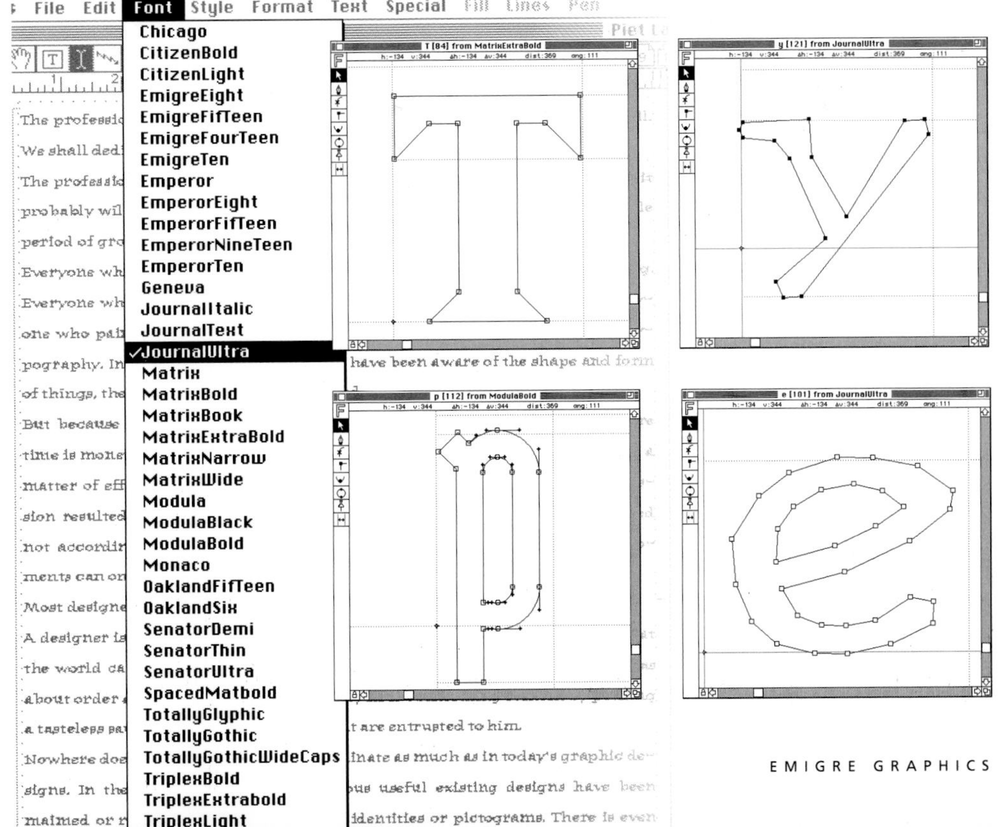

EMIGRE #17

Editor/designer: Rudy VanderLans
Editorial consultant: Alice Polesky
Distribution, promotion and editorial assistance: Elizabeth Dunn
Typeface designs: Zuzana Licko

Emigre is published four times a year by Emigre Graphics. Copyright © 1991 Emigre Graphics. All rights reserved. No part of this publication may be reproduced without written permission from the contributors or Emigre Graphics. Emigre magazine is a trademark of Emigre Graphics. ISSN 1045 - 3717. For information about Emigre write to Emigre Graphics, 48 Shattuck Square, #175, Berkeley, CA 94704-1140, USA. Phone (415) 845 9021, fax (415) 644 0820.

"A dangerous element." Hans Van Kampen

"Abominably bad." Helmut Salden

Piet Schreuders

"A soul-less, imitative, grease-stained 'typographical' joke that doesn't work." Karel L. Zwart

"A friendly man who poses, with no justification, as a designer." Gerrit Noordzij

Piet Schreuders was born in the Mathenesse polder (Rotterdam), Holland in 1951. He studied Dutch in Amsterdam, but soon after established himself as a self-taught graphic designer. He has worked for the Rijksmuseum in Amsterdam, various publishing and record companies, the VPRO (a national television broadcasting station) and a host of other clients ranging from local printers to government sponsored cultural organizations. In 1975, he became involved in founding the magazine *Furore*, "The Most Sophisticated Magazine in the World," taking charge of editorial matters and design (20 issues, 1975-1983). His booklet *Lay In Lay Out* (1977) sent a shock wave through the Dutch graphic design establishment.

With *Paperbacks, U.S.A.* (1980), he charted the history of American paperbacks of the 40s and 50s. He is managing director of *De Poezenkrant* (41 issues published up to now), editor of *Radiovisited*, and on the staff of the typographic magazine *Quarry*. Since the end of 1985 he presents the weekly VPRO radio program *Vrije Geluiden*, "Holland's Littlest Radio Program." In 1991 he will publish the book *The Beatles' London* with co-authors Mark Lewisohn and Adam Smith.

All text on the following 15 pages was set in Journal Text, Journal Italic and Journal Ultra, a new family of faces designed by Zuzana Licko for Emigre.

Thank you

Vanderlans refined the design, and proofed each iteration as it developed by printing reduced pages on a LaserWriter. Once the design was refined, final proofing and editing was done on full size pages, by tiling the pages to the LaserWriter and pasting them together. Finally, each page was printed to film on a Linotronic 300 imagesetter. These films were sent to the printer, who stripped in all halftone images.

The profession of graphic design is criminal and really ought not to exist at all. We shall dedicate a booklet to this notion.

The profession did not exist a hundred years ago. In another one hundred years it probably will not exist anymore. However, today it is experiencing a remarkable period of growth and development.

Everyone who writes a letter and uses a one inch margin on the left is designing. Everyone who sets the dining table in a certain way is creating a layout. Everyone who paints revolutionary slogans in huge letters on walls is practicing typography. In this sense, as long as people have been aware of the shape and form of things, the profession has always existed.

But because design developed over the years into a commercial entity, where time is money and business is big, the design of printed materials became more a matter of efficiency than of clarity and beauty. This degradation of the profession resulted in, among other problems, certain new typefaces being designed not according to typographic but commercial considerations. Such developments can only be explained as criminal.

Most designers are criminal.

A designer is criminal because his profession is one of those specializations that the world can easily do without; he is criminal because he sells contrived ideas about order and objectivity while in reality he is obliterating content by pouring a tasteless sauce over the assignments that are entrusted to him.

Nowhere does chaos and subjectivity dominate as much as in today's graphic designs. In the name of "design," numerous useful existing designs have been maimed or replaced by logos, corporate identities or pictograms. There is even an organization for designers; in other words, organized crime.

It is this graphic crime that I am so attracted to in graphic designers, much as I was attracted to the cowboys and gangsters of long ago. Probably in another thirty years we will reminisce about Jan van Toorn, Wim Crouwel and Pieter Brattinga, just as we do now about Billy the Kid, Al Capone and the Godfather. Designers: you'd rather not have anything to do with them, but at a distance they can be quite entertaining.

from *Lay In, Lay Out* (1977) by Piet Schreuders

PIET SCHREUDERS

(the original)

My most vivid memory of Piet Schreuders is of him kneeling down to study the typeface on a manhole cover in Los Angeles. I still remember it because this happened on Dutch national television. As an avid admirer of American culture (and in particular its typefaces), Schreuders was given the opportunity by the VPRO (a Dutch television broadcasting company) to do a video documentary about typefaces in Los Angeles. For this program, titled "Hollywood at Last!" Schreuders interviewed sign painters, checked out street signs, talked to the managing editor of the *Los Angeles Times* newspaper about the origins of its headline type, and visited locations that were used in Laurel and Hardy movies.

This documentary was an example of only one of Schreuders's many idiosyncratic interests. It was also evident of his need and ability to research topics and compile them into formats that are insightful, entertaining, and most of all, original. The different formats that he has utilized to present his research include television documentaries, radio programs, books and publications including *Furore*, *De Poezenkrant* and *The Explorer*. This prolific output combined with his outspoken criticism of the established graphic design scene in Holland has earned Schreuders a reputation varying from brilliant archivist to charlatan designer.

Regardless of these contradictory labels, many consider Piet Schreuders to be quite influential in Dutch graphic design, although he will modestly disagree. For instance, about the design of his publication *Furore* he said, "With my work, I never wanted to make a statement about graphic design; I wanted to make a magazine. The design was secondary to that." Nonetheless, it cannot be denied that he was one of a handful of people who provided a much needed alternative to the regimented purity of Wim Crouwel and Total Design, the dominating graphic design studio in Holland during the seventies.

Hard Werken founder Henk Elenga does not especially see Schreuders as an innovator. "Schreuders is more like an archivist," Elenga says. "He can detect trends and graphic phenomena and he will use the ingredients quite creatively in his own work, often to such a degree that people think it is his original invention. Then many designers actually end up copying him!"

Either way you look at it, the body of work that Schreuders has produced is impressive. And not just graphically speaking. *Furore* magazine was passionately written and entirely edited by Schreuders and his booklet *Lay In, Lay Out* displayed his mordant yet humorous critical writing. In it, he accused the graphic design profession of being criminal.

Piet Schreuders's design work is very different from many of his Dutch contemporaries. His work represents a part of Dutch design that has almost been forgotten. Over the past years, most of the attention that Dutch graphic design has received usually focuses on the lavishly printed, dye cut, razzle-dazzle graphics produced by such studios as UNA, Studio Dumbar, ProForma, and others. In stark contrast to these designs, Schreuders's work is often produced with little or no available budget and relates more to the experimental, self-taught approach of Hendrik N. Werkman or the early work of Hard Werken, which was strongly influenced by writing and the craft of simple, yet effective printing techniques.

It just so happened that as we were planning this issue, Piet Schreuders was participating in the symposium "America-Holland: Overseas Visions" held in The Hague in October 1990. The symposium centered around the approach of Dutch and American graphic designers in regard to various areas in graphic design. These included socially oriented graphic design, fine art and graphic design, graphic design and the computer, and the vernacular in graphic design. The latter topic was covered by Tibor Kalman and Piet Schreuders, who represented the United States and Holland respectively. In this issue we have reprinted the lecture that Piet Schreuders presented during that symposium.

Rudy VanderLans

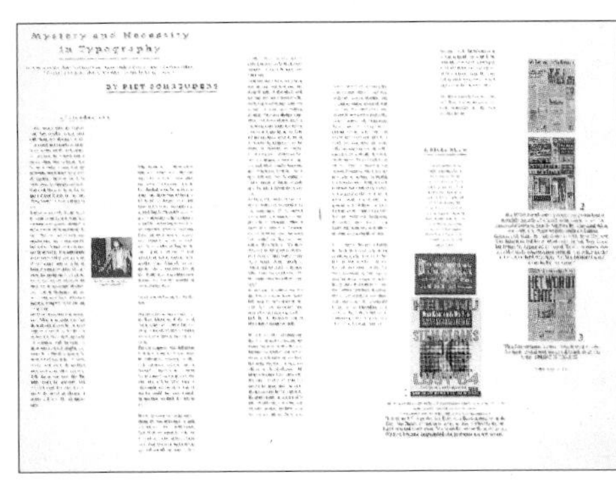

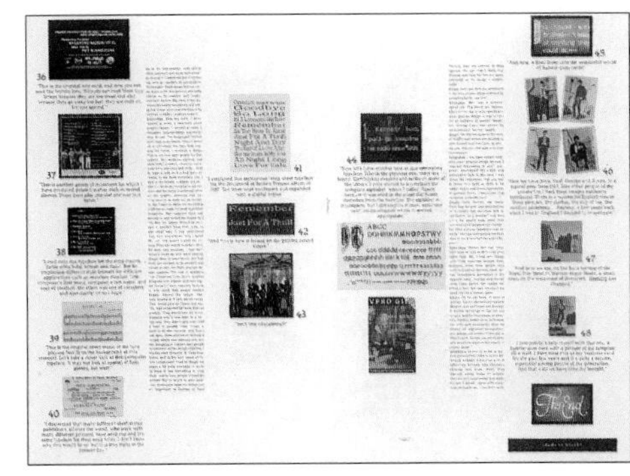

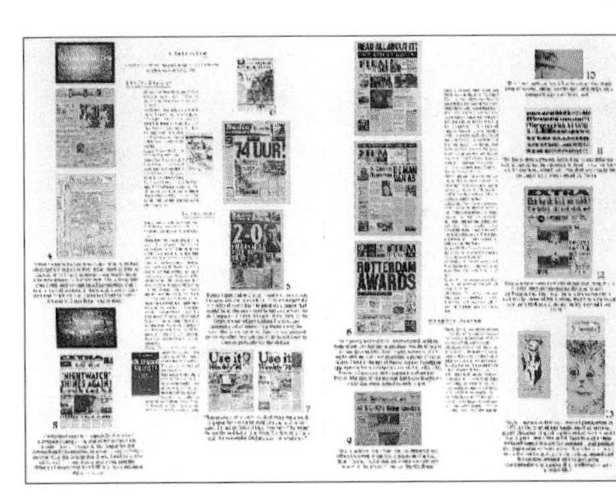

Portfolio

1

2

3

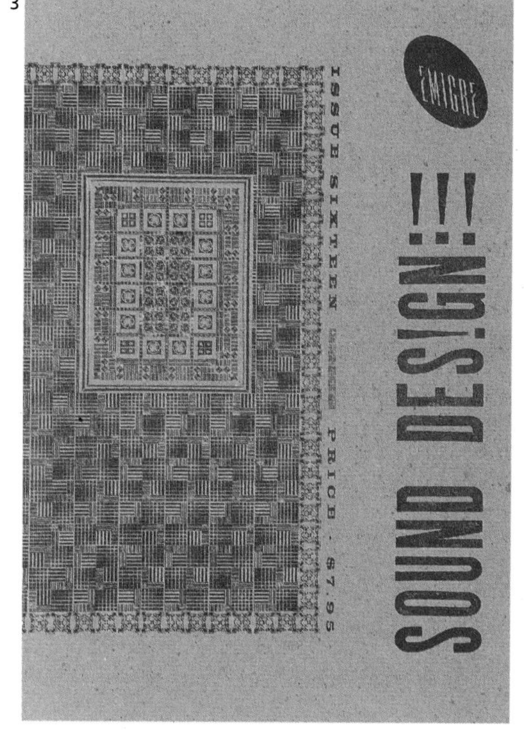

4

5

This spread and the following page:

1-3 Magazine covers, 1990
Emigre #14, #15, #16
Emigre Graphics
ReadySetGo, MacPaint, MacVision

4-9 Magazine spreads, 1988-90
Emigre #9, #11, #13, #16
Emigre Graphics
ReadySetGo, MacPaint, MacVision

3 Designed and printed by Bruce Licher

4 Illustration by John Weber

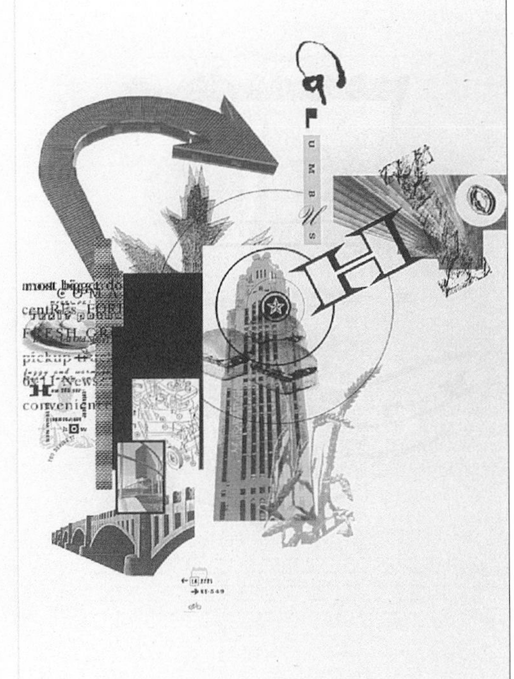
COLUMBUS, OHIO / John Weber

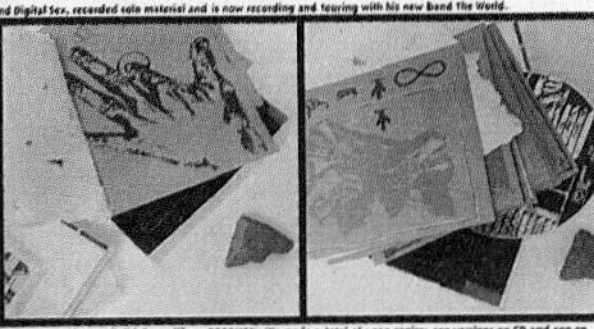

6

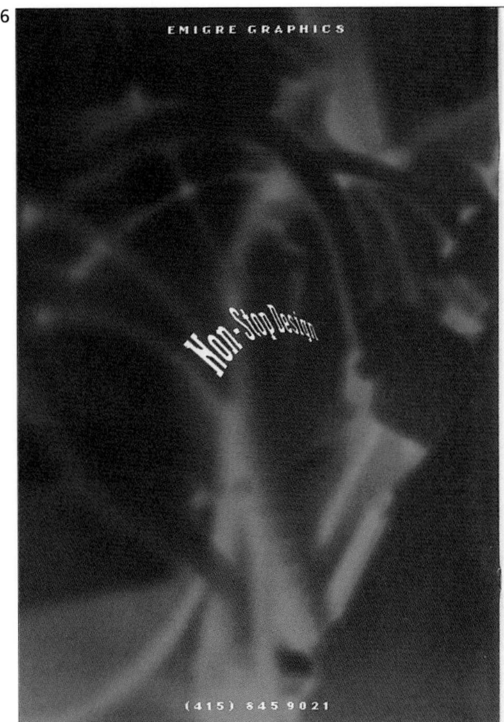
EMIGRE GRAPHICS
Non-Stop Design
(415) 845 9021

7

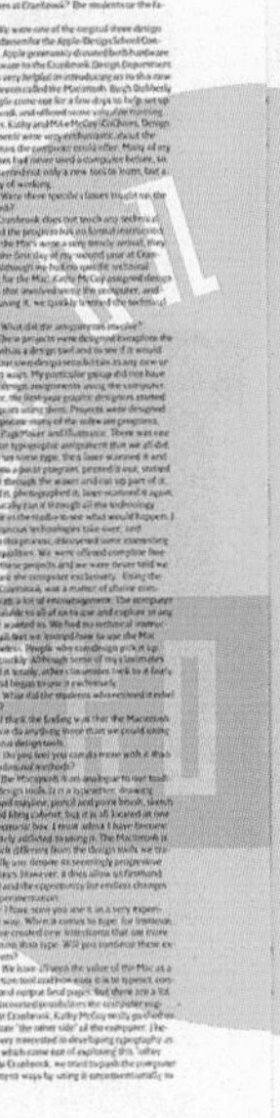

8

Nigel Grierson

Vaughan Oliver

22

23

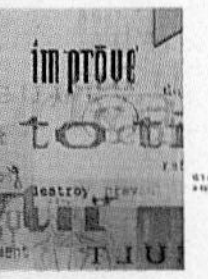

…n you are off on a whole new idea. This pioneering, **where you don't have an** … **you don't have tradition,** is both time-consuming and wonderful. **To feel** … ere are only a few areas in this very controlled industry that you can feel like that. **Emigre:** … tations lead to? **April:** There are two ways that we are pushing this technology. One is by … **eding up normal processes** of different disciplines, such as production and … **nology is a slave** and is simulating what we already know. But I think that, if we … going and other people jump in, all desperate for **new textures/new languag-** … hich it's going to advance is a **new design language.** Rather than get the language … u in English, you say, well, I know it can speak English, it does that very well, but there's … digital words really mean and say? There is a **natural language in that ma-** … in finding out what that is, and where the boundaries are. **Emigre:** How come you haven't … Macintosh? **April:** There just isn't enough time to do everything. I am such a fanatic about … such a perfectionist about it, and there are so many great typefaces that exist. It would take … ything decent and I just don't have the time. **Emigre:** Do you think that there will be an in- … ing due the Macintosh? **April:** Sure, but that happens with any new technology.

… t that. The Mac's so easy to use. It's going to be very scary. It'll be interesting to see what … years or so. Kids know how to use this now and everybody will be **modeming** and us- … **etin boards** and what not. So yes, there'll be a lot of mimicry and copying, but it will … onal design backgrounds and the people with the high-end equipment who know what they are … er. For a while, communications may be really ugly and bad. There are going to be large cor-

9

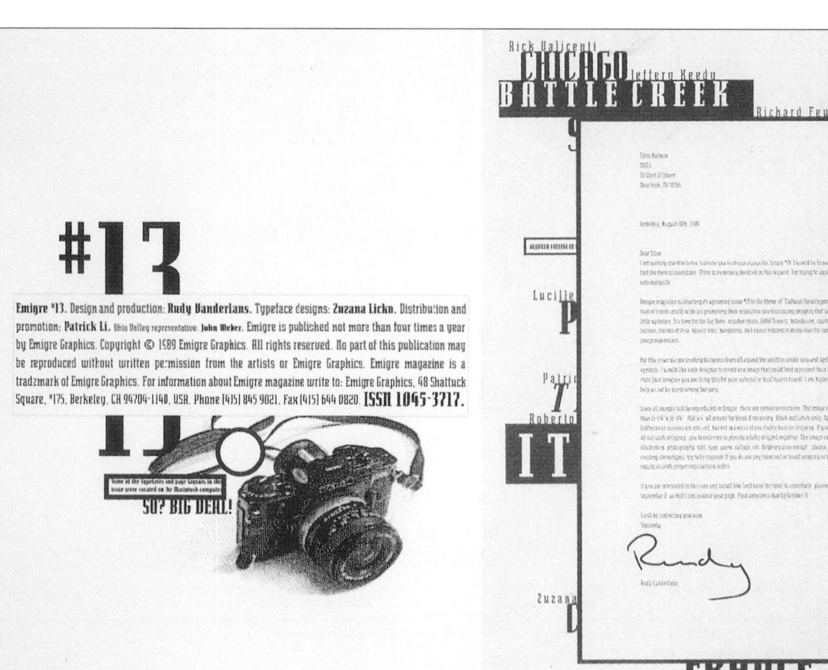

Emigre #13. Design and production: **Rudy VanderLans.** Typeface designs: **Zuzana Licko.** Distribution and promotion: **Patrick Li.** Ohio Valley representative: **John Weber.** Emigre is published not more than four times a year by Emigre Graphics. Copyright © 1989 Emigre Graphics. All rights reserved. No part of this publication may be reproduced without written permission from the artists or Emigre Graphics. Emigre magazine is a trademark of Emigre Graphics. For information about Emigre magazine write to: Emigre Graphics, 48 Shattuck Square, #175, Berkeley, CA 94704-1140, USA. Phone (415) 845 9021, Fax (415) 644 0820. **ISSN 1045-3717.**

Poster, 1988
Conpac 88
ReadySetGo, MacPaint, MacVision

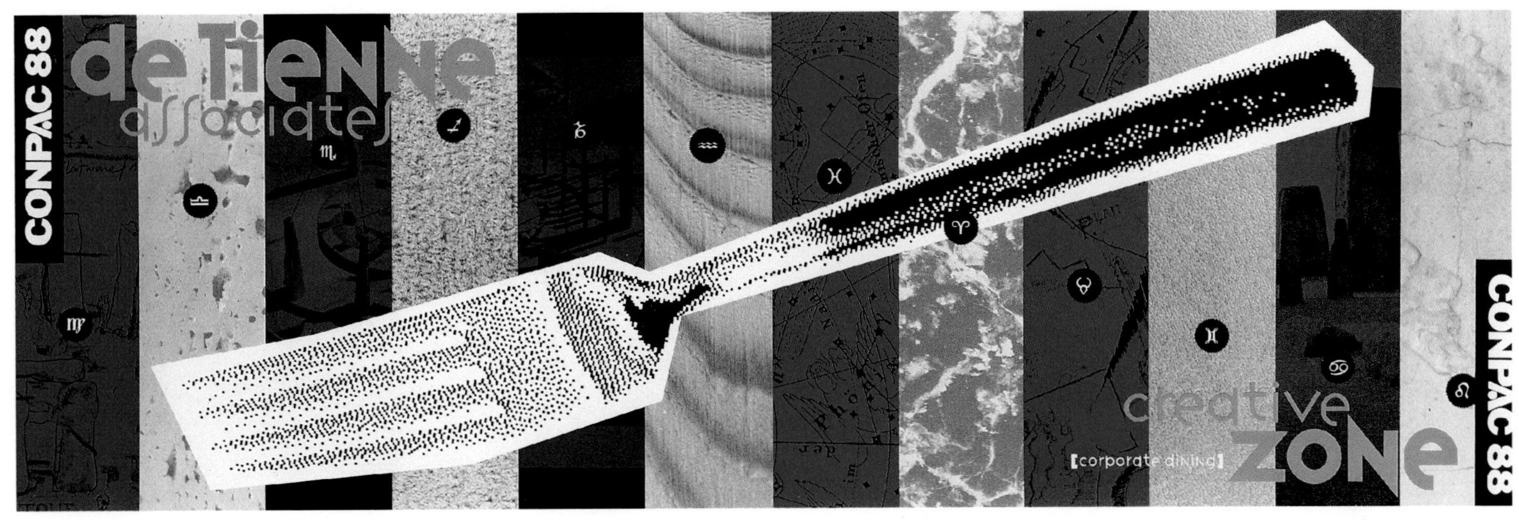

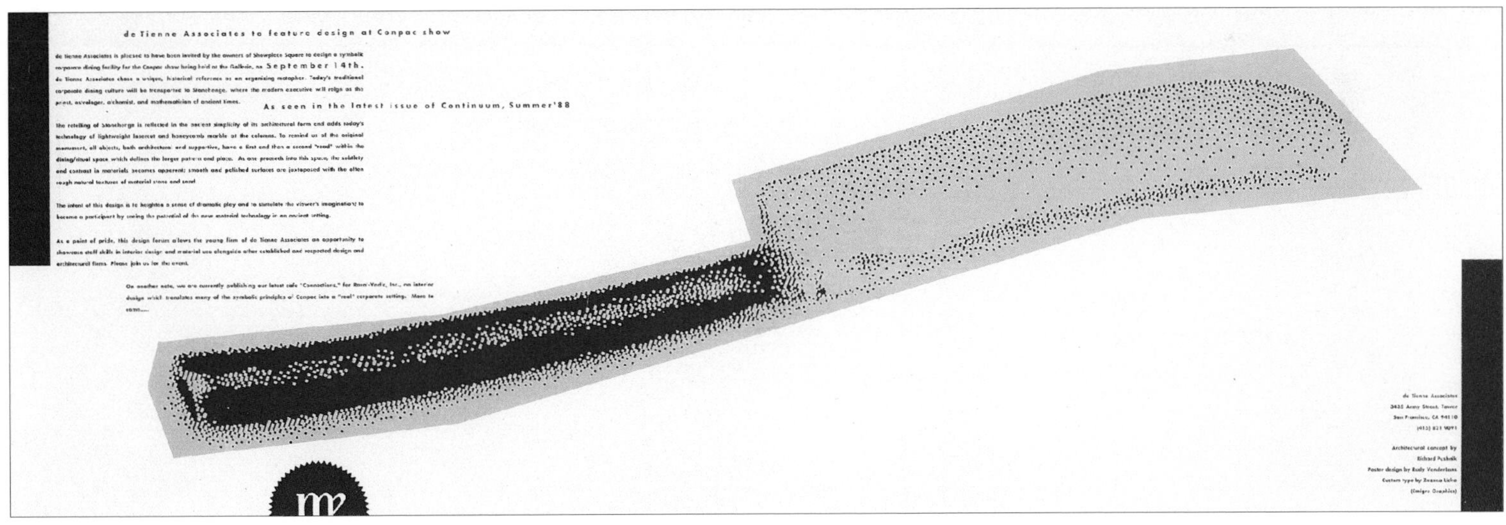

EMIGRE

Compact Discs

(Music!)

Graphic design never sounded this good.

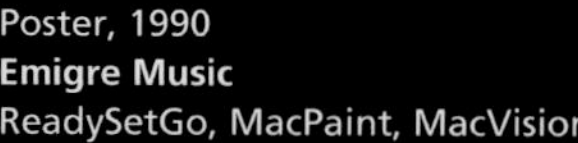

Poster, 1990
Emigre Music
ReadySetGo, MacPaint, MacVision

Poster, 1991
"Fact Twenty Two", Emigre Music
ReadySetGo

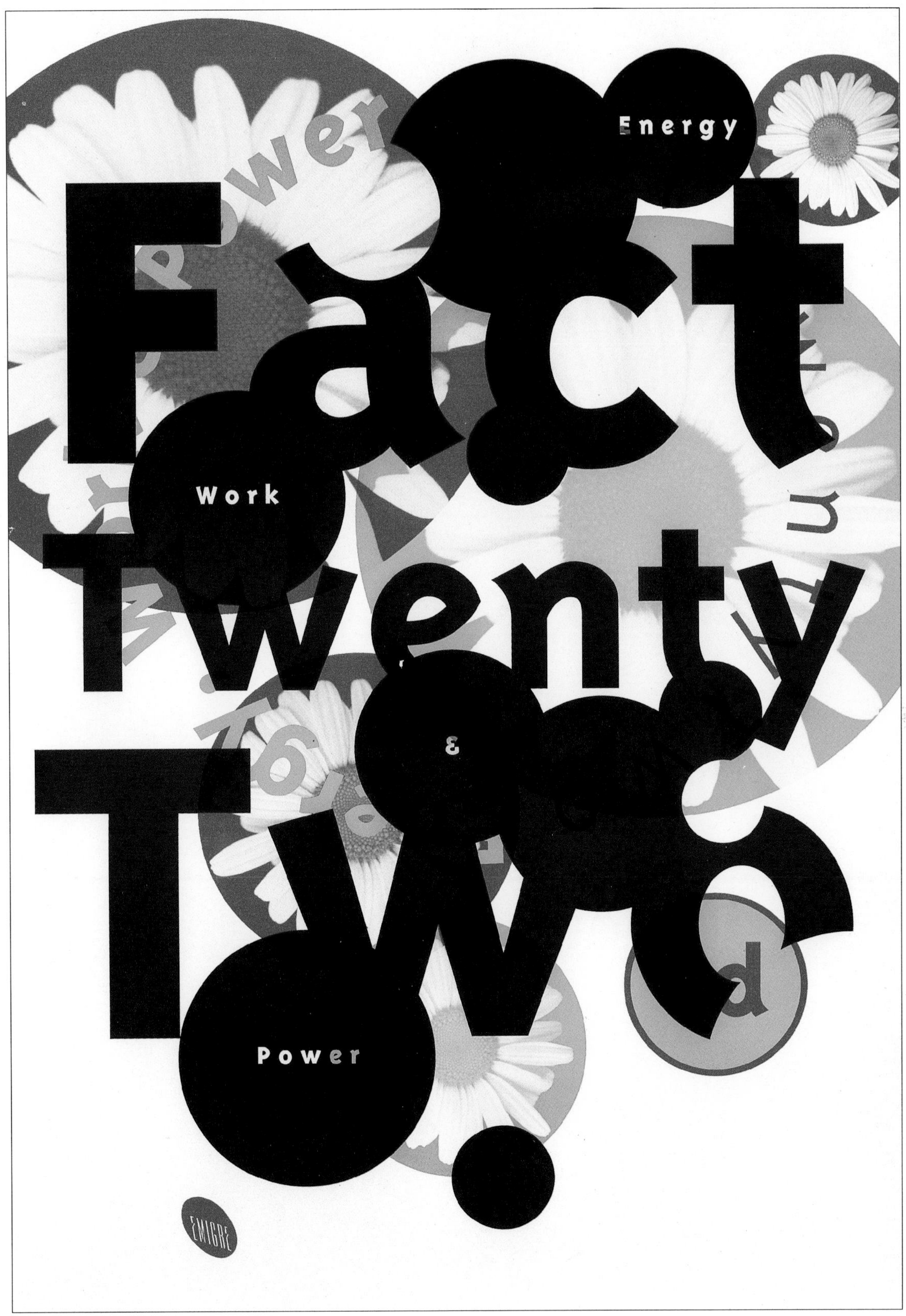

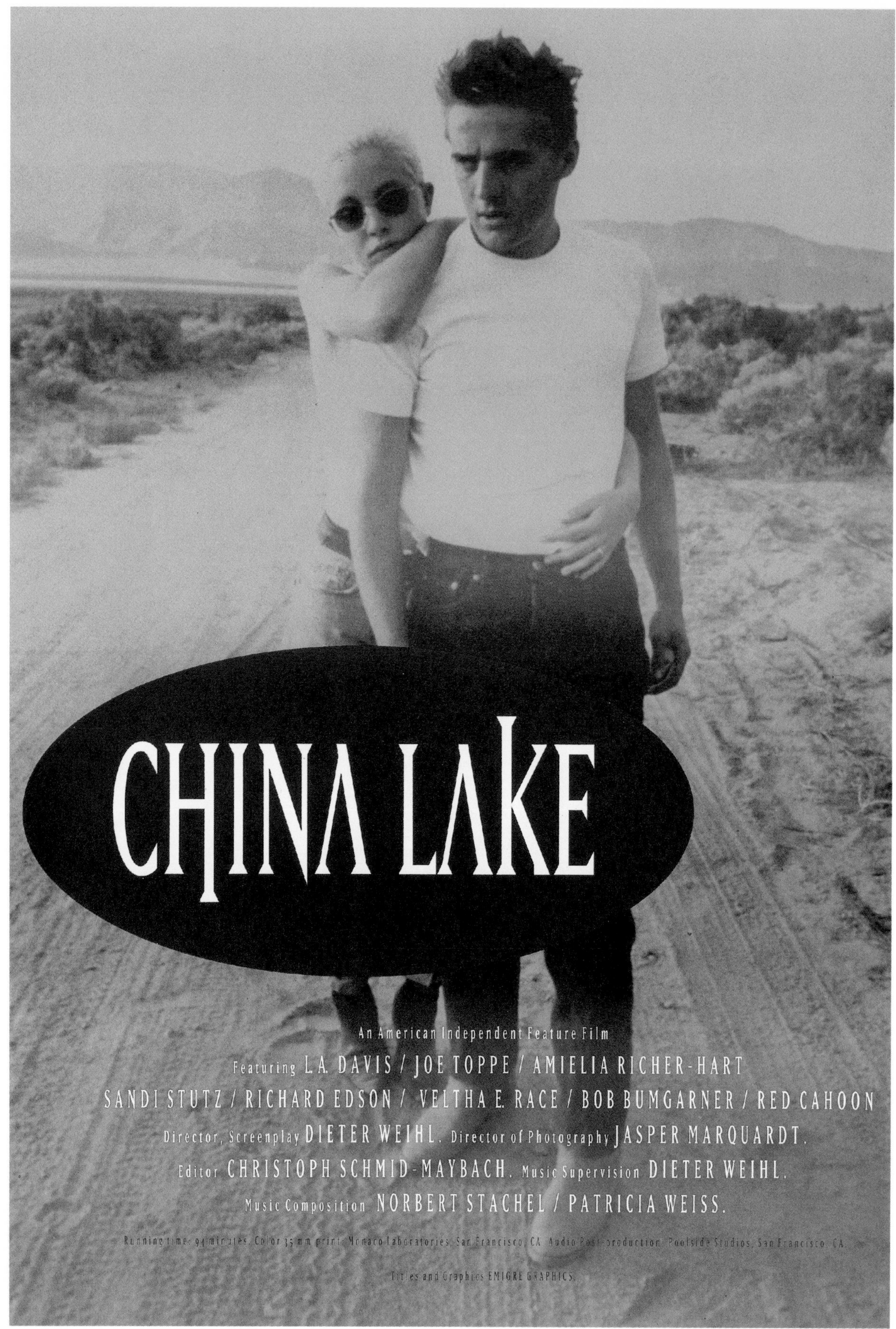
CHINA LAKE
An American Independent Feature Film
Featuring L.A. DAVIS / JOE TOPPE / AMIELIA RICHER-HART
SANDI STUTZ / RICHARD EDSON / VELTHA E. RACE / BOB BUMGARNER / RED CAHOON
Director, Screenplay DIETER WEIHL. Director of Photography JASPER MARQUARDT.
Editor CHRISTOPH SCHMID-MAYBACH. Music Supervision DIETER WEIHL.
Music Composition NORBERT STACHEL / PATRICIA WEISS.
Running time: 94 minutes. Color 35 mm print: Monaco Laboratories, San Francisco, CA. Audio Post-production: Poolside Studios, San Francisco, CA.
Titles and Graphics EMIGRE GRAPHICS.

1

2

1 **Poster**, 1989
Cairo Cinemafilms
ReadySetGo and
conventional paste-up

2 Postcard, 1989
Cairo Cinemafilms
ReadySetGo and
conventional paste-up

3 Business card, 1989
Cairo Cinemafilms
ReadySetGo and
conventional paste-up

3

1 Anouncement, 1988
Emigre Graphics
MacPaint

2 Anouncement, 1990
Emigre Graphics
ReadySetGo, MacVision

1

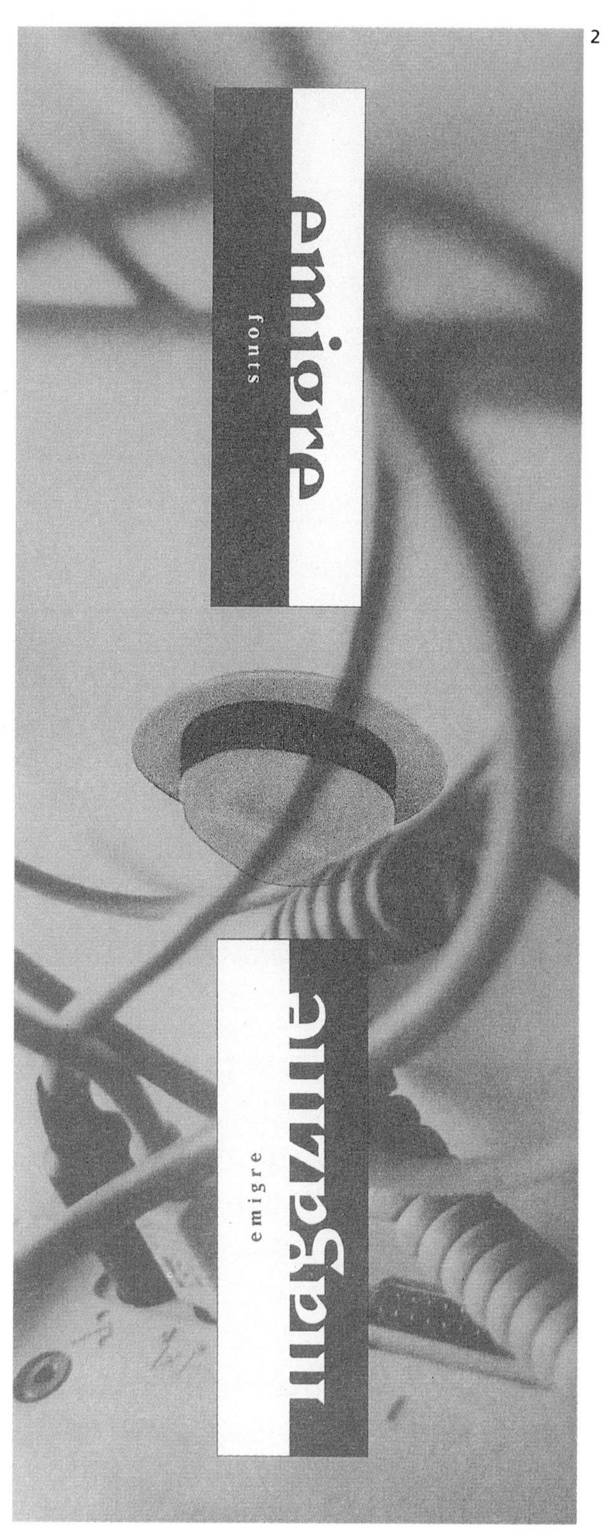

2

Poster, 1988
"The Lion Rampant", Artspace
ReadySetGo and
conventional paste-up

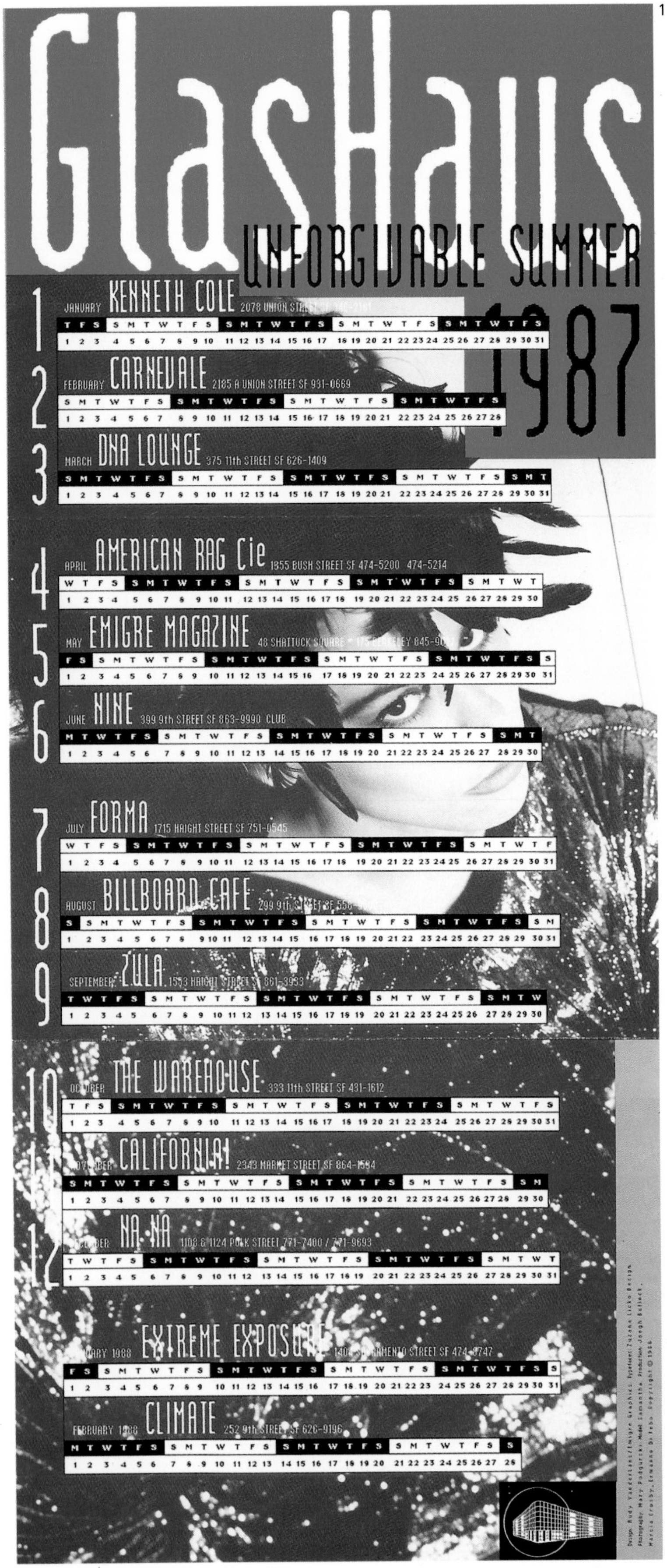

1

GlasHaus

UNFORGIVABLE SUMMER 1987

1 JANUARY KENNETH COLE 2078 UNION STREET SF

2 FEBRUARY CARNEVALE 2185 A UNION STREET SF 931-0669

3 MARCH DNA LOUNGE 375 11th STREET SF 626-1409

4 APRIL AMERICAN RAG Cie 1855 BUSH STREET SF 474-5200 474-5214

5 MAY EMIGRE MAGAZINE 48 SHATTUCK SQUARE

6 JUNE NINE 399 9th STREET SF 863-9990 CLUB

7 JULY FORMA 1715 HAIGHT STREET SF 751-0545

8 AUGUST BILLBOARD CAFE 299 9th STREET SF

9 SEPTEMBER ZULA 1553 HAIGHT STREET SF 861-3993

10 OCTOBER THE WAREHOUSE 333 11th STREET SF 431-1612

11 NOVEMBER CALIFORNIA! 2343 MARKET STREET SF 864-1554

12 DECEMBER NA NA 1108 & 1124 POLK STREET 771-7400 / 771-9693

JANUARY 1988 EXTREME EXPOSURE 1404 SACRAMENTO STREET SF 474-7747

FEBRUARY 1988 CLIMATE 252 9th STREET SF 626-9196

2

"If your feet are good it will teach you how to preserve them. If your feet are bad it will tell you why they are bad and help to save you from further agonies. It will do this because your feet are your shoes. In my life I have found that nature provides us with good feet. If your feet are bad it is because your shoes are bad. Your feet look like the shoes you wear, and if the shoes are wrongly designed your feet will be twisted, crushed, and pinched. Yet it is not necessary-not even for the sake of vanity-so to torture yourselves. We can all walk happily and be well shod, daintily shod, beautifully shod."

-Salvatore Ferragamo-

FERRAGAMO/Feet and the Famous

Continued on page 8

Continued on page 9

3

GlasHAUS

(The magazine)

The inevitable

4

1 Calendar, 1986
GlasHAUS
MacPaint and
conventional paste-up

2-3 Magazine cover and spread, 1986
GlasHAUS
ReadySetGo, MacPaint, ThunderScan
and conventional paste-up

4 Postcard, 1986
GlasHAUS
ReadySetGo and
conventional paste-up

(em'e grā)

"...THAT ODD THING, THE MIGRANT SENSIBILITY, WHOSE DEVELOPMENT I BELIEVE TO BE ONE OF THE CENTRAL THEMES OF THIS CENTURY OF DISPLACED PERSONS. TO BE A MIGRANT IS, PERHAPS, TO BE THE ONLY SPECIES OF HUMAN BEING FREE OF THE SHACKLES OF NATIONALISM. IT IS A BURDENSOME FREEDOM. ONE OF THE EFFECTS OF MASS MIGRATIONS HAS BEEN THE CREATION OF RADICALLY NEW TYPES OF HUMAN BEING: OF PEOPLE WHO ROOT THEMSELVES IN IDEAS RATHER THAN PLACES, IN MEMORIES AS MUCH AS IN MATERIAL THINGS; PEOPLE WHO HAVE BEEN OBLIGED TO DEFINE THEMSELVES – BECAUSE THEY ARE SO DEFINED BY OTHERS – BY THEIR OTHERNESS; PEOPLE IN WHOSE DEEPEST SELVES STRANGE FUSIONS OCCUR, UNPRECEDENTED UNIONS BETWEEN WHAT THEY WERE AND WHERE THEY FIND THEMSELVES. THE MIGRANT SUSPECTS REALITY: HAVING EXPERIENCED SEVERAL WAYS OF BEING, HE UNDERSTANDS THEIR ILLUSORY NATURE. TO SEE THINGS PLAINLY, YOU HAVE TO CROSS A FRONTIER."

Magazine cover, 1986
Emigre #6
MacPaint and conventional paste-up

Following page:

Business forms, 1987
Pam Pastrana
ReadySetGo and
conventional paste-up

PAMELA J. PASTRANA

CUSTOM WOOD WORK
P

PAMELA J. PASTRANA
CUSTOM WOOD WORK
P
1775 YOSEMITE STREET, SUITE E
SAN FRANCISCO, CA 94124
(415) 822 5144

PAMELA J. PASTRANA
CUSTOM WOOD WORK
P
1775 YOSEMITE STREET, SUITE E
SAN FRANCISCO, CA 94124
1775 YOSEMITE STREET, SUITE E
SAN FRANCISCO, CA 94124
(415) 822 5144

Annex
SF
ARTSPACE
SAN FRANCISCO ARTSPACE
1286 FOLSOM STREET
SAN FRANCISCO, CA 94103
[415] 626 9100

SAN FRANCISCO ARTSPACE
1286 FOLSOM STREET
SAN FRANCISCO, CA 94103

Previous page:

Business forms, 1988
Artspace
ReadySetGo and
conventional paste-up

variex light, varlex regular & varlex bold

a b c d e f g h i j k l m n
o p q q r s s t u v w x y z i
2 3 4 5 6 7 8 9 0

single line stroke characters (left) require fewer data points and therefore take up less memory space than double outline shapes (right) two separate outlines are usually needed to describe the delicate tapering shapes of traditional letterforms.

varlex letterforms have been reduced to the basic powerful gestures of primitive writing hands. elements from capitals and lower case are combined into a single alphabet. relying on a single set of characters eliminates the redundancy of upper and lower-case symbols. several alternative characters are provided for headline applications where optimal letter combinations are crucial. each character is defined by centerlines of uniform weight, from which the three weights are also derived.

varlex
varlex
varlex

varying the weight of a stroke typeface changes the thickness around the centerline and thus alters the alignment of some characters. varlex incorporates these variations of alignment in its design, making adjustments to the centerlines unnecessary when changing the weight.

Font catalog, 1990
Emigre Graphics
MacPaint, MacDraw

Susumu Endo

Susumu Endo has been called mysterious, a conjurer, a magician. His photographic images seem not of this world, but employ a skill and beauty that challenge our sense of reality. ¶ Though he finished high school in 1953, it wasn't until his graduation from Kuwasawa Design School in 1962 and the subsequent five years spent in a small design studio that his real work began. The first notice of his work came from a calendar he produced for Audio-Technica, an audio equipment company, and still one of his leading clients today. Since that time, his images have appeared commercially and in the collections of museums throughout Europe and Japan. ¶ After years of spinning his magic using manual photographic techniques, in 1982 Endo began using the Scitex Response System, allowing this computer system to aid in the technically complex task of creating his photographic works. With Adobe's revolutionary new software, Photoshop, the Macintosh became capable of performing the tasks required to reproduce the images that live in this sorcerer's mind.

The studio.

How is it that you came to use computers in your work?

My work is often used commercially in calendars, for example, or in advertising. At the same time, I am a lithographer, using the same images, but reproducing limited lithographic editions. The subject is the same, but the final products are quite different. Photographic images are the main element of my graphic design. I am a self-educated photographer and I used to do everything from the very beginning to the final stage of graphic design by myself, using photographic techniques only.

My basic concept of design is "space and space." I feel there are different levels of consciousness that we can have of space, all coexisting at once. This is the concept that drives all the work I create. My main theme is the relationship of two different dimensions in space: the real and the imaginary. I feel a strong image can give us entrance to the other, unseen world. All my works are "space and space"; only at the very last stage of a piece do I create a title. I don't use romantic titles very much and often name works simply, like the name of the objects in the picture.

In the early days, ideas often stayed in my mind for two or three years, until I could figure out how to produce them. Sometimes it took several years until I finally found the way to photograph an object to obtain the desired effect. For example, some of my work may appear to be airbrushed, but it is not; I often use a 4 x 5 camera with a piece of white paper placed in front of the lens to blur the image. Or I might arrange an object, a bottle, for example, on one side of the composition area and take one photograph, and then move it to the other side and take another photograph. Finally, I might combine the two, three, or sometimes four transparencies to produce the finished print.

Even though I was not using computers in creating my early work, people thought I had, since my images included many touches and devices that seemed only a computer could create. I had a reputation as one who designed in a strange and mysterious way. Friends and other designers recommended that I start using a computer in my work. So when the Scitex Response System was first introduced in Japan, about 10 years ago, I accepted it quite naturally.

At that time, the first project for which I used the Response System was to create a calendar for the West German paper company, Zanders. Zanders had invited leading graphic designers from around the world to submit a design, and I decided to create my contribution with the aid of the Scitex Response System.

The original engineers for Scitex, in Israel, had never thought about the Response System being used creatively; to them, the system was just a matter of convenience. They were astonished to see my work with it.

The Response System made it much easier to combine films for printing, but there are certain effects that are still better to create photographically. For example, the computer cannot create really subtle, natural-looking gradations. Or sometimes you have to use the whiteness of photograph itself; otherwise the finished art looks very unnatural since the whiteness of a computer image does not have the same texture as that of a photographic image. So in some ways my work was very far from being computer-like. Yet the Response System made it possible to do certain things more effectively.

To me, the most important thing was to understand how I could make a good mix between the computer's abilities and traditional photographic solutions. My previous manual technique, before I used the Response System, was based on the same principle as the Response, in the sense that they both combined images.

Susumu Endo's son, Etsuro, hard at work.

How did you first learn about the Macintosh?

I had been using the Scitex Response System to produce a lot of work since 1982. So in my case, the Macintosh was brought into my office because its capabilities, and especially those of Adobe Photoshop, were really suitable for my design expression, and I could naturally switch from the Response to the Macintosh. The reasons that I started using the Macintosh were the very same reasons why I had started using the Response System — it was conducive to producing the types of images I wished to create.

My son was very interested in computers and he introduced me to the Macintosh. Most of the technical information on how to make the Macintosh and Photoshop work for me came from my son. As you know, Photoshop requires a high level of knowledge about printing techniques, especially for my type of application. So at first, I asked my son to show me all the functions of the Macintosh and Photoshop. We tried to create simulations of what the Response System could do, and we found the two were comparable.

Even now, very often I am busy and have to take a fairly long time to think about the technical aspects of how to express an element on the Macintosh rather than thinking about the element itself. So I needed, and still need, a lot of help from my son. He may be the one of the most knowledgeable people in Japan about Photoshop.

There are more and more people who are now using the Macintosh in Japan. Some designers bought the Macintosh because they were interested in the new things the Macintosh could offer them. In my case, the Macintosh was brought into my office because it was especially suited to creating my images as I had been making them for years.

What's different about the Macintosh from the Scitex Response System?

First of all, I think the Macintosh is in some ways more advanced than the Response System. The monitor of the Macintosh is better than that of Response. The monitor of the Response System has too shiny a glare; the Macintosh monitor is more natural. When using the Response System, I had to constantly keep in mind that the color of its monitor was completely different from that of the printed piece. I felt that the difference between the Response monitor and the colors it reproduced in print was too large. But the color of Macintosh is, by comparison, very close to the actual printed color. More conveniently, on the Macintosh, I can check the approximate percentage of each process color on the screen.

Another basic difference between the Macintosh and the Response System is that Response is based only on CMYK, cyan, magenta, yellow and black, the three primary printing colors plus black. However, the Macintosh uses RGB, that is, red, green, and blue, which are the three primary colors of luminescence. So I can control the color balance, the contrast, or other finely-tuned color characteristics, as I like. And the newest version of Photoshop has added the capability, for the first time, to edit CMYK directly.

Finally, as you know, the hourly cost of working on the Response System with a qualified operator is very expensive compared to working on the Macintosh. With the Macintosh I can work right here in my own office; I don't have to go out to a special studio.

Some of Endo's preliminary sketches.

How exactly do you work with Adobe Photoshop on the Macintosh?

I am always drawing rough sketches, day and night, throughout the year. Sometimes these sketches are fairly rough, but I always start with a sketch. Once I'm through with these sketches, I make a decision on what kind of final image I should make. Then I start to write out all of the production steps of the process from beginning to end, just as I did for the Response. However, this process review still is based in imagination only, as I can't always detail the exact steps required to get the "final" image, which at that point is living only in my mind. Sometimes I have had to fine-tune my ideas once I was working at the computer, but I do try to figure out the correct general order of the production process before I start, or I may never get exactly the right result.

Basically, if you don't have a firm idea of the concept, you will never be able to create your desired final image. The computer provides a wide variety of attractive possibilities. It shows you a lot of interesting things. You must, however, simplify it as much as possible. If you want to try a new effect that would take you away from your original idea, I think it's best to try it in another piece. I don't want the computer to take the initiative; the computer's temptations are unlimited, especially in the choice of colors you can create on the screen.

The first production step is taking the photographs. As I do so, I have an image of the finished art in my mind. I always had it, even when I used the Response, or even before that, in the days when I employed a variety of photographic techniques, such as putting two films together and having them scanned in together.

After the photographs are taken, I have the transparencies scanned in on the Scitex system; this ensures the highest quality image. Each photograph is scanned in separately.

When I was ready to combine images on the Response System, I had to make really complex, detailed color indications for the Response operator. When using the Macintosh, this is not necessary. You can simply work directly on the screen. Often I take notes while simulating one effect that will be useful for another part of an image.

From time to time, I do make a last minute change to my original idea, but these changes mainly relate to the colors, as opposed to the composition, since the computer offers an almost unlimited selection of color hues. But I try to concentrate on the initial image created in my mind. It's great to be able to see colors change directly on the screen; it's so different from the Response System, for which you had to go to the printing company to check, or just hope you were right until press proofs were ready. I know how to indicate the right colors through long experience, but being able to look directly at the colors and see them instantly is a big difference.

I work with the images in many ways. As for the colors, I sometimes change the color of the plates in Photoshop; for example, by changing the yellow plate to the magenta one, or making one plate negative. Many of the effects I wish to create are done by changing parts of an image from positive to negative.

In the beginning, one of the problems we had was that my way of thinking, or my technique, was not described in the Photoshop manual. We could only come up with what we wanted by guessing, using the explanations in the manual just as a basis.

Once we have completed the image in Photoshop, we send it on optical disk to be output to film on the Scitex Visionary System. Often we have at least five films; for example, cyan, magenta, yellow, black, and silver, which will often be printed under the process colors. Of course, you can't make silver on the

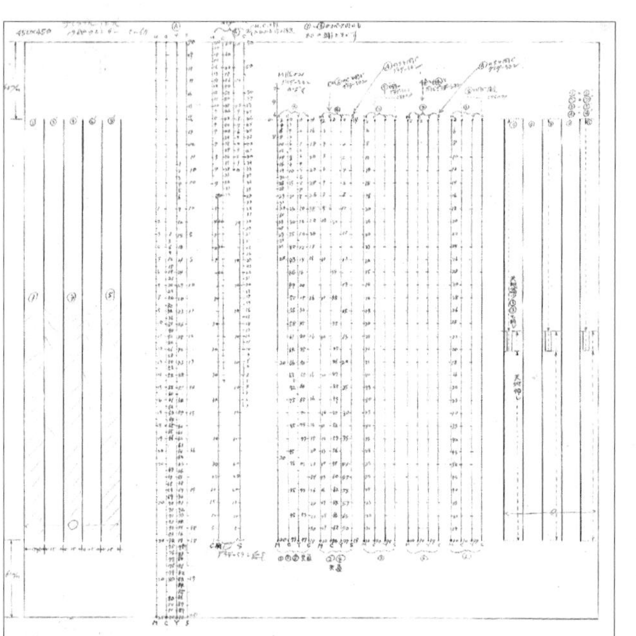

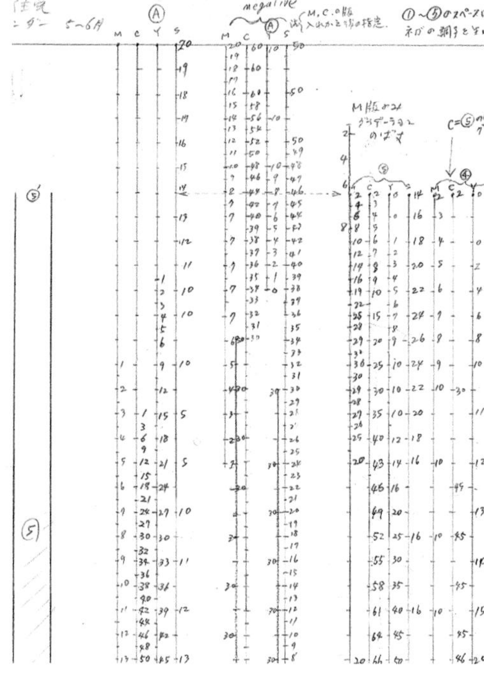

Detail from the complex specifications that were needed to communicate Endo's ideas to the Response operator before he began using the Macintosh.

Macintosh screen, but we use a special channel in Photoshop to simulate silver, based on my experience with what the final effect will be when they are all printed together.

What are some of the problems you encounter using the Macintosh for your work?

One of the biggest problems we had with Photoshop 1.0 is that it does not address the color black in the way Japanese printers use it. The way of thinking about black is completely different between Japan and the United States. In the case of Japanese printing, the basic idea is to try to specify black mainly as cyan, magenta, and yellow, and use black only to supplement CMY. But in the United States, black ink is used much more, especially in magazine publishing. So for my work, I create my own black curve and change the balance of black.

Also, I was not entirely pleased with the appearance of gradations in the earlier versions of Photoshop; it didn't satisfy my sense of how they should look. If you looked carefully, you could see the discrepancy in gradations, especially in gray tones. Once I even had to create the gradations in an image on the Response System, and the rest was done in Photoshop. Now, with the recent version of Photoshop, however, this problem has been almost entirely eliminated.

What's would your advice be to other designers who don't like the idea of using computers?

I always try to convince other designers to use computers. Maybe the younger generation is different, but people of my generation are very hesitant. They simply don't like it; they don't understand what's happening, what's going on. Possibly 90% of my generation has doubts about using computers. I think that maybe they feel have no control over it.

I have young staff in my office, and young staff in general show an interest in computers. Showing an interest is the most important step in starting something. When the younger staff encounter a computer, they think it is great. At this moment, the major percentage of the top Japanese graphic designers of the older generation don't use computers. But in some studios, where there is a young staff working for an older graphic designer, the young designers will start using the computer, and this might arouse the older guy's interest. I actually haven't mastered every operational, technical detail of the Macintosh myself, but this won't be a problem as long as I have young people in my studio.

My work hasn't changed since I brought the Macintosh into my studio. However, since the computer has many advantages, such as the rich variety of colors, or making it easy to create compositions, designers can profit from these to improve their designs. These advantages help the designer like me a lot. The basic flow of the job, though, has not changed.

With or without the computer, my way of thinking has always been the same. I try to think about ideas all the time, day and night. It's like I having a film library in my mind that I can explore.

Step by Step

As part of a series of work, Susumu Endo created "Space & Space / Nature / Branch 2." The theme of this series is the exploration of new dimensions of space in nature. "Space & Space / Nature / Branch 2" was first created as a limited edition print. Later, Endo was commissioned by Chemiway-Maruzen, a chemical company, to use the image for a promotional calendar.

Once a transparency of Endo's original photograph was scanned, Endo used Adobe Photoshop to create the image he envisioned. The original was changed and saved in several different versions, then all were combined to create the final. Photoshop's ability to control fine nuances of color, including hue and lightness, to create masks, and to combine various images made it possible to produce this complex work from one photograph.

Endo's images always begin with a small sketch, in which he notes the overall idea that resides in his mind. The way the image should look is fixed prior to beginning its production.

For this image, the original transparency was scanned at 100 pixels per centimeter on a Crossfield Scantex Scanner. It was then opened in Adobe Photoshop and cropped slightly.

Endo then began preparing different versions of the image that would be merged together to create the final. The first version was made by using the original image file and making a negative of it using Photoshop's Invert command. Various adjustments were made to the hue, contrast and brightness settings of the inverted image, and the file was saved as "Step 1".

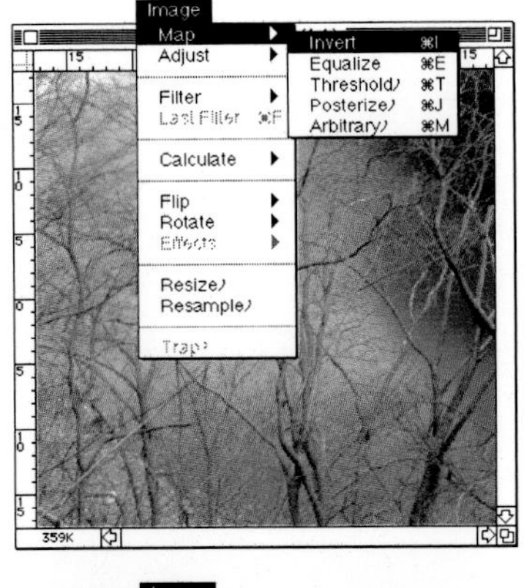

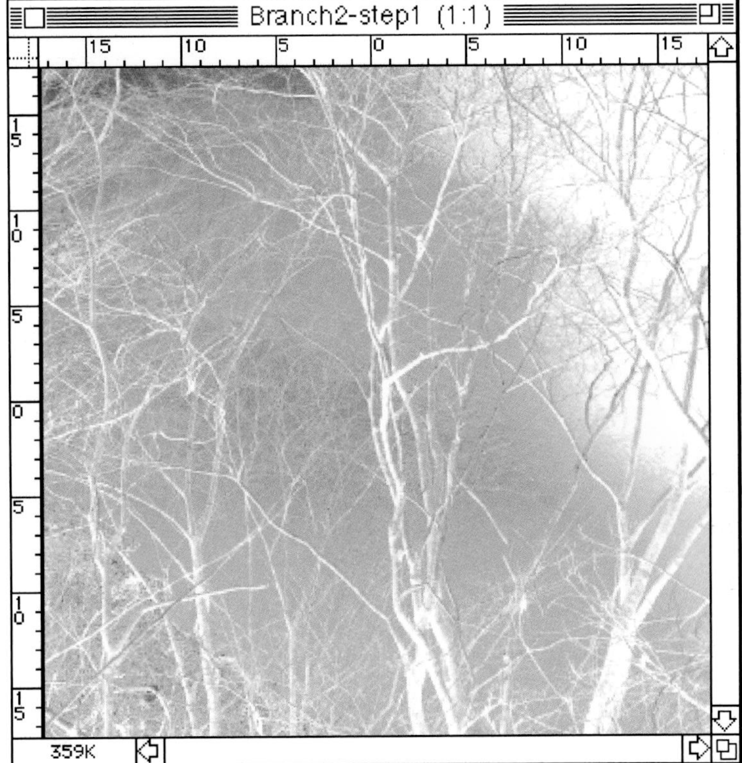

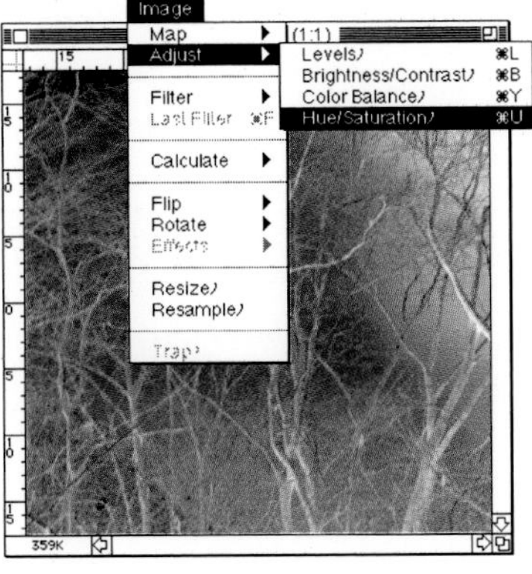

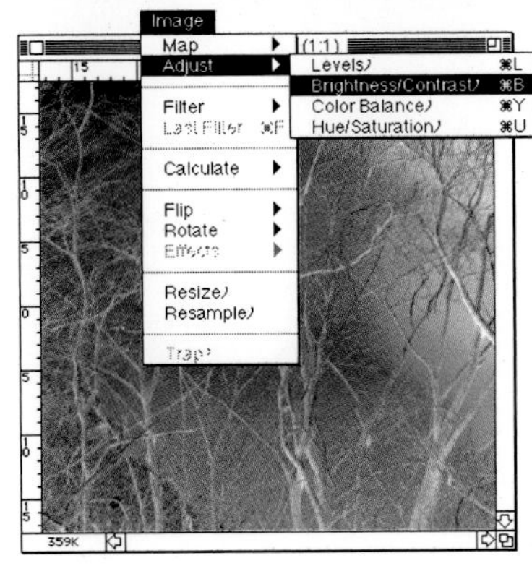

The second version of the file was created by again opening the original image, and adjusting the lightness setting. Endo then selected the top half of the image precisely using numerical settings in the selection tool dialog box. The selected top half was made negative using the Invert command. The bottom half of the image was selected, and various adjustments to hue, saturation and brightness were made.

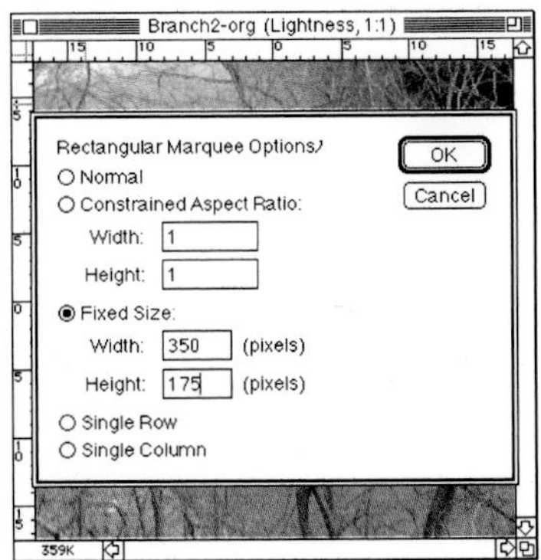

The next step was to create a mask that would be used to combine the previous version of the image, "Step 1", with the current image. A new channel was made, and the blend tool was used to create the desired mask.

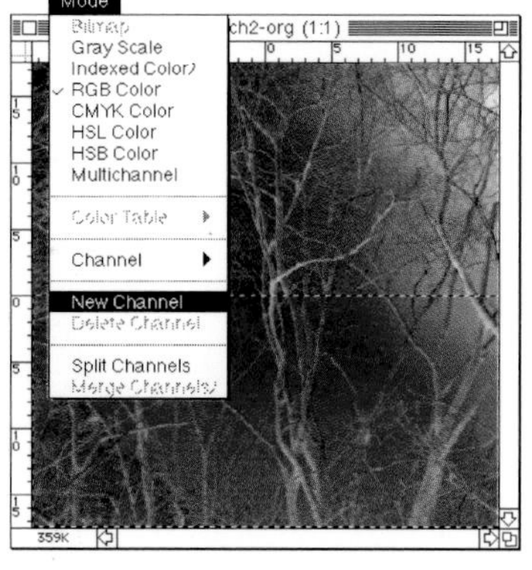

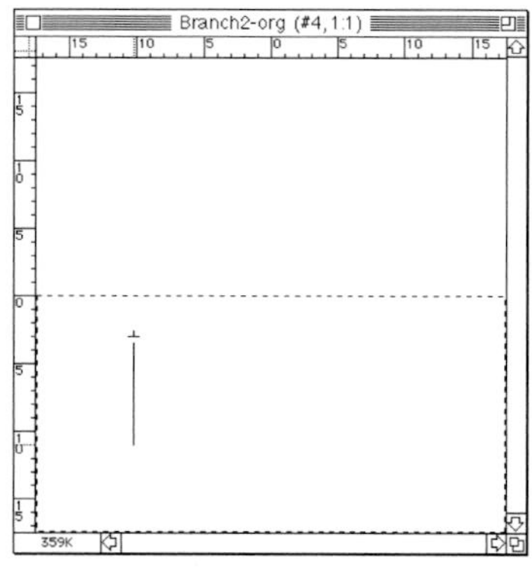

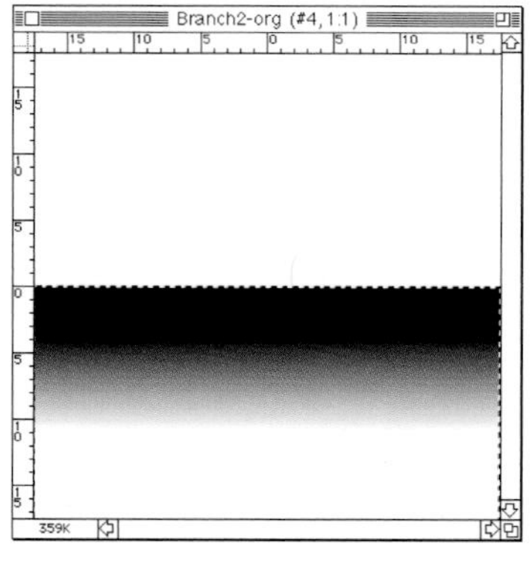

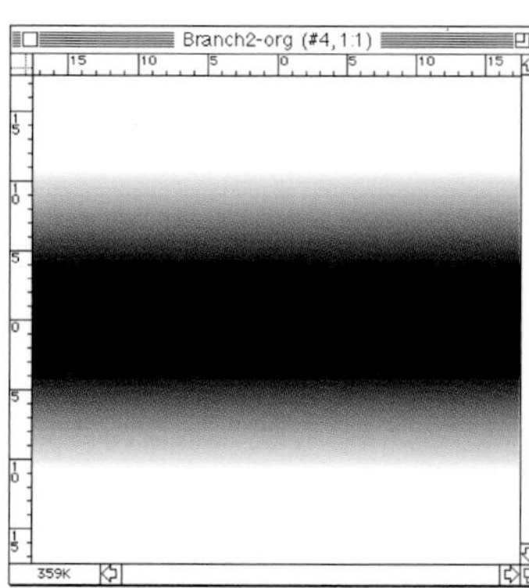

The Composite command was used to combine the "Step 1" file with the parts of the second file that would show through the mask. The resulting image was saved as "Step 2".

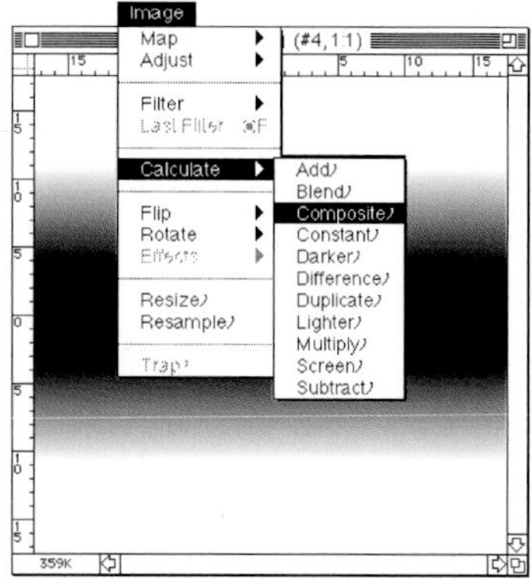

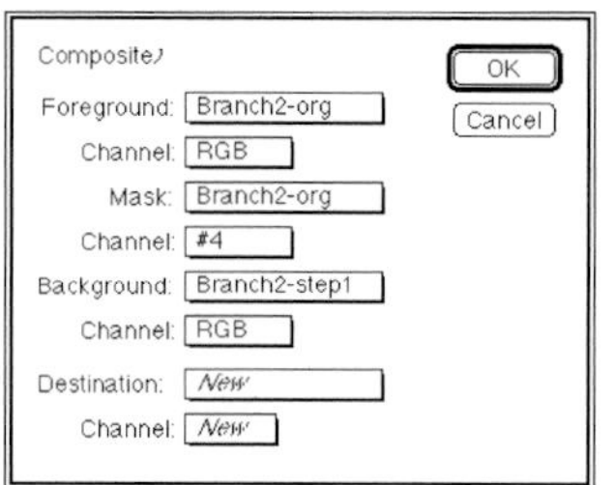

The next image was prepared by selecting the outer edges of the original and changing the brightness and contrast settings. Another mask was created in preparation for combining the images. The file was then combined with the file "Step 2", which produced a new composite, called "Step 3."

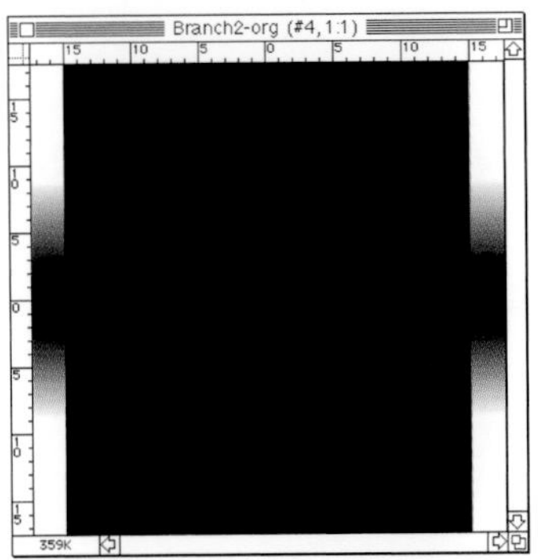

The final image was prepared by once again opening the original image. This time, the center of the image was selected and adjustments were made to the hue, brightness and contrast of the selected area. A mask was created, and the current image was combined with "Step 3" to produce the final composite image. Slight adjustments were made to hue settings to fine tune the final color. The file was then sent on an optical disk to a printing company where it was output directly to film on a Scitex Raystar imagesetter.

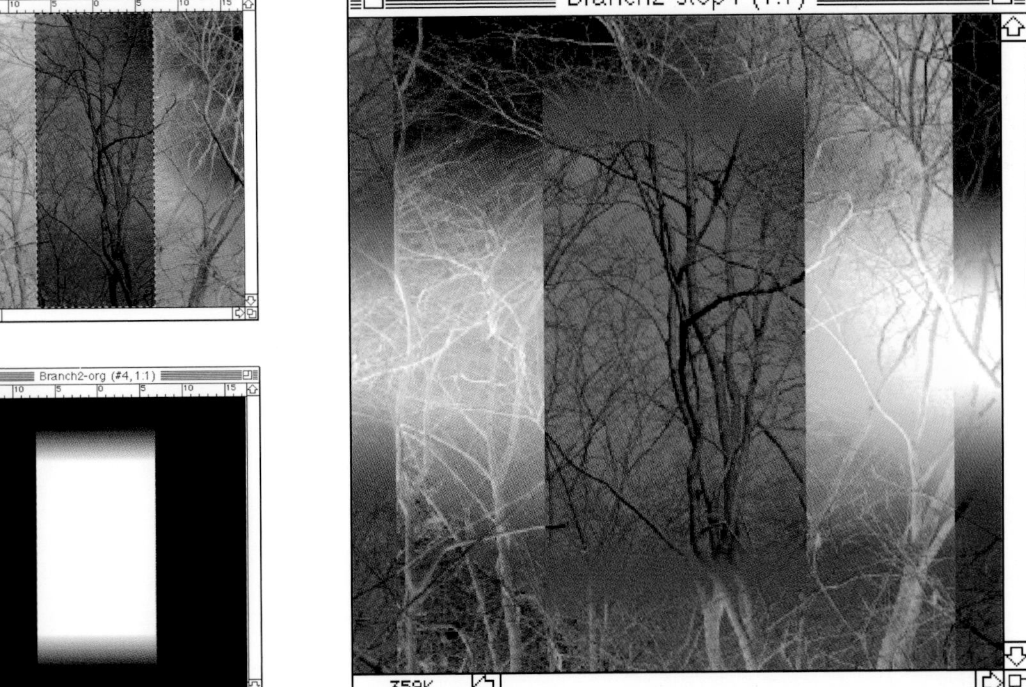

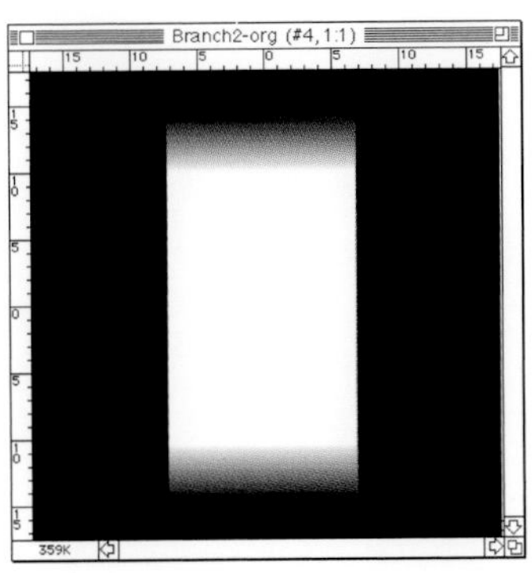

Portfolio

Book cover, 1990
Rikuyo-sha
Adobe Photoshop and conventional paste-up

Book cover, 1990
Rikuyo-sha
Adobe Photoshop and
conventional paste-up

Adobe Photoshop™
PostScript

Previous page:

Poster, 1991
Adobe Systems Incorporated
Adobe Photoshop, Adobe Illustrator

This page:

Calendar, 1991
Audio-technica
Adobe Photoshop, Adobe Illustrator

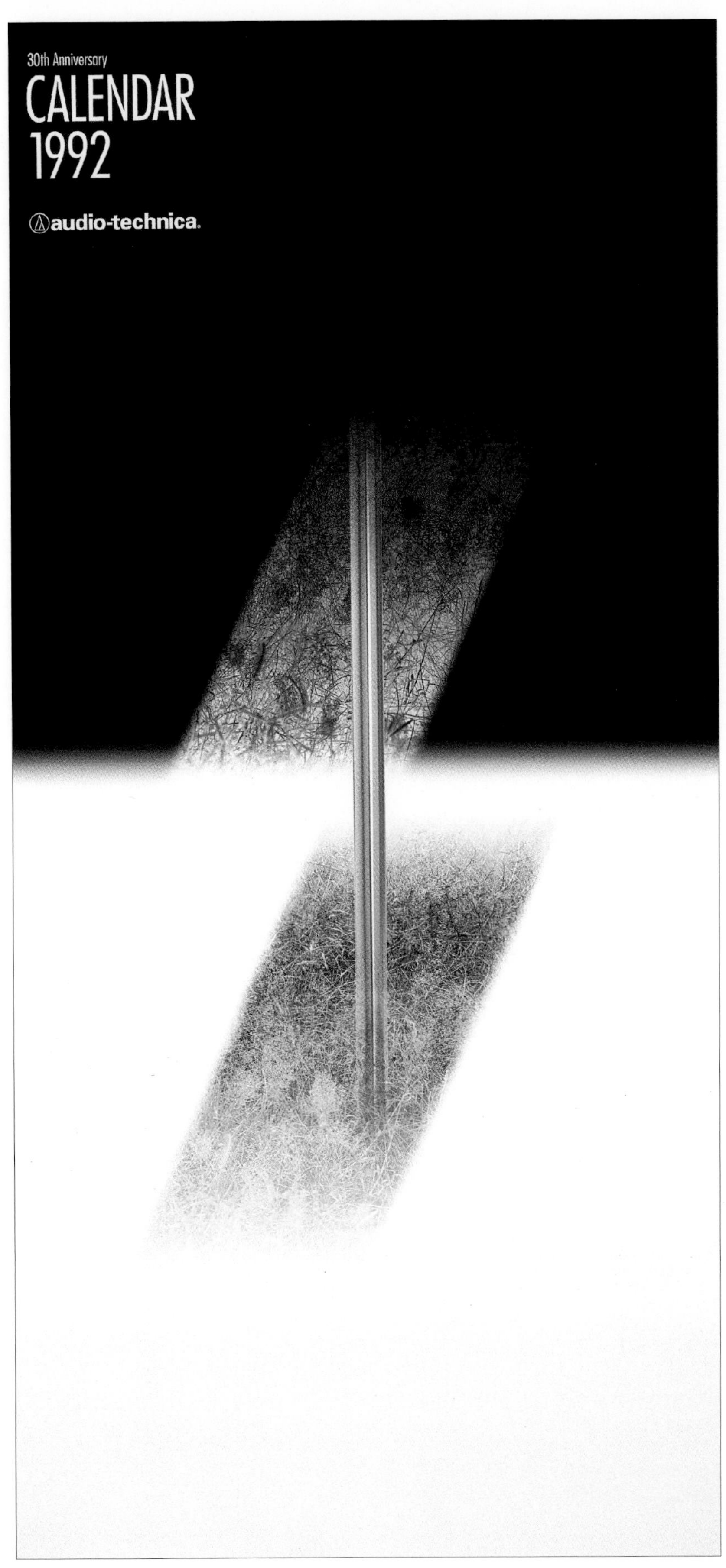

"Space & Space / Wood 3", 1991
personal
Adobe Photoshop

"Space & Space / Forest 91E", 1991
personal
Adobe Photoshop

"Space & Space / Forest 91A", 1991
personal
Adobe Photoshop

"Space & Space / Egg 6", 1990
personal
Adobe Photoshop

"Space & Space / Bottle 10", 1991
personal
Adobe Photoshop

"Space & Space / Forest 91C", 1991
personal
Adobe Photoshop

"Space & Space / Light Bulb 7", 1990
personal
Adobe Photoshop

"Space & Space / Forest 91B", 1991
personal
Adobe Photoshop

April Greiman Inc.

April Greiman is often associated with the movement known as "California New Wave." Her education, however, took place in the traditional world of the Swiss Basel Allgemeine Gewerbeschule, after which she joined the faculty at the Philadelphia College of Art. In 1976,Greiman visited Los Angeles and within a few months relocated. The early days included work for a variety of progressive clients and in 1982, Greiman became Director of Visual Commnication at the California Institute of the Arts. Not one to fall into and remain part of a single movement or look, Greiman's work has continued evolving over the years as she has served a diverse assortment of clients, from developing identities for trendy Hollywood clubs to creating television spots for Esprit and Lifetime Television. ¶ Today, April Greiman Inc. is a leading international design firm. Greiman's aesthetic, which she has dubbed "Hybrid Imagery," has developed as a result of her daring, her intuition, and her experimental use of a variety of technologies, including the Macintosh.

You've worked with a lot of different technologies, but was the Macintosh the first computer you worked with?

Before the Macintosh came along, I was involved in experimenting with video in print. But as for computers, the Macintosh was the first one I used, except for working on a mainframe a bit at the California Institute of the Arts in 1982, where I was the Director of the Visual Communications Program. I can't remember exactly what kind of computer it was, but I do remember it had some kind of color synthesizer. I was using a video camera to enter images on video tape, then layering them and re-coloring them using a bigger computer. It was one of those single-task, bozo pieces of equipment that you could do a couple of things with and then call it a day. The problem with high-end technology is that it really is, nearly, single task oriented, so it obsolesces quickly. Who wants to spend a year or two learning how to use one program? And who wants to spend a year or two just doing one thing?

That's one of the good things about the Macintosh; it's very profound in that it can do so many different kinds of tasks, and these also integrate with other technologies into one digital language, one common weave. We just created some television spots for Lifetime Cable Television. We did all the sketching on the Macintosh, using MacroMind Director, and we actually completely designed two of the five and ten second spots on the Macintosh. We then went directly from the Macintosh to the Harry. The Harry is a high-end video editing and animation tool, which is what is usually used for broadcast quality video editing. The Macintosh is a lot easier and less expensive to use.

Soon we'll start using the sound capabilities on the Macintosh and incorporate them into our video work. We'll probably make mistakes along the way, but then, I've built an entire career on "mistakes." In our studio we may call something an error; meanwhile others call us "authorities."

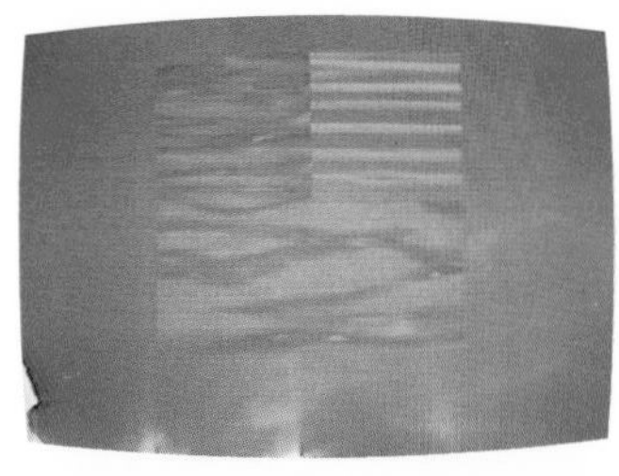

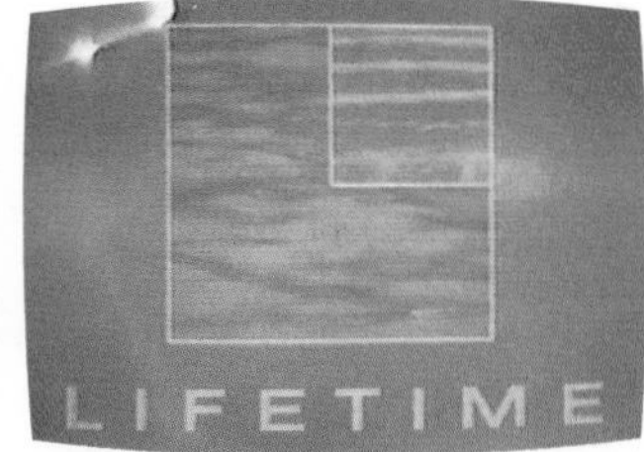

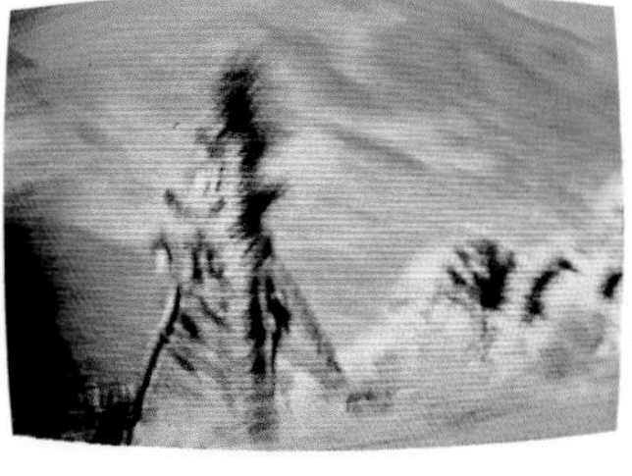

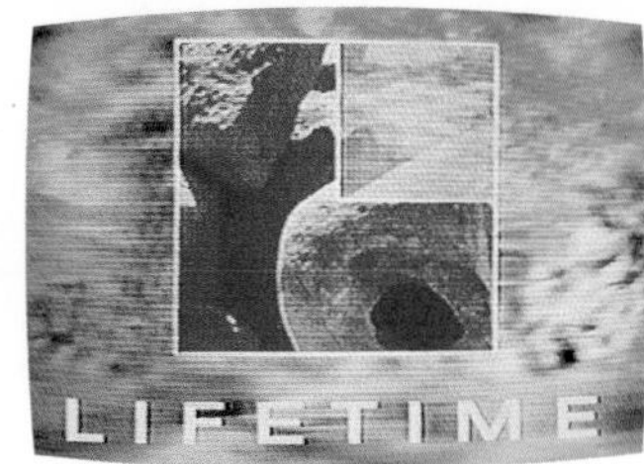

These two Lifetime Cable Television sequences originated on the Macintosh, and were then transferred to the "Harry" for broadcast quality.

How did you happen to first encounter the Macintosh?

I just got hooked early. I went to a conference, Technology Entertainment Design, called TED, the first one in 1984. One of my best friends is Harry Marks, who is a mogul in all of this, and the day after the conference ended, he and some friends dragged me to Macy's department store, and said: "You've got to see this amazing box." That's where I first saw the Macintosh, at Macy's department store in Carmel, California, sitting in the middle of calculators, answering machines, cordless phones and all types of consumer electronics stuff. I just started playing on it, and without anybody showing me, it just started. And then they said: "Come on, Greiman, you've been here an hour — other people want to use this thing," and they dragged me out of there.

Then around 1985 my colleague, Eric Martin, got a Macintosh. In the evenings, when I'd get back from the studio, he'd show me how to do things on it. I had just bought a video camera, and we attached the video camera to it. Before I knew it, we were having problems, because he was trying to get some work done and I was playing on the thing. So, as an attempt to save the relationship, I got my own Macintosh.

The Pacific Wave sculpture in Venice, Italy, was built from drawings faxed from Los Angeles.

In the beginning, I didn't think it was a profound tool; I thought it was just an interesting object to know about. I was more interested in video at that time. I treated the Macintosh like it was a Polaroid camera, the kind that gives you instant prints, or an Instamatic, or a color Xerox. Something that, if you were into making images, you had to know about, and you had to experiment with to see it's potential.

After a while, we started experimenting with it extensively. For the most part, we were not trying to imitate traditional disciplines, but were trying to explore the real texture of the computer — the digital, pixelized look — and attempting to combine that with other traditions, even hand-set type, along with a variety of other non-digital textures. Later, when the software became high quality and professional enough, we became serious about using the Macintosh and made an investment in purchasing a few of them.

A whole new world opened up when color became available on the Macintosh. I actually won my first Macintosh II for the "Pacific Wave Sculpture," which I entered in the fine arts category in *Macworld* magazine's first art competition. As jobs became more demanding, we purchased more color Macintosh computers. We still have two Macintosh Plus computers for production and business management.

How is the Macintosh used in your studio now?

I'm still the same person who was trained in Basel, and I still use pencils; or I may very often use a camera to generate an image. Usually, I make a sketch and turn it over to one of the other designers in the studio. I'll give them a direction, either in pencil or verbally, and then I let them work on things up to a point. Usually this means they create a file on the Macintosh. Often I sit with them and they're the operators.

I can literally work on several projects at a time, because we have several computers, and I can go from one Macintosh to the other. While one person is working on something, I can move over to the next and work with that person. Frankly, it's impossible for me to have the level of expertise that my staff has, because they use the computer all day long. I'm out in meetings, I travel a lot and I've got seventy-two irons in the fire. But I like what happens this way. I have the final say over what is done, but when I work with someone, my aesthetic blends with theirs, and vice versa. We make one aesthetic together. If you work on something alone, it's not better, it's just different. Sometimes my staff will do something I wouldn't have necessarily done; sometimes I'll refine it and

April Greiman Inc., Los Angeles.

they'll work around that. I like the refinement process that happens when I work with others. I also like the things I do by myself.

I'm pretty quick at learning the software, and if I need to, I can usually fudge my way through. I've had a Macintosh for seven years, and I've found its simple, iconic language makes it possible to work your way through, even if you're not a technical wizard. The good thing about not being too knowledgeable is that accidents occur, and I've built an entire career on accidents.

I'm lucky that, relatively speaking, the Macintosh is low-end, because I'm kind of a big supporter of the low end. I feel low-end, low resolution images can be more profound than images that have little or no texture. These days, though, it seems the Macintosh is also a kind of central figure in a lot of different sophisticated technologies, including high-end prepress.

I would say about 50% to 60% of what we do currently ends up in print. We still create corporate identities, stationery and logos, and we've done a few books and catalogs. I've designed a lot of posters, many of which are in an exhibit currently touring in the United States. But we're also doing a lot more environmental and architectural projects. We've designed custom fabrics and etched glass facades and different types of signage. The last area we're involved in is video; I think it's an area that will really grow fast for us.

In all of this, the real workhorse is the Macintosh, but it doesn't start there and it doesn't end there. We use everything we can get our hands on. We use a lot of traditional and manual processes. The point of it for me is not the box, it's the process. After all, the new tools, including the Macintosh, don't replace one's intuition, they merely inform it. We weave the computer in and out of our working process; that's why we call it "hybrid imagery."

The idea that currently inspires me the most is that this technology provides continuing expansion of creative opportunities. I've just begun to explore the rich possibilities of being able to design in space. By this, I mean that a document, a file, is not "site dependent" but rather is a global object capable of simultaneous creation from many different locations and sources. I am convinced of a future for collective expression. As long as we tie design to familiar tasks and tools, we fail to see that these new tasks and tools are in fact forming our future role as designers.

For your design jobs in print, do you often output your own film?

While I think ultimately the most important role the Macintosh plays is that of a conceptualizing tool, we have, in fact, more and more, taken our print jobs all the way to final film; if we couldn't, it would cause a significant change in our business. Of course, for a long time we couldn't do that. We'd just send LaserWriter output to a typesetter and have them match it.

But the fact that we can output to film makes certain tasks more efficient. The designer has almost total control now, even over the prepress. That control is important. At the same time, it brings a lot of headaches. We are not intended, nor qualified, to be typographers, strippers, and color separation experts. Sometimes files crash or really inexplicable things happen technically. Sometimes it's a little scary that we're so locked in, everything is in the computer, in that box.

Do you use Macintosh-generated products for presentations to your clients?

Absolutely. We very often take a Macintosh to a client, or bring them here to the studio, and have work sessions with the client, right on the Macintosh. This is a practice I began when I worked on a Quantel Paintbox. It was so expensive to rent time, at $500 per hour, that if I had a fixed budget when I got in there, I would feel safer if a client came to the session with me. Even though my clients knew roughly what was going to be done, and they knew what the concept was, it was better if the client could be there and directly approve an increase in budget due to a change in direction. Not all clients want to do that, by the way. But then I realized that the ones who did come felt very comfortable working with us more and more. They realized I was some sort of Communist, in that I liked sharing ideas and directions collectively, so there were no surprises. I really like collaborating with people. I'm always the one that signs off on a design, and it's my aesthetic, but the client has already come to me based on that, so that's not really an issue. I like working as part of "collective" decision-making, collective consciousness and collective unconsciousness; it's very Jungian, but I think that this process indicates a new metaphor, among other possibilities, that you can work globally.

We work with international clients and we use these tools to communicate, and we develop new languages that are iconographic, and that give new texture to communication. Sometimes we'll make a presentation, and leave them a hard copy, like a 300 dpi color printout. The interesting thing is that these printouts are usually terrible and vulgar compared to the subtlety of what you can really do on the Macintosh. But the client is familiar with the intentions, so color printouts are simply a graphic gestural representation. Just as a color photocopy represents a color photograph, it's two different things, but if you've seen the color photograph, the photocopy will do. That's the way we work.

I think the beauty of this is that you see more and explore more ideas, rather than do more, like spending hours preparing comps. The doing, then, becomes based on appropriateness; it's based on what you see.

What do you think is most important for the education of young graphic designers today, given that technology has come to play such a key role?

Given my reputation for experimentation, it may be surprising to some that I think immediately of the use of type. My sensitivity to typography came from exercises in hand-setting type at the Basel Kunstgewerbeschule, from putting little pieces of type into a composing stick. Once you do that and address the formal problems of typography, that background never goes away. The computer provides such immediate results in type composition that subtlety is easily lost, and in typography, subtlety is a key part of the expression, of the communication. In our case, ordinary laser proofs are so different from output on an imagesetter, like the Linotronic, that we commonly output at high resolution the same type with different leading and kerning settings and choose from those.

The studio here is a bit like a school, because some of my staff learned typography using phototype, rub-down lettering, or a Macintosh. So I spend a lot of time controlling and patrolling that; I'm the typo-police in the studio. It's funny, because young people today have a real feeling for electronics because they were brought up on television; but they can be really set in their ways, really fixated on certain approaches to design problems. I feel like I'm very free because I learned in the Old World, in the traditional ways of doing things, and I have a lot more options than they do. In some ways, I feel like that traditional training has helped make my world view larger.

I'm training young designers to discriminate in ways they seem not to have learned in their education, trying to perpetuate Old World standards. Hopefully other designers are doing that, too, so that a craft that transcends technology will be passed on.

Step by Step

The University of California at Los Angeles (UCLA) asked Greiman to design a poster for their summer program that would also appear as the cover to a catalog of summer classes. Greiman and designer Noreen Morioka used Adobe Photoshop, Adobe Illustrator, and Aldus PageMaker to create the piece.

Photoshop enabled manipulation of images and their color to take place dynamically onscreen as part of the design process. Illustrator was used to create hard-edged images that contrasted to the photographic images. PageMaker was used for type and to bring the various graphic elements together on the page.

The "L" image was created by typing the letter in Photoshop. Next, a file containing an image of clouds was opened. With both files open, the "L" outline and the clouds, Photoshop's clone tool was used to paint clouds inside the letter "L". By selecting the outline of the letter first, the clone tool could be used to paint the clouds inside the letter without going outside the boundaries of the letter.

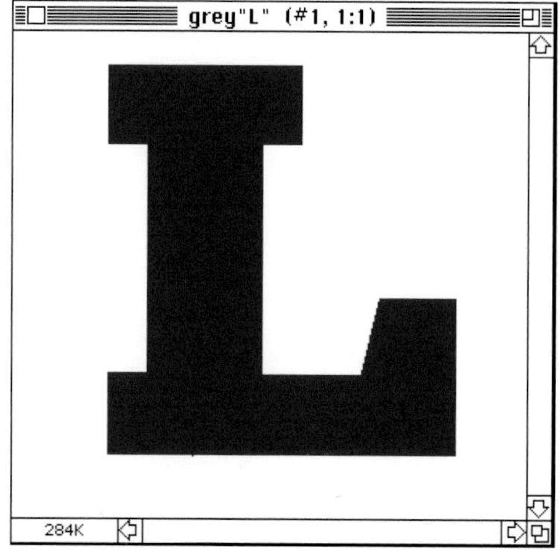

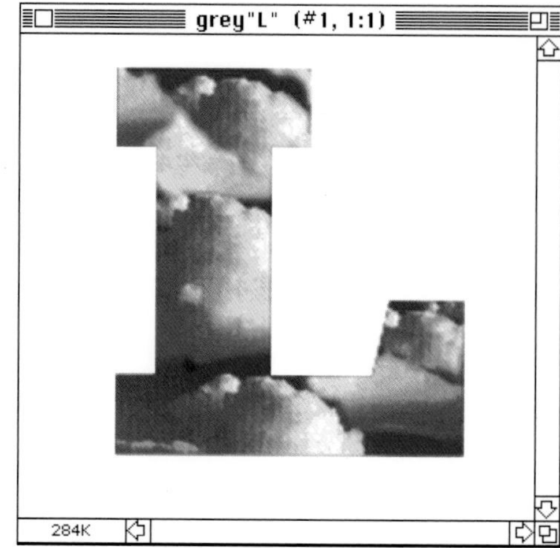

The image of hands holding a sheet of paper was created from a Polaroid snapshot taken in Greiman's studio. The Polaroid was scanned in on a Microtek color scanner, and taken into Photoshop for further manipulation.

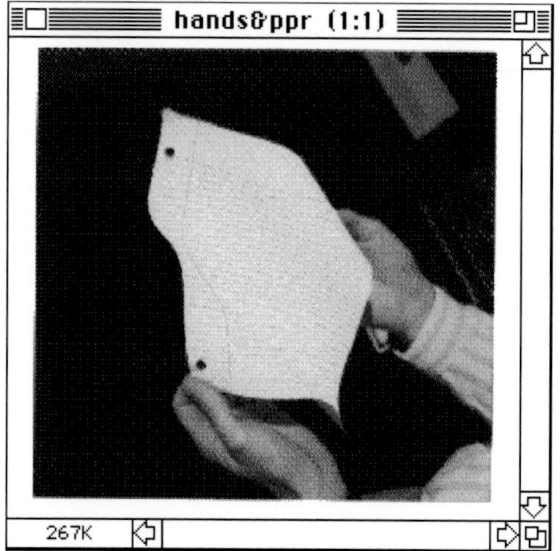

The background of the image was removed by selecting the image using the magic wand tool. It was determined that the paper image was not of high enough quality, so it was removed in order that a better quality paper image could be put in later.

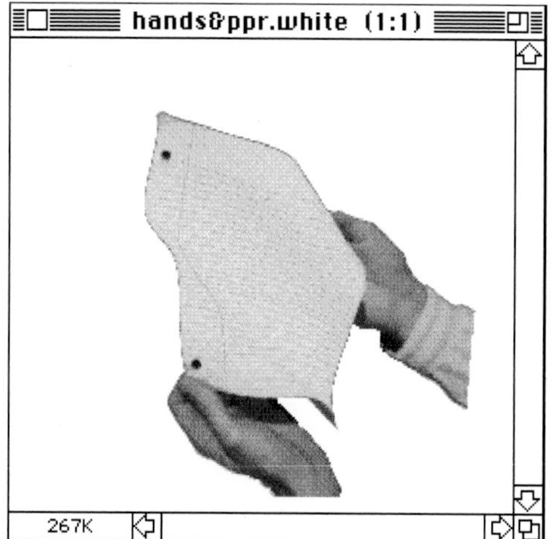

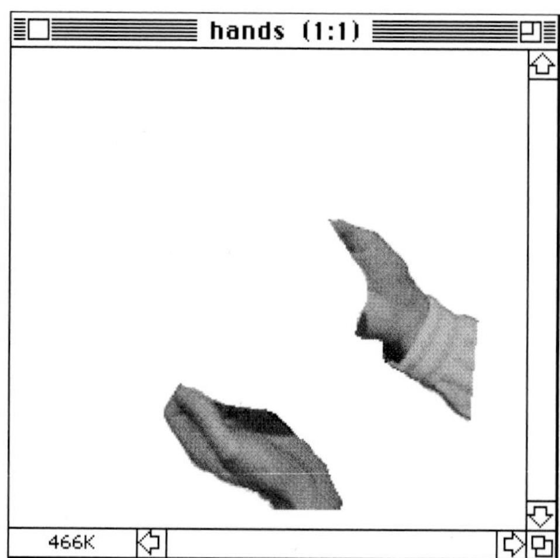

The paper image was shot in a separate studio session. A 3"x 5" transparency was sent out and scanned in using a Scitex system. A low-resolution scan of the paper was created in Photoshop to be merged back into the hands as a position only image.

Using Photoshop, the water was pasted into the paper image, with opacity set at 60% for transparency. Greiman's Studio sent three files to the Scitex system: the hands only, the water only, and the composite shown here.

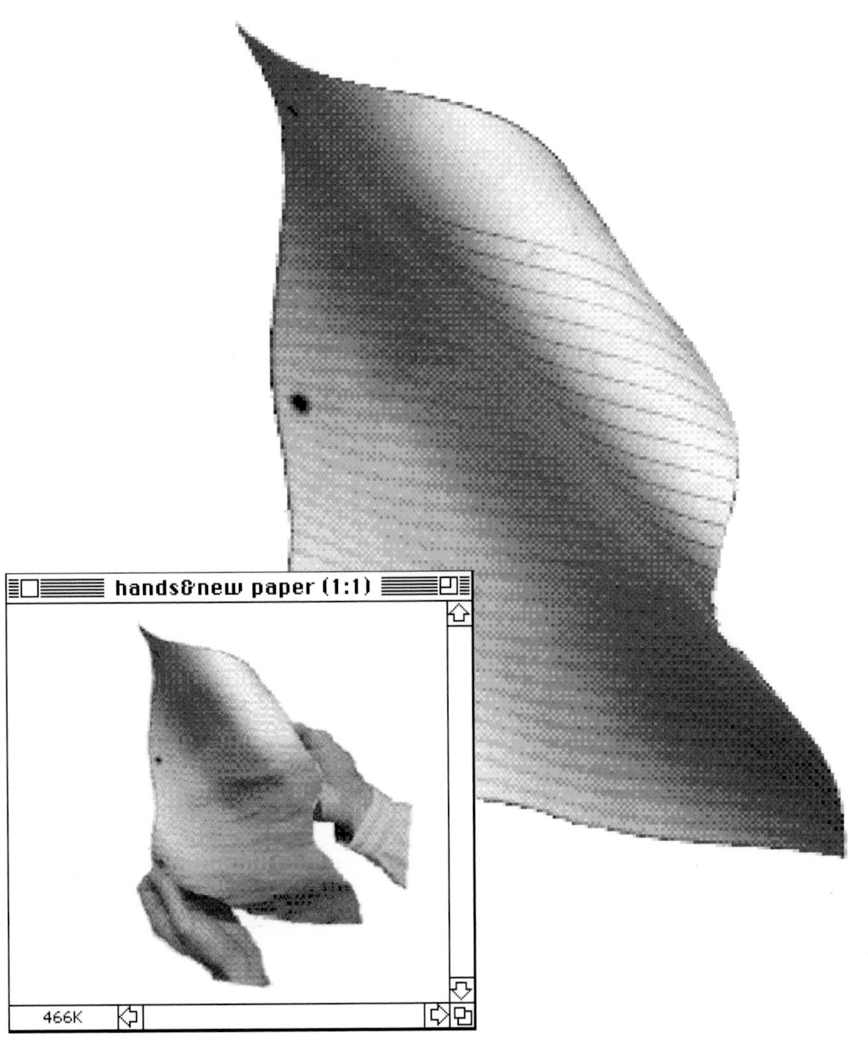

The various elements were put together in a Photoshop file.

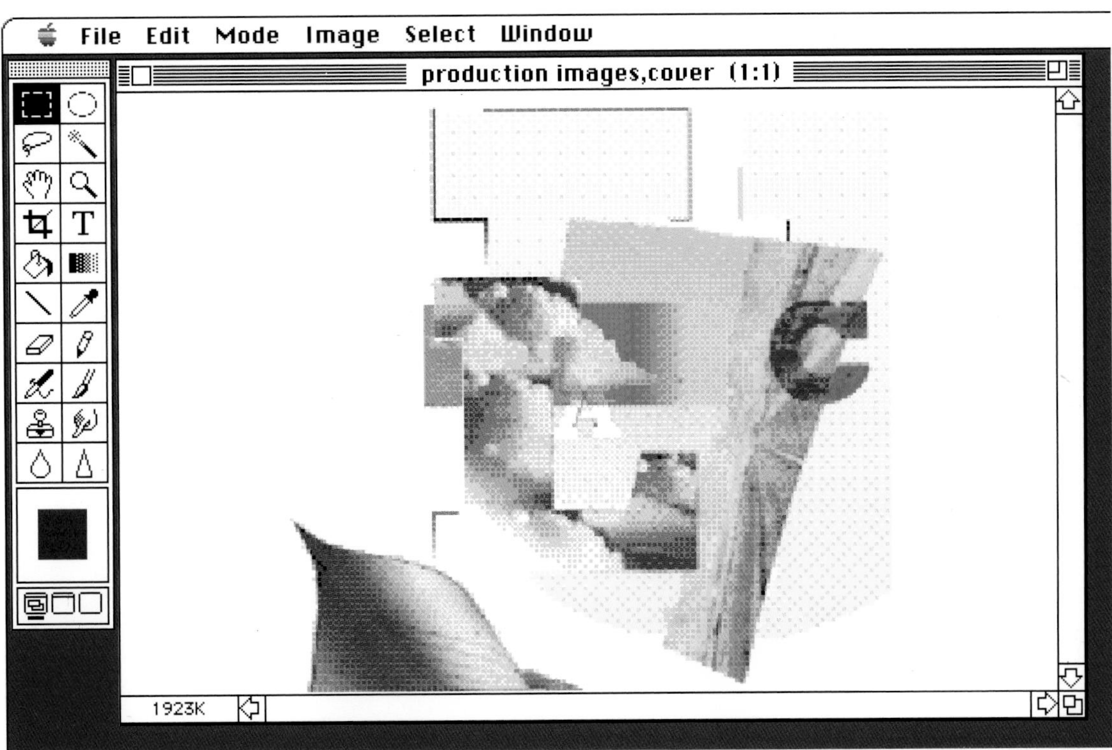

Other elements in the file were created in Adobe Illustrator, to obtain a clean, hard edge. The Photoshop image was placed in the Illustrator file temporarily, so that items in Illustrator could be positioned correctly. Type Align was used to create the type on a curve.

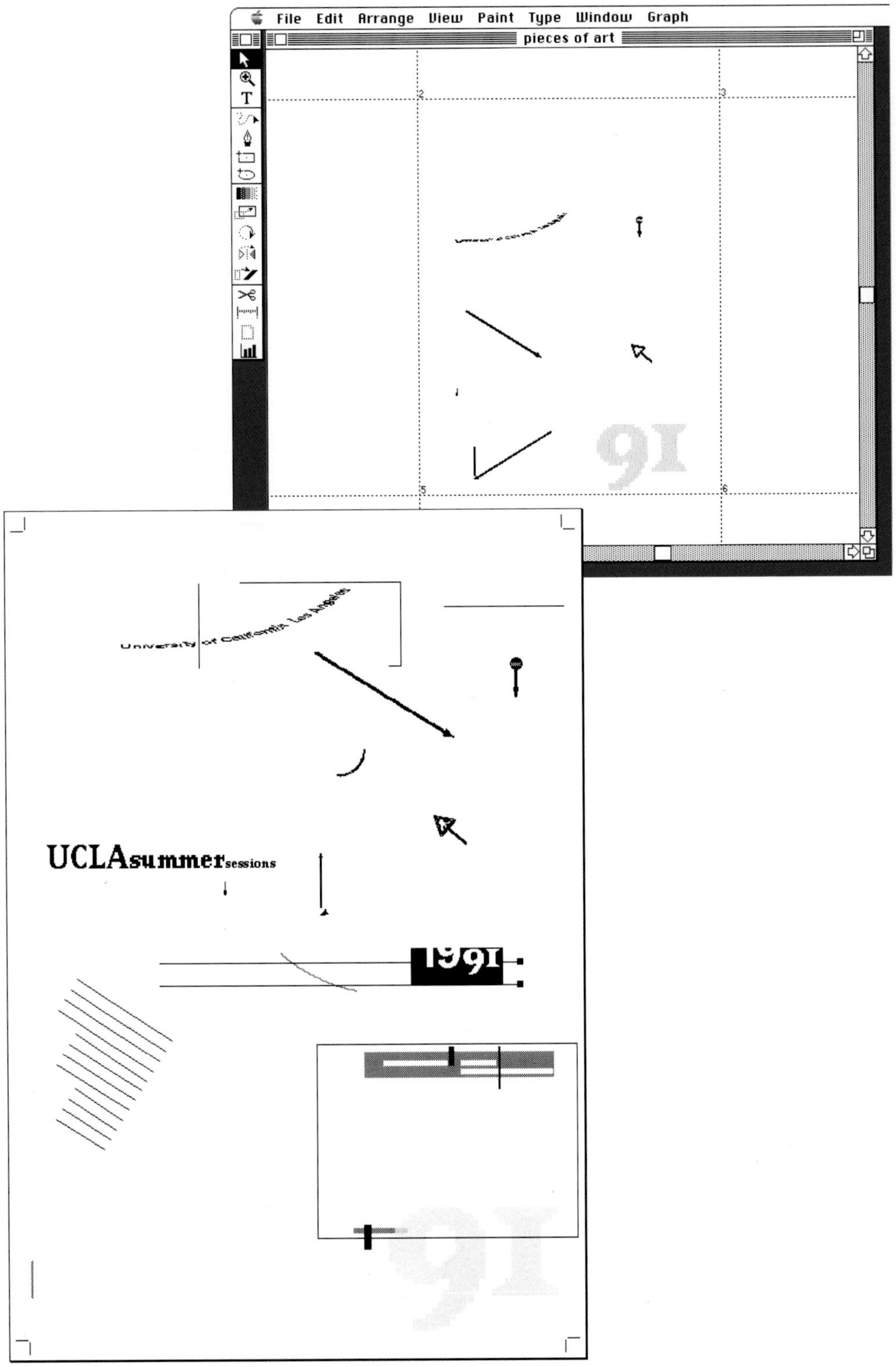

The Illustrator file was placed on a page in PageMaker. Type elements were added in PageMaker. Film was created from the PageMaker file and the Photoshop file; the high resolution image of the hands was digitally stripped in using a Scitex system to produce the final poster.

Magazine, 1988
Vitra International
Aldus PageMaker, Adobe Illustrator,
Microsoft Word, Image Studio,

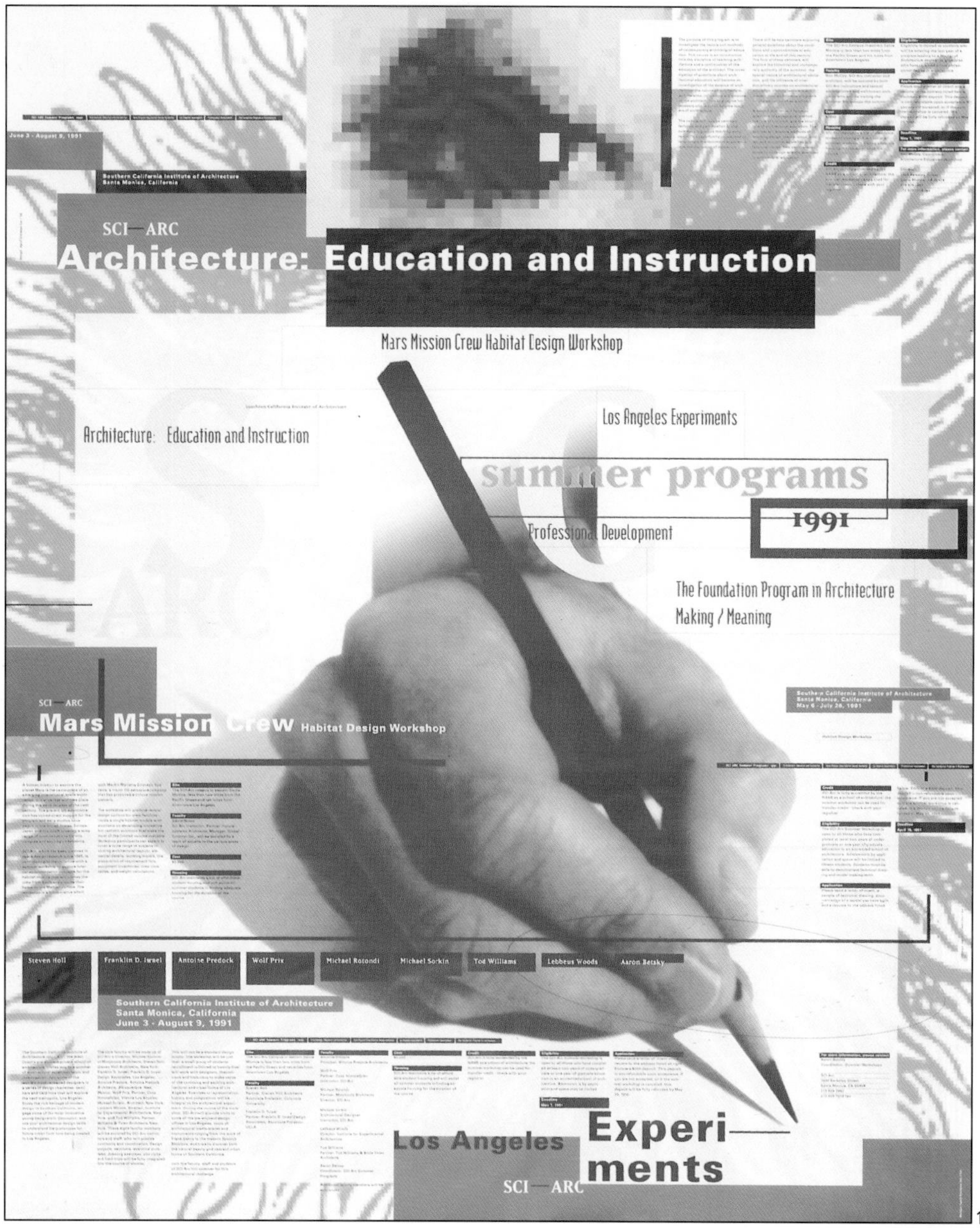

1

2

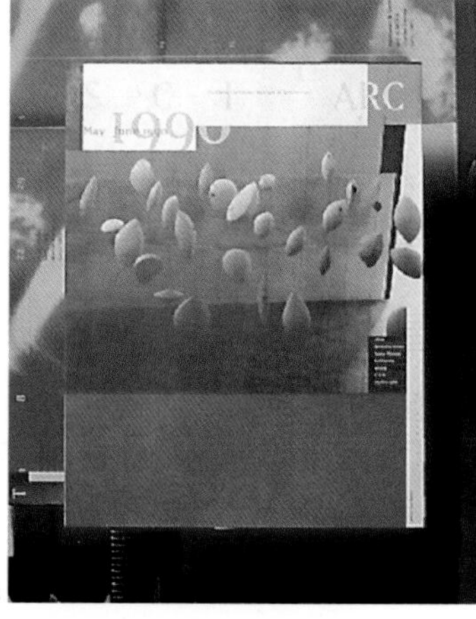

3

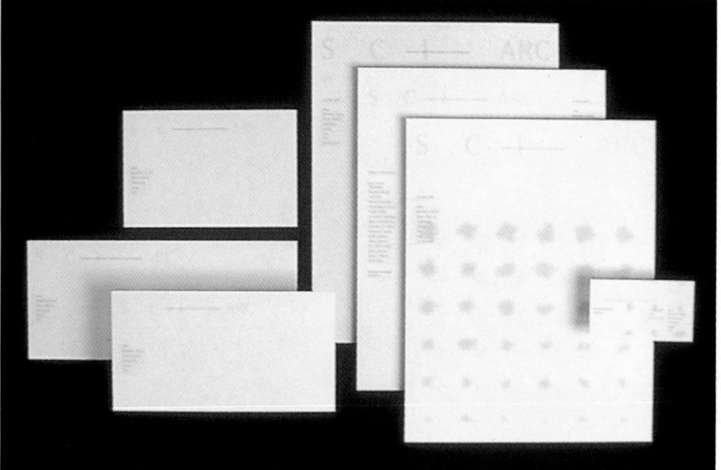

4

1 Poster/catalog, 1991
Southern California Institute of Architecture, Summer Programs
Aldus PageMaker, Aldus FreeHand, Adobe Illustrator, Photoshop, Microsoft Word

Designed with Sean Adams

2 Newsletter, 1990
Southern California Institute of Architecture
Aldus PageMaker, Aldus FreeHand, Adobe Illustrator, Photoshop, Microsoft Word

Designed with Sean Adams and Mike Ellison

3 Newsletter, 1990
Southern California Institute of Architecture
Aldus PageMaker, Aldus FreeHand, Adobe Illustrator, Photoshop, Microsoft Word

Designed with Sean Adams

4 Stationery system, 1989
Southern California Institute of Architecture
Adobe Illustrator, Image Studio

Poster, 1987
Southern California Institute of Architecture, "Making/Thinking"
Aldus PageMaker, Aldus FreeHand, Adobe Illustrator, Photoshop, Microsoft Word

Designed with Sean Adams

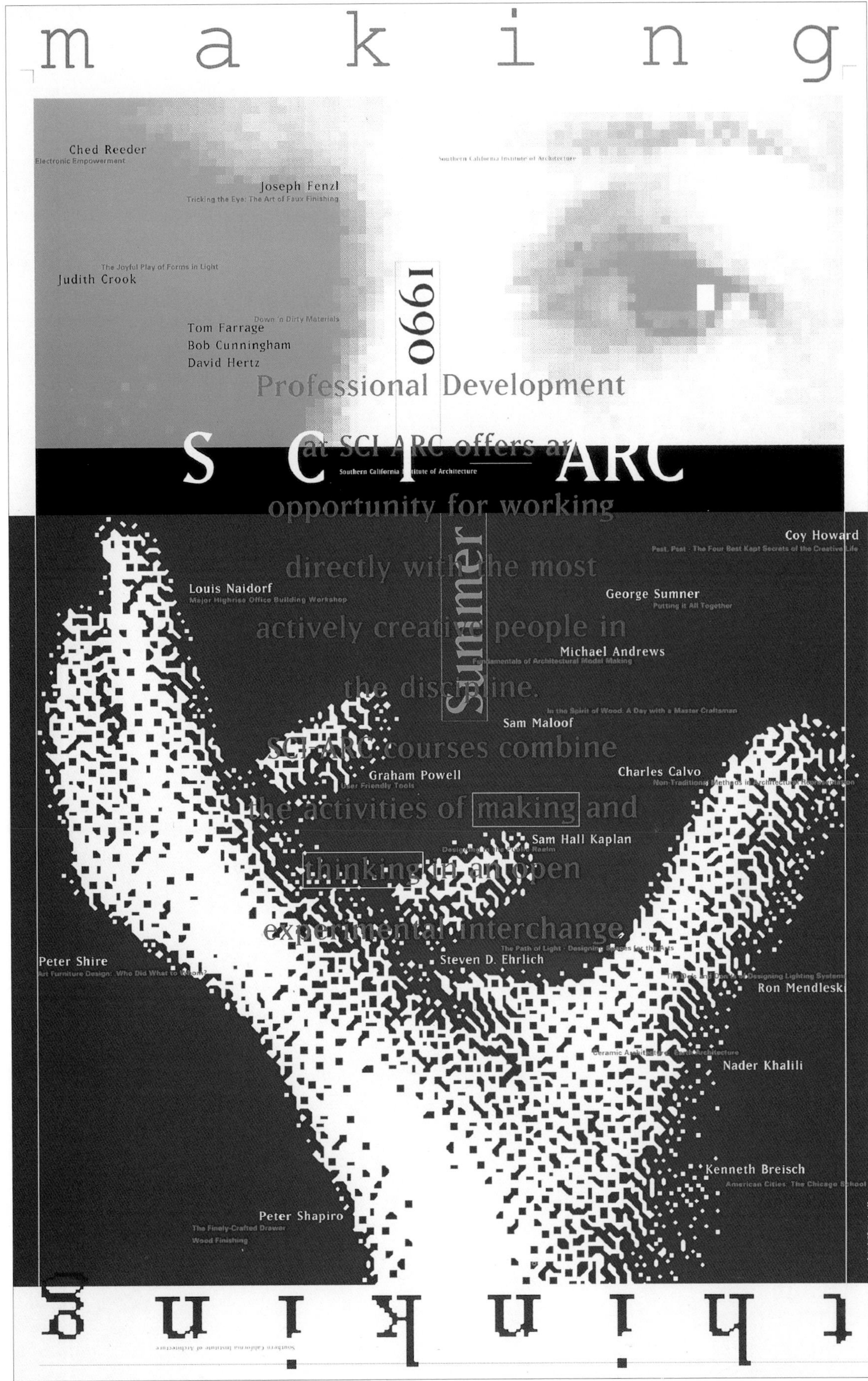

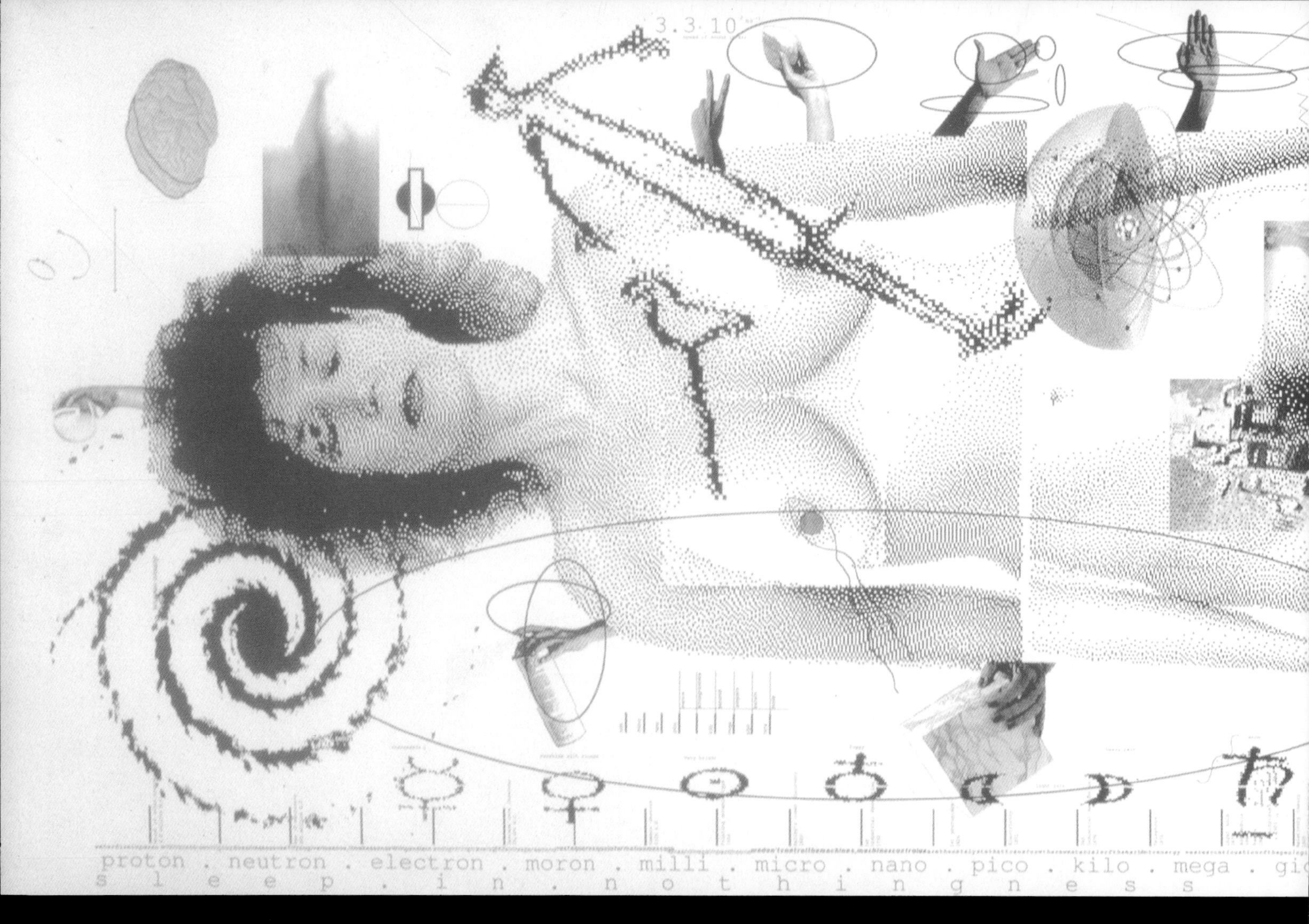

Poster/folder with slipcase, 1986
Walker Art Center, Design Quarterly,
"Does It Make Sense?"
MacPaint, MacDraw

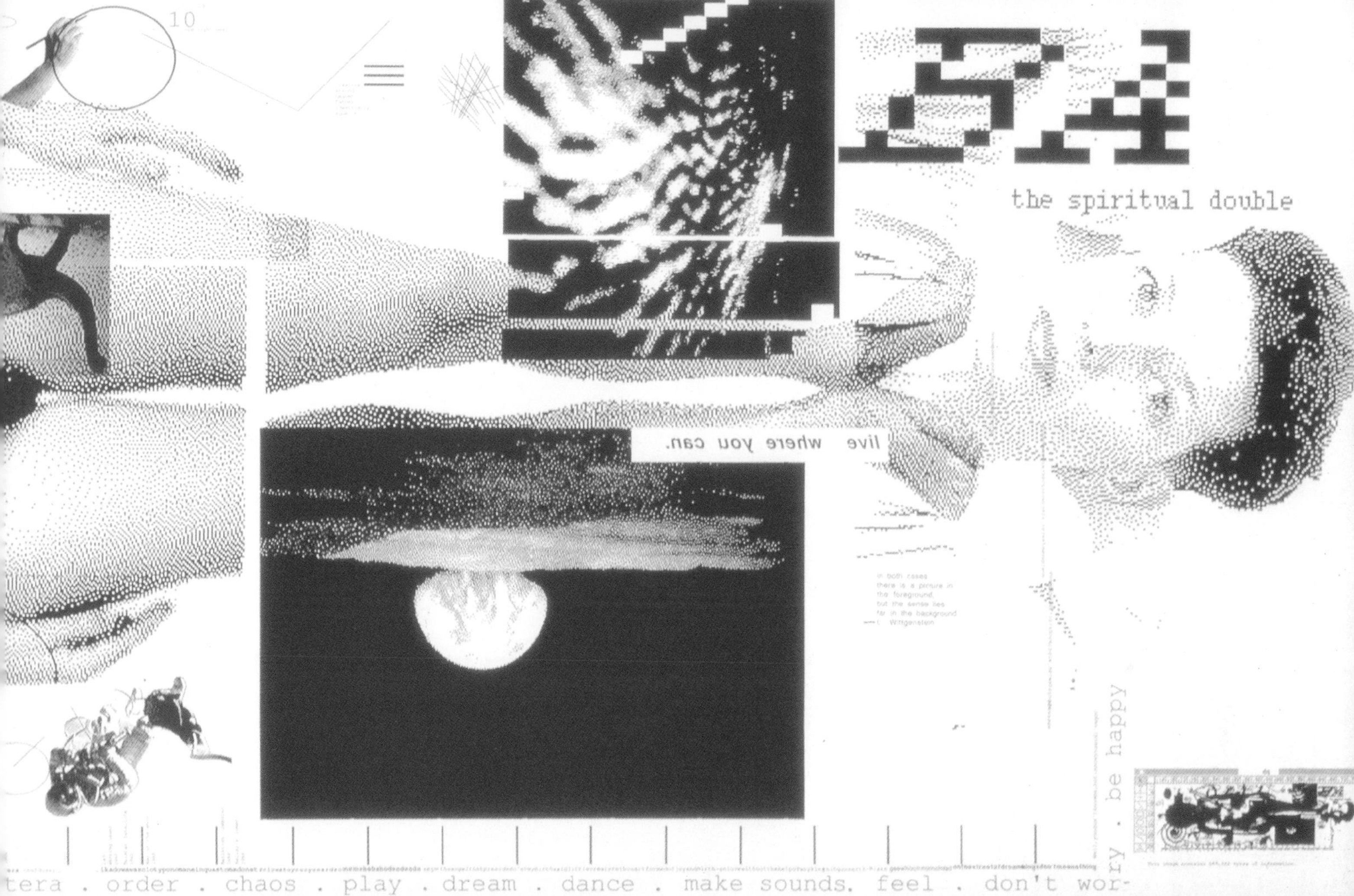

the spiritual double
live where you can.
in both cases
there is a picture in
the foreground,
but the sense lies
far in the background
L. Wittgenstein
tera . order . chaos . play . dream . dance . make sounds. feel . don't worry . be happy

Poster, 1986
Los Angeles Institute of Contemporary Art
MacDraw and conventional paste-up

Advertisement, 1987
Di-Zin opening exhibition
MacDraw and conventional paste-up

Poster and billboard, 1989
Graphic Design in America exhibition,
Walker Art Center
Aldus PageMaker, Adobe Illustrator,
Quantel Graphic Paintbox

Hybrid Imagery book design, 1990
Watson Guptill Publications
Aldus PageMaker, Adobe Illustrator,
Image Studio, Microsoft Word

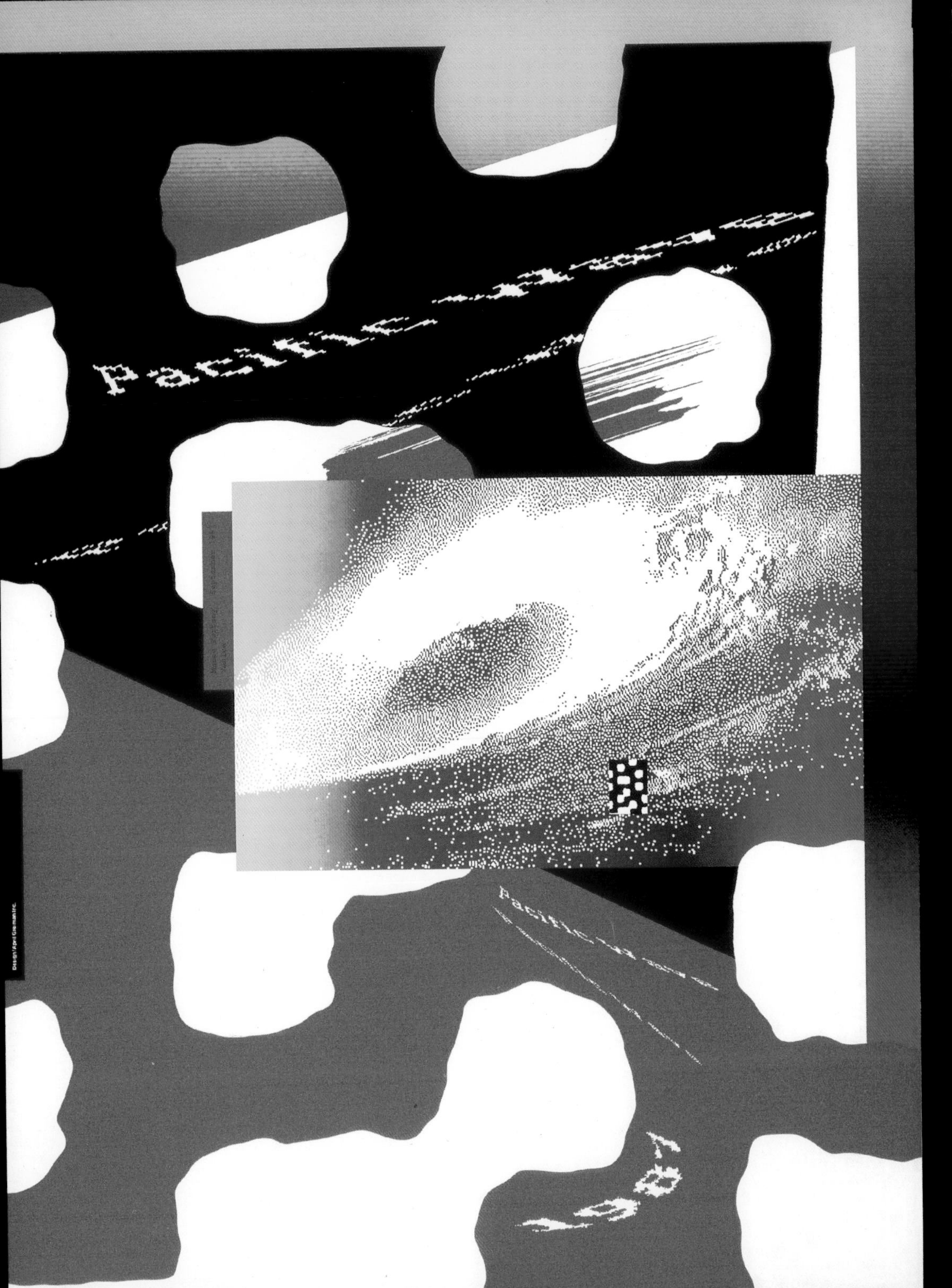

Fortuny Museum, Venice
"Pacific Wave" exhibition
Full Paint, MacDraw,
Quantel Graphic Paintbox

Poster, 1987
"The Modern Poster" exhibition, Museum of Modern Art, New York
Aldus PageMaker, MacVision, MacDraw

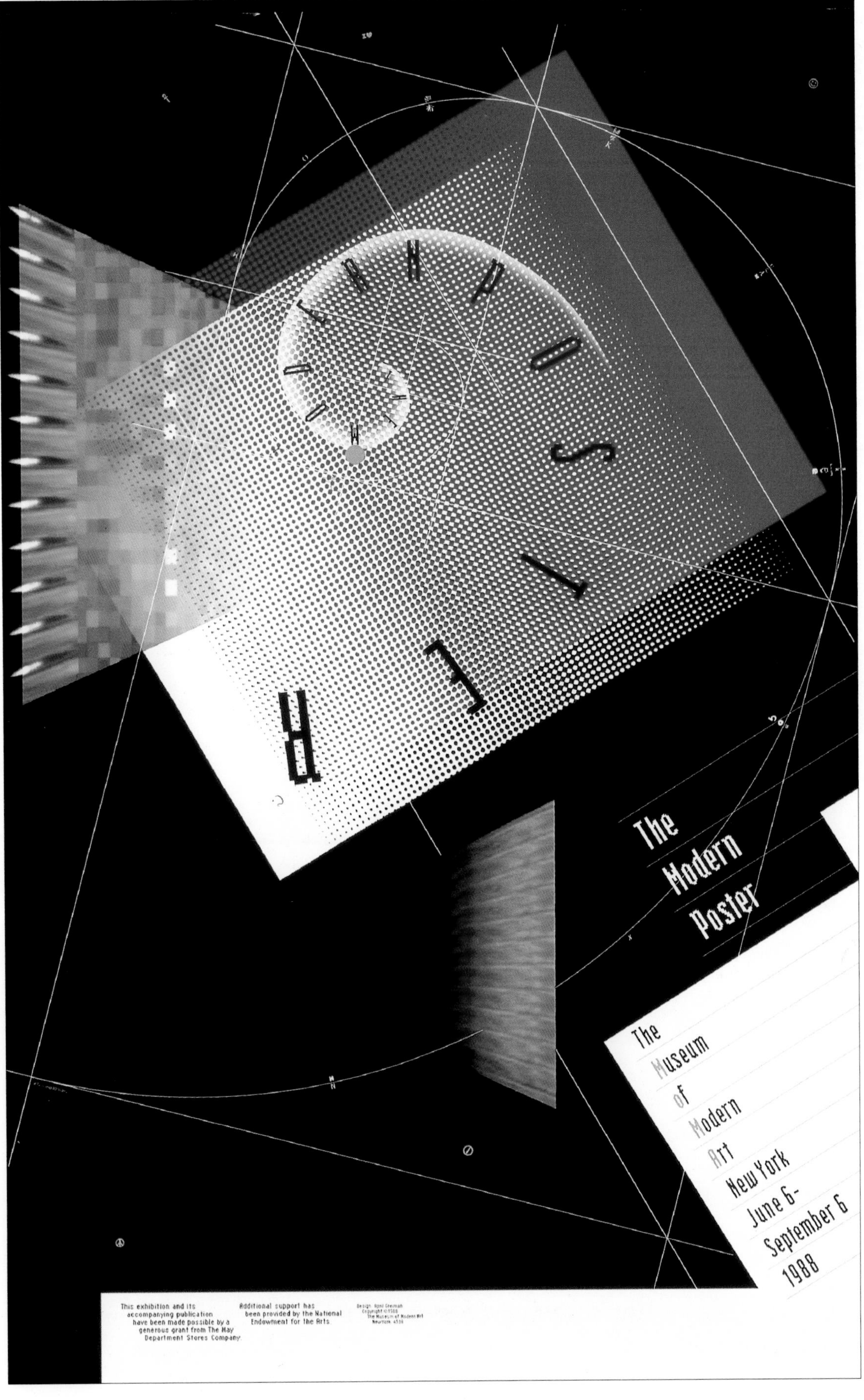

Kazuo Kawasaki

Kazuo Kawasaki is one of Japan's leading industrial designers. Following his graduation from Kanazawa University of Art in 1972, he became a designer in Toshiba's Industrial Design department. Seven years later, he formed his own design firm, eX-Design, Inc., based in Fukui, a town of about 250,000 people some 200 miles north of Tokyo. Since that time, his genius has turned ordinary daily objects, from clocks and scissors to ashtrays and eyeglasses, into the extraordinary. ¶ Kawasaki is a recent recipient of the Mainichi Design Award, one of Japan's most esteemed honors for design. The award was granted for two simple yet revolutionary products: an ultra-lightweight wheelchair and a computer-aided suspension bed. One of Japan's earliest Macintosh enthusiasts, Kawasaki's studio is not only a busy center for design, but is also an important learning center for young designers as they move into the 21st century.

Some of Kawasaki's earlier pre-Mac designs for Toshiba.

How did you first come to use the Macintosh?

After I graduated from the university in 1972, I worked for Toshiba Electronics. My education was in industrial design with an emphasis on electronics, so at Toshiba I designed audio equipment and high fidelity audio systems. My role there was to provide concepts to the engineering staff and to be responsible for the specification of both the internal electronic design and the outer design. In addition, I worked as a creative director, responsible for product management from concept to marketing. While at Toshiba, I designed using traditional drafting equipment.

In 1980 I left Toshiba to form my own company. About that time I began to use various computers, including the Sinclair Z80, made in Britain, and the NEC Handheld PC8201, which I used primarily for telecommunications. Later, I began using the Canon AS 300, producing some drafting work on it that was output to a plotter.

In 1984 I saw a 128K Macintosh in Fukui. It was a great surprise to me. I borrowed it from the local computer shop and tried to create a few things using MacPaint; I was very impressed. A little later, I bought a 512K Macintosh and began using it to make rough, but very interesting, product sketches.

In 1985 I had an exhibit at a Soho gallery in New York. Many designers attended the exhibit and they all were surprised and impressed because much of the work I created was animated on the Macintosh using VideoWorks 1.0, the program that has now become MacroMind Director. This exhibit showed mostly product design.

Eventually one of the directors of Canon Sales, Inc., the distributor for Macintosh in Japan at the time, came to my studio and asked me to create another exhibit showing how the Macintosh could be used for design. The exhibition was held in 1986 at the Axis Gallery in Tokyo and was called "Mac the Sketch." In this exhibit, there were works by myself and one other industrial designer named Shouhei Mihara. It was the first exhibit in Japan showing how the Macintosh could be used for design.

When I first started using the Macintosh, I was very inspired by the computer and I felt my work actually changed. But more recently, I've come to think of the computer as simply a tool. And, because I am an industrial designer, I became more and more interested in designing a computer, rather than just working with a computer as an end user only. So for the past two years, I have been an advisor to the development team for the Graphical User Interface of Toshiba's J3100 laptop computer, called the T3100 in the United States. I also was a consultant to Panasonic's computer division until only recently.

Many people say I am an early pioneer of the Macintosh in Japan. Last year I supervised an event in Sabae-shi, Fukui called "Mac the Design." I brought in 100 Macintosh computers and invited 150 designers from all over Japan to the seminar. It was very successful and was actually overbooked, a remarkable event for the small town.

How do you use the Macintosh in your studio?

In my studio there are two sections, one for industrial design and the other for graphic design. Every designer in both sections has their own Macintosh. In general, I make a simple rough sketch by hand and give it to the staff. In the industrial design section, I usually have a meeting with my staff and explain the image or concept of the project, as well as the final size and other specifications. Then the staff creates initial sketches directly on the computer. After this, there are usually three different things that happen: we make a full-scaled

Kawasaki's Fukui studio.

model by paper or other material; we create detailed drawings using a CAD program; and we also prepare presentation materials for the client.

In the graphic design section, we primarily design logotypes and corporate identities. There are no output services in Fukui; no one has a Linotronic or any other type of high resolution printer. Therefore we usually use photo stats of images output by LaserWriter and indicate the position and other instructions on the mechanical boards, then give these to the printer. These instructions are sometimes for reducing the LaserWriter output, which for many things gives us quite satisfactory results. From the time I began using the Macintosh Plus, I gladly stopped using instant lettering and pasted up the letters from the LaserWriter directly on to the mechanicals.

I sometimes suggest to my staff to work out their ideas by hand, as I am aware of the importance of using one's hand. But they can't help using the computer; sometimes they use it without telling me. I don't think the computer is more important than using the hands, or vice versa. I think it's important that since we have both the opportunity of using the computer mouse and making rough sketches by hand, we should try to create a good balance between the two ways.

Basically, in the past, design was done with pen and paper. However, facing the computer screen directly, as we do in our studio, is a brand new idea for designers. A designer can confirm that his ideas are good or not by encountering these directly on the screen. And with the computer, it is no longer necessary to make separate, final drawings based on rough sketches.

Before making the final products, a product designer has to present the concept of his idea to his clients and the computer makes this job easier. Designers can use the computer to organize the entire process at once, from the rough sketch, to rendering the final drawing, to making a presentation to clients. Also, I discovered recently that in my studio, young designers don't seem to be able to draw a clean, straight line, so computers can help them make better presentations of their ideas to me and to our clients.

Can the Macintosh adequately produce the drawings necessary for product design?

You can make perfect and precise indications by computer. I am currently supervising the development of a project for making molds automatically from computer data. I am collaborating with a local manufacturer; the proposed machine is to produce molds by reading the data of drawings directly off the Macintosh. The most important stage of the product design is to make this mold, and this machine will read data from Claris CAD, a computer-aided design program on the Macintosh, and make the mold for the product automatically.

All of the eyeglass designs I create are done mostly by computer using Claris CAD, from drawing the initial sketches to the final drawings complete with all the specifications. These drawings provide all the necessary detail by the time we give them to the manufacturer. Even the sales catalog for most of the eyewear we design is produced on the Macintosh.

People are always saying that the Macintosh is a convenient tool for graphic designers, but that it cannot be used by industrial designers yet. We always disagree, because we think it actually makes drafting easier. Right now there are at least four good CAD programs in Japan: VersaCAD, AutoCAD, Claris CAD, and Mini CAD. Claris CAD is especially easy to use, because it's based on MacDraw, one of the first programs available on the Macintosh. In fact, I am planning to publish a book about Claris CAD, written especially for industrial designers. Quite often designers cannot understand how to use CAD programs only working from the software manuals, so I hope that this book will have a great impact on Japanese industrial design. I think that if Japanese industrial designers used Claris CAD, and other programs like it more frequently, it would make their drafting tasks so much easier.

Do you use the Macintosh to make presentations to your clients?

In product design, even though the designer may have an idea for creating something, it is not easy to present because it is very expensive to show the actual product to the client, much more expensive than trying to show an idea for graphic design, for example. If you cannot get a product manufactured, it will not exist. So the key is how a designer can persuade clients to invest their money. We've found using the computer for presentations to the client makes it easier to get approval. The presentation by Macintosh can be so impressive that clients sometimes have nothing to say except to agree to the proposal.

We often use HyperCard or Macro Mind Director animation to show the development of our ideas to clients. Recently, we made a presentation to demonstrate a bed designed for people whose movement is severely limited. The angle of each part of the bed can be controlled by a programmable IC card, or by a wireless remote commander. We are currently developing a bed that lets the position of the head of the bed be controlled by a person's breath using three different nozzles, so even a person who can only move his tongue and breathe can change the position of the bed to be comfortable. In the case of this product, we used HyperCard to animate how the bed would work. In order to make a presentation to our client for this product, Seibu Department Store, we installed 17 Macintosh monitors in

Some of Kawasaki's Claris CAD-originated eyeglasses.

the offices of the 17 different people taking part in the decision-making process. Each person could see the demonstration simultaneously. It was a great success. Client presentations are one of the most key aspects of product design.

In my studio in Fukui, we have a 100" Sony projector that we attach to the Macintosh for presentations and for conducting seminars. We also have 35" Mitsubishi monitors as well. When we can, we like to make presentations directly from the Macintosh screen. If this proves impossible, we make slides from the screen.

Design is, for better or worse, a business. Besides the pure process itself of designing a product, I have to think about whether or not the manufacture of the design is possible. Then I have to consider how to promote it. Without these kinds of political elements, the work of a designer would be far more enjoyable. It's sometimes kind of a pain to make deals with top executives of big companies. I would say almost 80% of my time is devoted to the business side of product design, and a great deal of that includes creating presentations for clients.

So not only the design work, but also the manufacturing aspect has to be considered, along with the sales and promotion. I'm often responsible for the names of products, for example. Fortunately, it gives me a chance to express the interest I have in mythology, and I often give products the names of mythological characters or gods, based on the product's nature or feeling and the nature of the mythological character. And I'm always thinking about systems for doing things, since I have to become so involved with a product all the way through to the manufacturing stage. So I have many projects in my mind, like designing more efficient transportation systems and developing a way to use computers in our political system. For example, even though there may be no particular political candidate who attracts you, you may still have strong political opinions; many people are this way, I think. So I'm thinking about a system where large numbers of people can more effectively voice their opinions to government officials using computers and a telecommunications network.

I'm also interested in designing tools and instruments that have no written labels on them, so anyone can understand or use them. I'm intrigued by expressing function through form, and I try to reflect this philosophy in my design based on product semantics, not just designing buttons with words next to them.

What should the role of the computer be in the education of young designers today?

Basically, to me, a good designer must have a rich imagination and an established consciousness of beauty, an aesthetic sense. In addition, the ability to use computers is becoming another essential one for designers. Especially for young designers now, who must be able to use the computer, and use it freely for all their ideas. If they don't have such an ability, they should not become designers. This means the computer is an essential tool for a designer, like pencils and inking pens; at the same time, the designer must have a specific philosophy about what it is he or she wants to create with a computer. Simply knowing how to handle a computer is not enough. A designer must have both a sense of design and expertise with computers; otherwise, we cannot call this person a designer.

The quality of design should improve because of the possibilities that the computer can provide. In this sense, I think that the computer is becoming critical. Designers should concentrate on what they can design using a computer, and not have to think about which computer functions they must use for the design.

But, I don't think design will ever be able to be done by computer only. To me, the relationship between paper and hands is still important. I can explain it using an analogy: most people are right-handed, which means they are able to use the right hand freely. This is analogous to using a pen and pencil. But some people are left-handed. And this left-handedness is equivalent to using a computer. Now people can have an option as to which hand they can use; they can be ambidextrous. Designers should have both abilities at the same time.

I think art schools should teach using computers first. As a first step, students should learn to design using the mouse. They will learn how to get along with the computer. After this, they must then discover the importance of using their own hand.

Design by computer is a very digital idea or action. On the contrary, something like drawing lines by pencil or sketching by charcoal is a very analog type of action. We need to know that we can use both at the same time. After all, both are realities of our world today.

Step by Step

The Seibu Saison Group, parent company of Seibu Department Stores, commissioned Kawasaki to refine the design of the original model of a computer-controlled air-suspension bed which was brought to Seibu by an inventor. Although based on the original idea, Kawasaki had to reconstruct, from conceptualization to actualization, the whole of this project.

There were many problems to avoid in the actual production. Seibu felt reluctant and informed Kawasaki to give it up. However, Kawasaki made detailed plans and offered a solution to each problem. He demonstrated his plans through a presentation using HyperCard on the Macintosh. Seibu finally agreed to make the Vivo Healthtec Bed a reality.

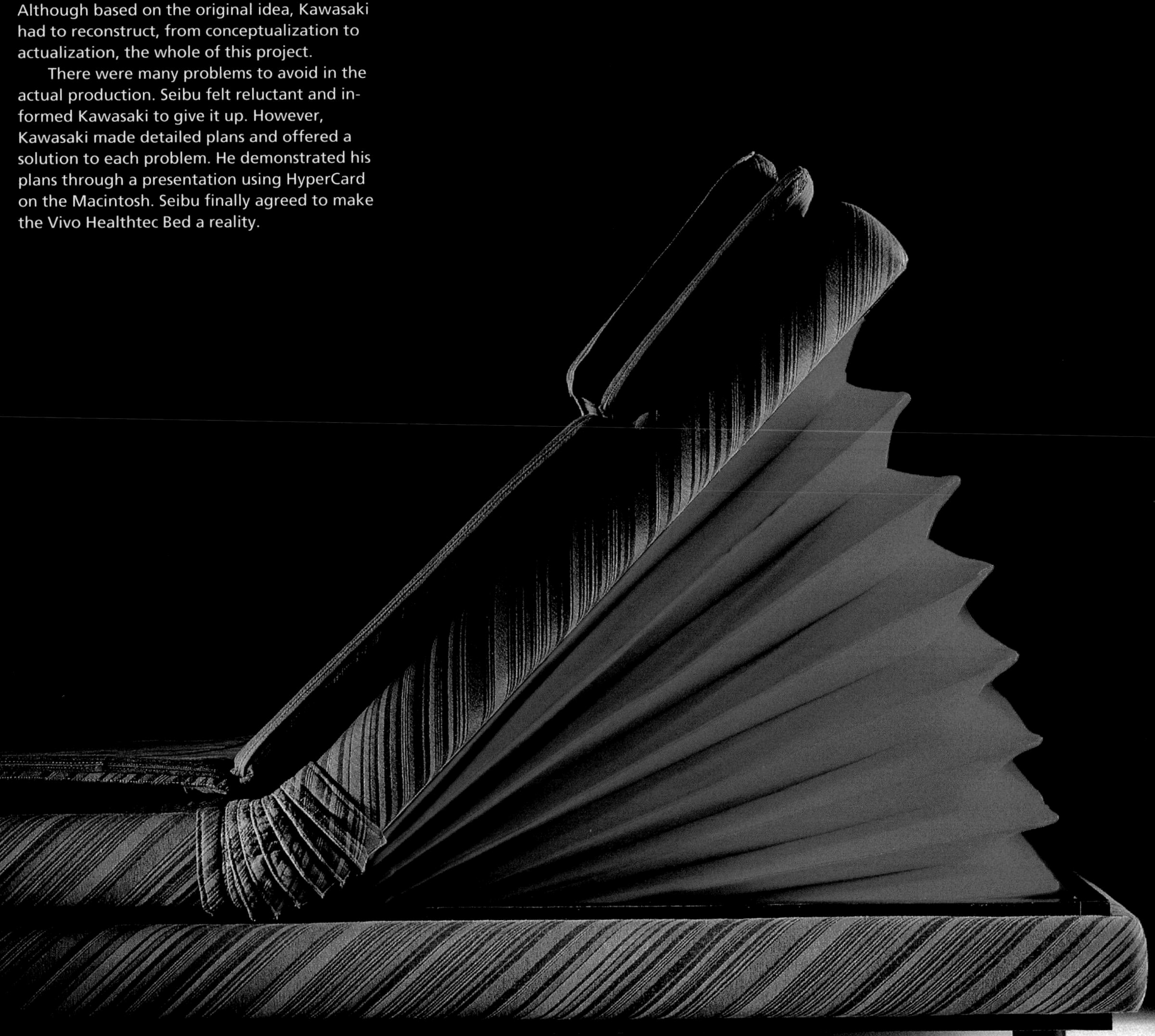

REMOTE COMMANDER

□NEXT
□END

Early presentations on how the bed would work were created in HyperCard. The bed is computer controlled and moves by pneumatic power. The bed is hinged in the middle, so the head of the bed can be raised or lowered by the force of one large air compartment under the head of the bed. The bed can also move by filling any one of 36 compartments in the mattress itself with air, using remote control. Hyper Card allowed Seibu executives at the presentation to click on buttons on the remote control and see an animated diagram of how the patient and bed would move.

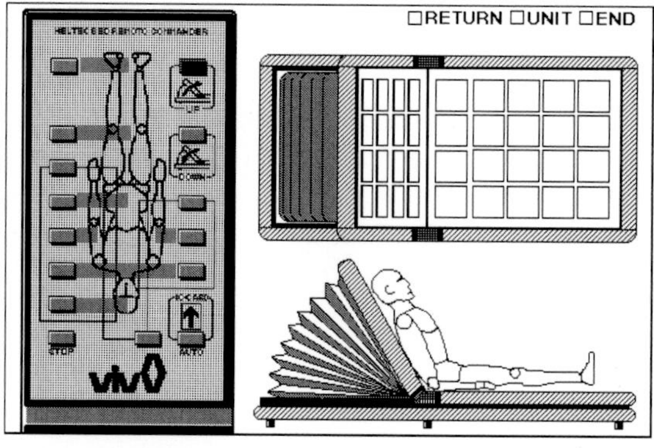

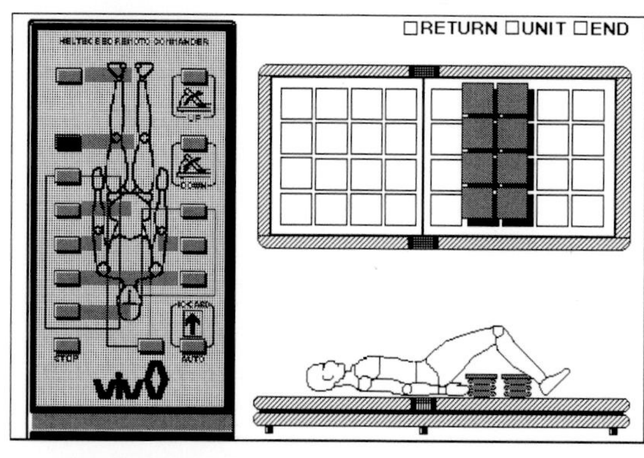

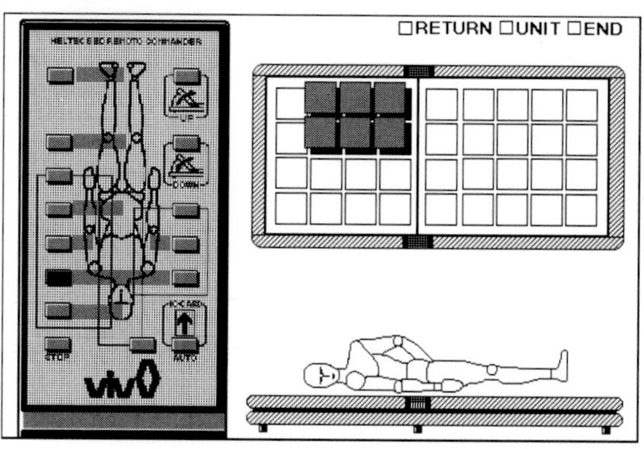

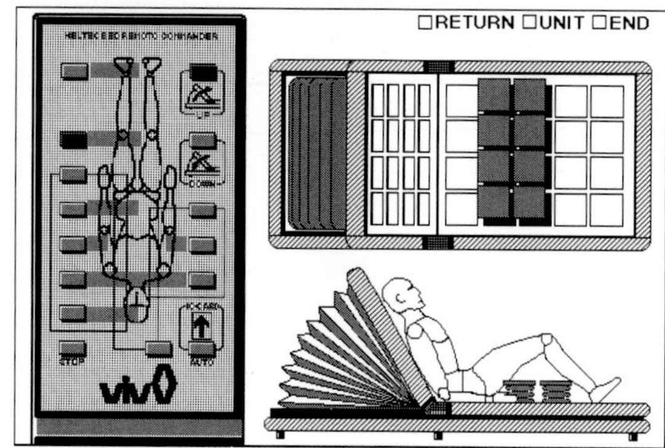

Information on any patient can be recorded on a credit card-sized IC card, and inserted in a controller that will adjust the bed to the needs of the patient. The bed can be programmed, for example, to raise the feet of the patient for two hours, or to raise the head of the patient at a specific time of day.

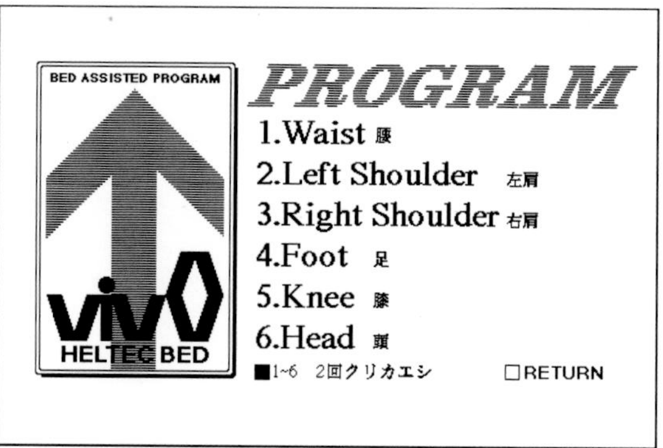

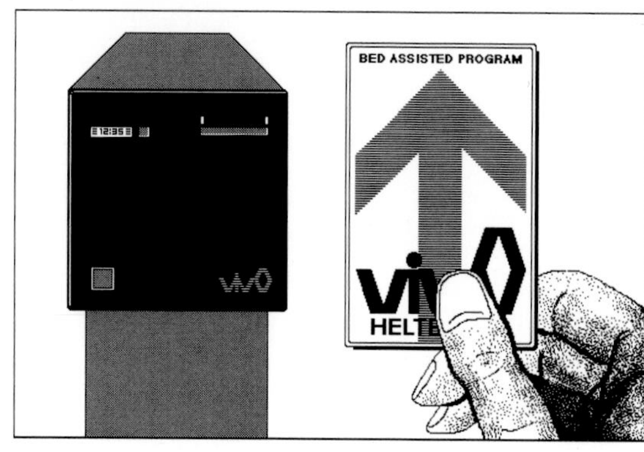

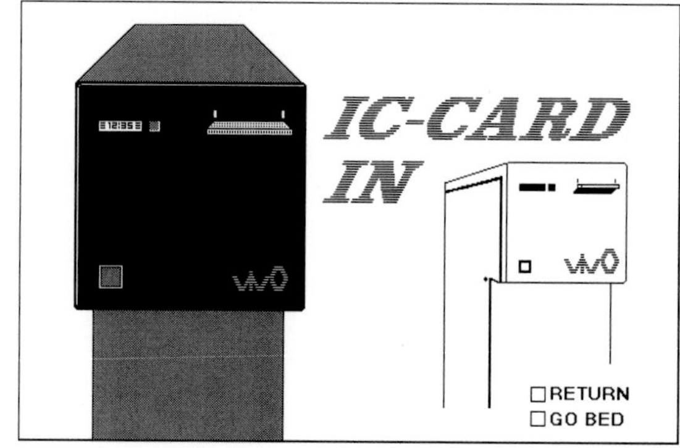

Once the project was approved, more detailed drawings of the bed were created with Claris CAD.

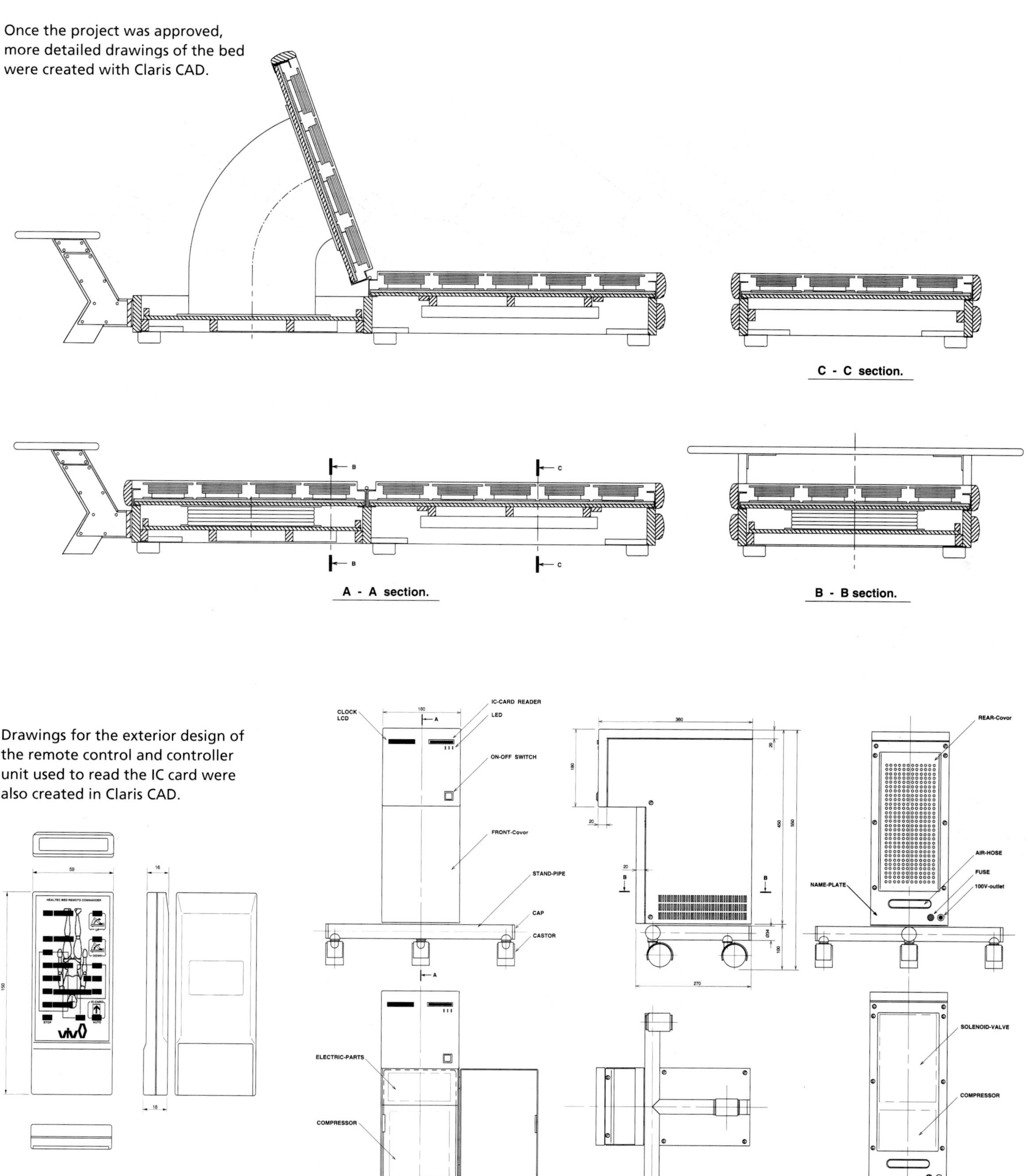

Drawings for the exterior design of the remote control and controller unit used to read the IC card were also created in Claris CAD.

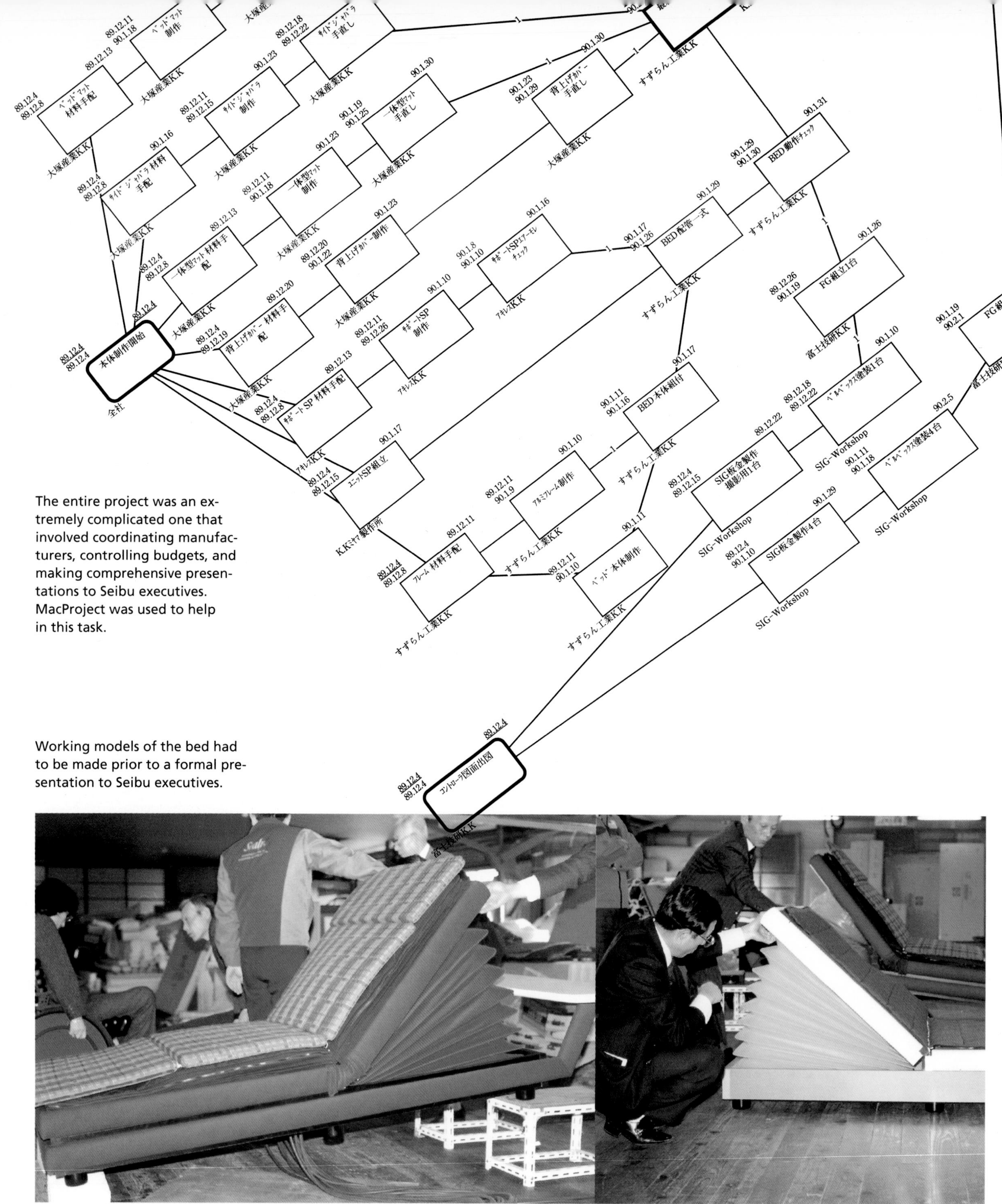

The entire project was an extremely complicated one that involved coordinating manufacturers, controlling budgets, and making comprehensive presentations to Seibu executives. MacProject was used to help in this task.

Working models of the bed had to be made prior to a formal presentation to Seibu executives.

Before permission could be obtained for the Healthtec Bed to be manufactured in quantity, a final presentation had to be made to Seibu. For this presentation, Kawasaki assembled a Macintosh for each executive to view a HyperCard and PowerPoint presentation created for this purpose.

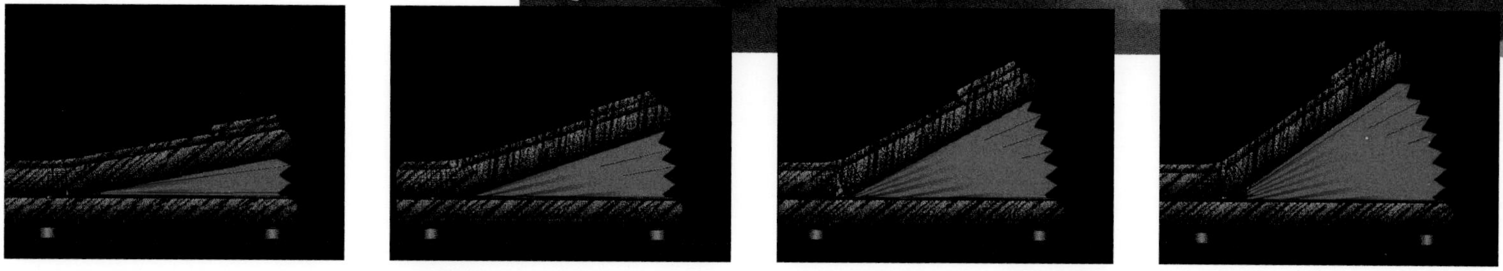

Kawasaki's presentation was a great success, and Seibu gave approval for the beds to be manufactured. Unfortunately, soon after manufacturing began, massive changes were made in the executive staff at Seibu and, as sometimes happens, the Vivo Healthtec Bed never reached the step of mass-production. To date, only 30 sets have been sold, and whether or not production should continue is a matter currently under discussion.

Portfolio

Desk Clock "Micros Hola", 1991
Takata, Inc.
Claris CAD,
MacroMind Director (for rendering)

Following page:

Wall Clocks "Hola", 1988
Takata, Inc.
Claris CAD,
MacroMind Director (for rendering)

Computer desk, 1990
Plus Corporation
Claris CAD,
MacroMind Director (for presentation)

Following page:

Flower vase series, 1991
Takata, Inc.
Claris CAD

Wheelchair, 1988
SIG Workshop
Claris CAD, PowerPoint and
MacroMind Director (for presentation)

Swinging chair, 1990
Tokyo Designer's Week Exhibition
"Kagu"
SIG Workshop
Claris CAD, HyperCard

Following page:

Floor chair "Ton Ton", 1987
Maruichi Selling
MacDraw

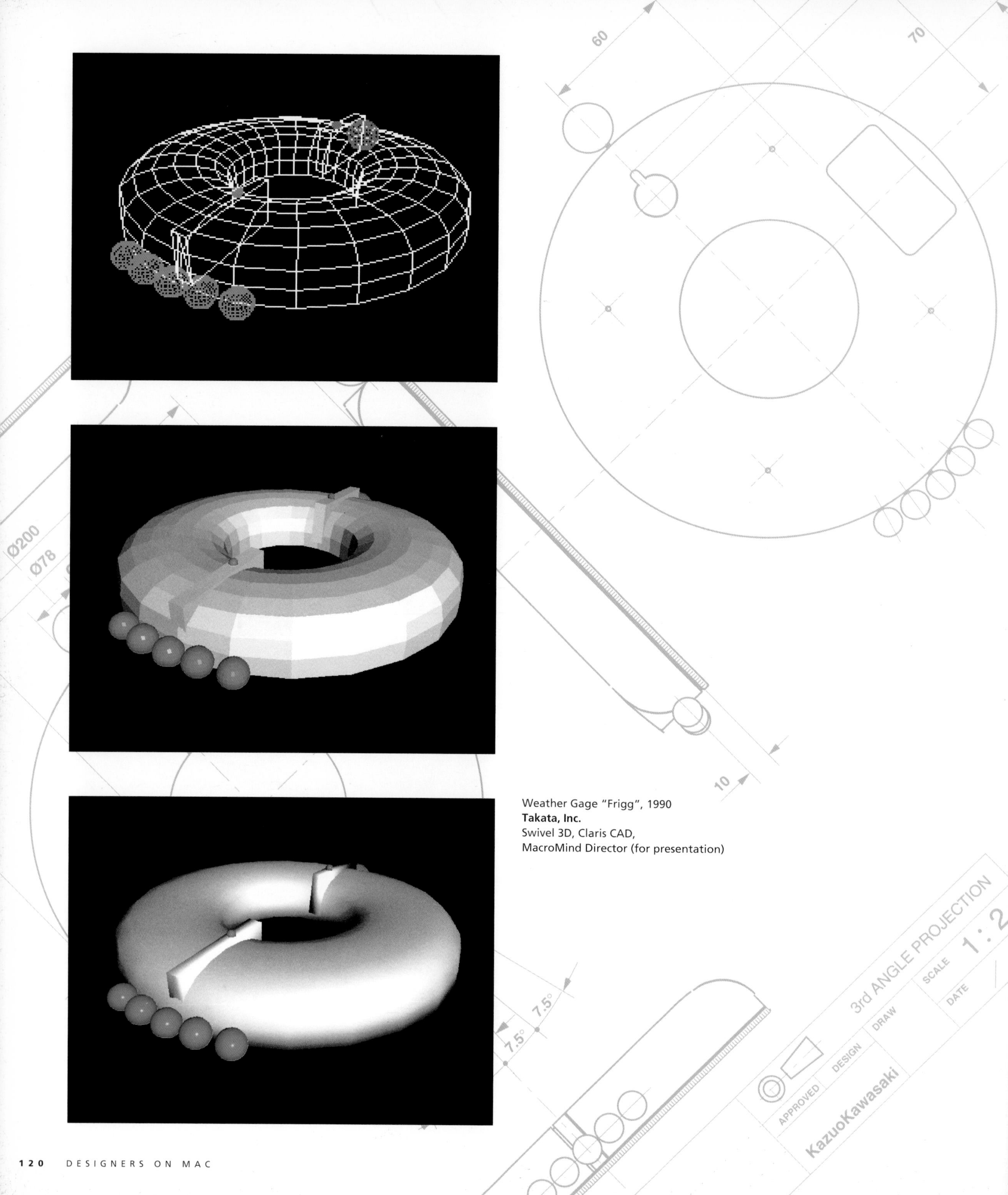

Weather Gage "Frigg", 1990
Takata, Inc.
Swivel 3D, Claris CAD,
MacroMind Director (for presentation)

Knife and cutting board, 1991
Takefu Knife Village
Claris CAD

Knife series, 1989
Takefu Knife Village
Claris CAD

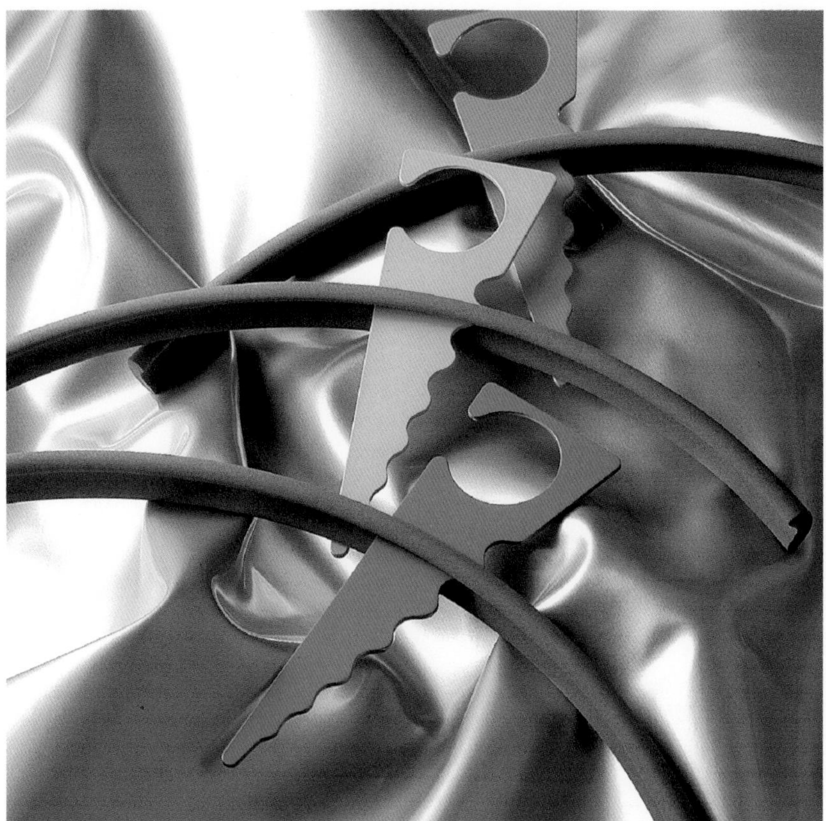

Coat hangers, 1989
SIG Workshop
Claris CAD,
MacroMind Director (for presentation)

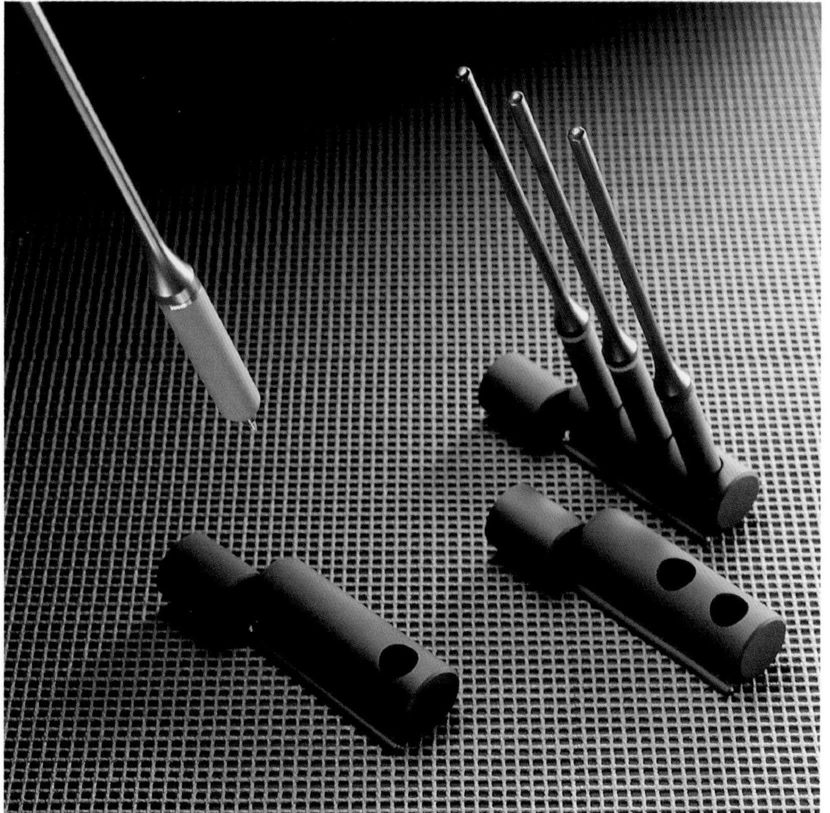

Pen set, 1989
Takata, Inc.
MacDraw, PowerPoint

Javier Mariscal

Javier Mariscal follows in the tradition of some of the greatest Spanish artists and designers. Born in Valencia, Spain, Mariscal began his creative career in Barcelona, drawing underground comics. For over twenty years, he has lent his playful sense of humor to graphics, textiles, and interiors. His furniture designs have been shown throughout Europe, including at Memphis: The International Style exhibit in Milan in 1981, and Nouvelles Tendances at the Georges Pompidou Center, Paris, in 1987. ¶ In 1988, Mariscal's character, Cobi, was chosen as the official mascot of the 1992 Olympics in Barcelona. Today, Mariscal's studio is bustling, with all the tools of the graphics trade — paints and brushes, modeling clay, and Macintosh computers. These tools serve the creativity of a man whose art has a childlike quality, on the one hand, and who is enormously commercial on the other.

A selection of Marsical's earlier work, including posters, fabric designs, and comics.

Your work is so happy, so free-flowing, and so painterly, how did you become interested in using computers?

As far as my work goes, some people, especially other painters, may look at it and say "When you're painting, you're smiling, and you look like you're having a good time. You are not creating real art because you're so happy; in real art, you must suffer a great deal. Your art is always smiling art." But the thing is, I like it. Some artists create art that people don't understand until they read about it in a book, then they think they understand it, so suddenly, they like it. I hate this kind of art.

If you look at my career over the years, you can see that I've always been willing to try many different things. My first exhibition, Gran Hotel, which took place at Barcelona's Galería Mec-Mec in 1977, is a good example. The entire gallery was designed as a 1950's hotel, and displayed many different kinds of work. Of course, these included my comics and posters, which I had been doing for awhile, but there were also papier mâché sculptures, paintings on glass, sweaters, and even videos. Soon after, I began working with Marieta, one of Spain's leading fashion houses, designing textiles. Since then, I have worked in a variety of media. The computer was simply another new thing for me to explore.

How did you first become involved with the Macintosh?

A friend of mine bought one very early, back in 1984 or 1985. It was, of course, black and white only with a tiny, tiny screen. The first time I used the Macintosh was to draw an invitation for my daughter's birthday party. It seemed to me that the Macintosh was like a new kind of pencil, and I knew I wanted to understand more about it.

I've always enjoyed the experience of change. I had seen the Macintosh in one or two studios, around 1985 or 1986. I saw that it was not so complicated and I thought about it. I wanted to know exactly what a computer was; to understand its process, its way of thinking, and its language. I also wanted to know how it could be used by someone like me. So I tried to see how the Macintosh could fit into the studio. I knew I would have to experience it for awhile before I could understand it thoroughly. I thought it was best to start very slowly and so for the first year, I expected nothing. You know, it's just like when you come to a swimming pool for the first time; first you have to learn how to swim. You can't just start without going through the learning process.

In some ways, though, my early experience with the computer was very negative, because it had so little memory and a such a tiny screen, and I actually didn't learn how to use it as quickly as I expected. There were many things that took hours to do using the Macintosh that I could do in five minutes by hand.

During that learning process, I tried to observe the computer's process, then I began to observe my own process of work. I tried to see how the two could be merged. It became very interesting for me to grasp my own way of working, and to look at why I cut here, or why I photocopied this thing, or how the work actually became produced and printed. Understanding this was necessary for me to make any significant transition to using this new tool, this new pencil called "Macintosh."

It was quite a long process, learning how to use the computer in my work, because my work is not like, say, a tomato-packing factory, where many different people do the same thing, and put the same kind of tomatoes in the same box. My work requires many different things of the computer, not just the same thing all the time. It's important to know why you're using the computer each time.

Last year, we worked with a Silicon Graphics workstation to create a 3D animated commercial for TV. We created an animated logo, but we also spent days experimenting and trying to use the technology in a different way, playing with the textures, the lines, and the colors; even the movement itself. It really made me realize that with the computer, you have a special kind of problem. If you're using a pen or a brush on paper, you have maybe three different ways of doing something, but with the computer, you have 3,000 different ways. With a computer, you have so many different choices, it's easy to get lost. It's important to keep thinking about what you're doing, and what it is you really want to express. You must keep the end result in mind, and never forget it. It's important not to change the end just because the machine gives you so many options.

Another major consideration in our bringing Macintosh computers into the studio was to determine the right people to work on the computer. We had to find people who had an understanding of both graphics and how to make the computer work. It's especially hard in a country like Spain, which is not as technology-oriented as some other countries, like the United States or Japan. We did find one person in particular who was really able to bring us from the theory of what the Macintosh could do to showing us the details of how to make it work for the graphic results we wanted. She brought the computer part and the graphic part together. She could train others in the studio, too, which was really critical.

The Macintosh is now a key element in the way I work now, but it's taken a couple of years to evolve to this stage.

This television commercial for Onda Cero Radio involded 3D models, Chinese ink paintings on couche paper, and a variety of software including Scanner 2D, Scanner 3D, Wavefront, and Photoshop. It all finally came together on a Silicon Graphics workstation.

How exactly is the computer used in your studio?

Well, right now we use the computer in three different ways. One way is to all archive images, whether they were originally created on the computer or not. We can then use these images in presentations about our work to various clients by creating a demonstration of these MacroMind Director.

The second way we use the computer is to sketch with. We'll use the computer to work out an idea, but then we may use traditional techniques to produce a final mechanical for printing. For example, yesterday I was working on a cover for a textile catalog. I decided to hand-draw some letters and then put them in the scanner. Once in the computer, we applied colors, and experimented with various ideas for the cover. It's very similar to how I might have used a photocopier and colored pens in the

Estudio Marsical.

past to work up a rough sketch of an idea. The computer just makes it easier to try different ideas and colors out very quickly. Once we have "sketched" various ideas with the computer, we produce an original in the traditional way, with pen and ink, and the separations will also be done traditionally.

The third way we use the computer is to sketch with it and then create the final process color separation film directly from the Macintosh disk file.

Your work is so colorful. Do you find it a problem that the color on the Macintosh monitor is often quite different than the final color that will be produced by the offset printing process?

Well, when we work on those pieces for which we ourselves want to produce the final film, we follow a number of steps to alleviate the problem of the difference in monitor colors from actual printed colors. First, I often start with a pen drawing. I like to use Japanese brush painting for letters and shapes. We then scan this painted image in, convert it to an encapsulated Postscript file using Adobe Streamline, and then use Aldus FreeHand to apply various colors, usually PANTONE colors, until we find the colors we like.

As you know, the monitor colors have nothing to do with the final printed color, and if we create four-color process film from this file, the colors will not match the colors on the monitor. So we make a copy of the file and apply the correct process color percentages. These are determined by matching the screen color to a color book, which gives us the right CMYK breakdown for the color, as it appears to the eye on the computer monitor. That file is then sent out to produce four color process film separations.

I think the lack of a consistent color model on the Macintosh is a big problem. You can even see the same color change on the screen just by switching from one program to another, even if you use the same machine, with the same monitor. This is one of the many reasons I feel like we're in a cave making primitive cave drawings using the computer. The Macintosh is, in many ways, a very primitive machine right now. It's crazy to have these problems with something as important as color, and to spend so many hours doing things only to run out of memory. It makes me feel like Buster Keaton or Charlie Chaplin in the early days of cinema-making. Like them, I feel like I'm in the beginning of a very new process.

Tell us about Cobi, the 1992 Olympic mascot — did the Macintosh play a role in your development and subsequent production of the many different images of Cobi?

I think the Olympics are a great thing, because people from around the world come together. It's competitive, but people like it because it's like a big party, the "Fiesta Mundial," the world party. We made a character that has many different expressions, but mostly happy ones. Cobi was the chosen character in the competition for the Olympic mascot, and though he is "official," he's deliberately not serious, as so many official things are.

We did not use the Macintosh for the development of the original Cobi, nor did we use it for the hundreds of pages of the Mascot Variations Manual that had to be produced, showing Cobi participating in different sports. Now, however, we are using it to produce the official comic books of "The Cobi Troupe" for the Olympics.

The Macintosh did play a big role in the development of Petra, one of the characters from the cartoon series "The Cobi Troupe." Petra was chosen as the official mascot of the IX Paralympic Games. The IX Paralympic games will be held in Barcelona soon after the regular Olympic games. Petra is just like any

Petra, the official mascot of the IX Paralympics.

other person except she has no arms. I didn't want to portray her in the more typical way of being in a wheelchair, because that's always used. There are so many other types of handicaps — there are people who are blind, who are very intelligent but who have motor control problems, for example. Also, it's more of a surprise because the first time you see Petra, you think she looks normal, but then, she tries to drink a glass of water, and she cannot, because she has no arms.

We ended up making a lot of color changes for Cobi as late as the printing stage, and, as you know, it costs a lot of money to change something once it's printed. With Petra, I could see all of the Petras, in each of the different sports, all at once. After looking at these for three or four days on the computer, I could see very quickly if a color was wrong; we didn't have to wait a month for it to get back from the printer.

We produced the *IX Paralympic Games Barcelona '92 Graphic Standards Manual* for Petra completely on the Macintosh, using both FreeHand and QuarkXPress. It made a tremendous difference, because I could make color decisions more quickly, and we could move through the actual production of so many pages much faster.

Do you use the Macintosh to show clients new ideas as they are being developed?

We're beginning to do so now, and have had many successful presentations using the Macintosh. Sometimes we use the screen for presentations, and sometimes we use printouts from our color printer, the QMS ColorScript. Both provide a perfect way for me to discuss the graphics, the drawings, the type; everything about a particular piece.

Also, I find that leaving the drawings in the computer is like leaving them in a drawer, where they are sleeping. They are more "alive" than if they were stuck on a piece of paper where they're not so easily changed.

Do you think you'll ever stop painting and use the computer exclusively?

You're asking me? I really don't know — painting, or working with computers, or making videos — it depends very much on your feelings, doesn't it? Also, I think it depends on your evolution. At different periods in my life, I've done quite different things. Right now I don't know if I'll only be painting in the future, or never paint again. But if I stopped painting, it would not be because I thought painting is a very old — too old — way of doing things; it would be because it no longer interested me.

I think that people will always paint, because it's a very natural exercise. There will always be people making things with their hands, because it's normal. It's like eating; it's something you do with your hands, your eyes, with your brain, and sometimes, with your heart.

Step by Step

The Feria de Valencia, Valencia's Department of Events and organizers of Valencia's 28 Feria Internacional del Mueble de Valencia, the 28th Annual International Furniture Show, asked Mariscal to design a poster for the event. Mariscal began with a sketch, and his studio staff used Adobe Photoshop and Aldus FreeHand to produce the piece.

Mariscal drew black and white sketches of furniture using Japanese sumi ink and brushes. The sketches were scanned in, and converted to PostScript outlines using Adobe Streamline. FreeHand was used to apply the colors to the furniture and background tile shapes. Photoshop was used to indicate the color and position of the large brushstrokes in the background of the painting.

Mariscal began working out his ideas for the poster with crayons and paper. This sketch became the guide for the production of the poster.

Mariscal drew pieces of furniture using Chinese ink and brushes. These black and white illustrations were scanned in at 500 dpi and saved as TIFF files.

Adobe Streamline was used to convert the TIFF files to Postscript outlines. Streamline's default settings were used to trace the high resolution images, producing accurate rendering of the brush-stroke feeling.

Conversion method:
Outline
Centerline
Centerline & Outline
Noise level 8 pixels
Reverse image
Select image area
Convert image using:
Curved & Straight lines
convert long lines as:
1 2 3 4 5
straight normal curved
Curved lines only
Straight lines only
Match bitmap (tolerance):
1 2 3 4 5
tight normal loose
Cancel
Defaults
OK

Mariscal wanted to use pastel colors in the poster, with a feel reminiscent of swimming pool tiles. Colors were set up in a FreeHand file, thus allowing Mariscal to make decisions about colors and change them interactively onscreen. Colors were applied to the furniture drawings, and one by one, they were placed on square tiles. The pattern of the background tiles began to evolve during this process.

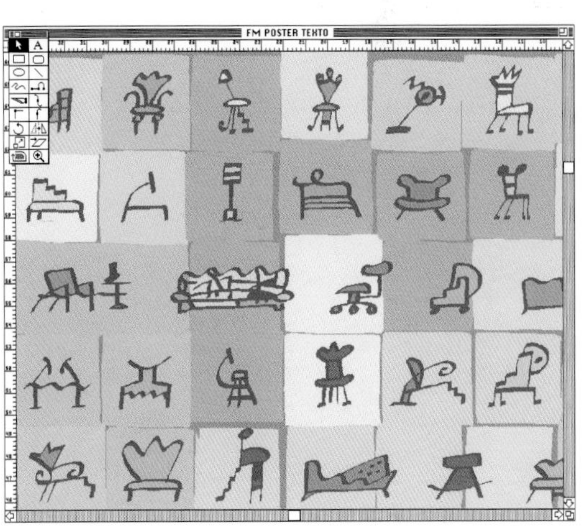

A scan of the type from the previous year's poster was scanned in at full size to begin to explore the type treatment. Final text was typed in FreeHand.

The last touch to be added was the large brush strokes in the background. Mariscal painted a brushstroke, and it was scanned in. The scanned brushstroke was opened in Photoshop, where the brushstroke was saved in an alpha channel so it could easily be selected for placement in the poster.

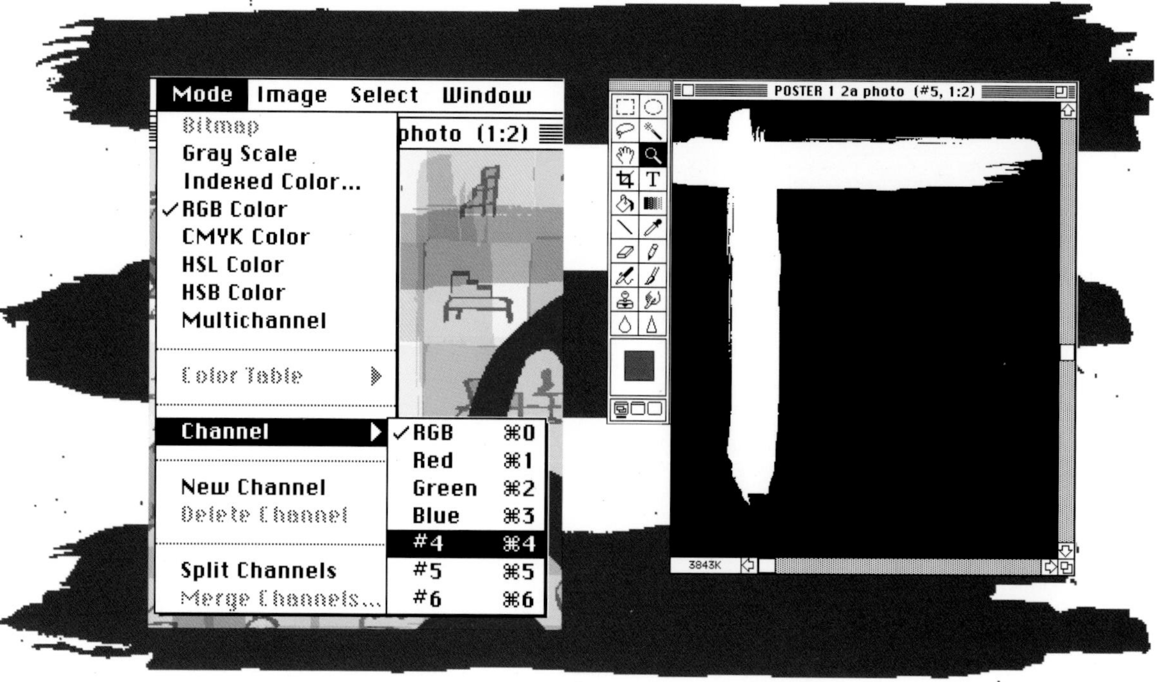

The FreeHand file was opened in Photoshop. The brushstroke was filled with a transparent color, and positioned in the poster. The Photoshop file allowed Mariscal to work out the details of color and position onscreen. The FreeHand file was later used to output four-color process film, but the brushstroke had to be scanned in on a Scitex system and digitally stripped into the film created by FreeHand.

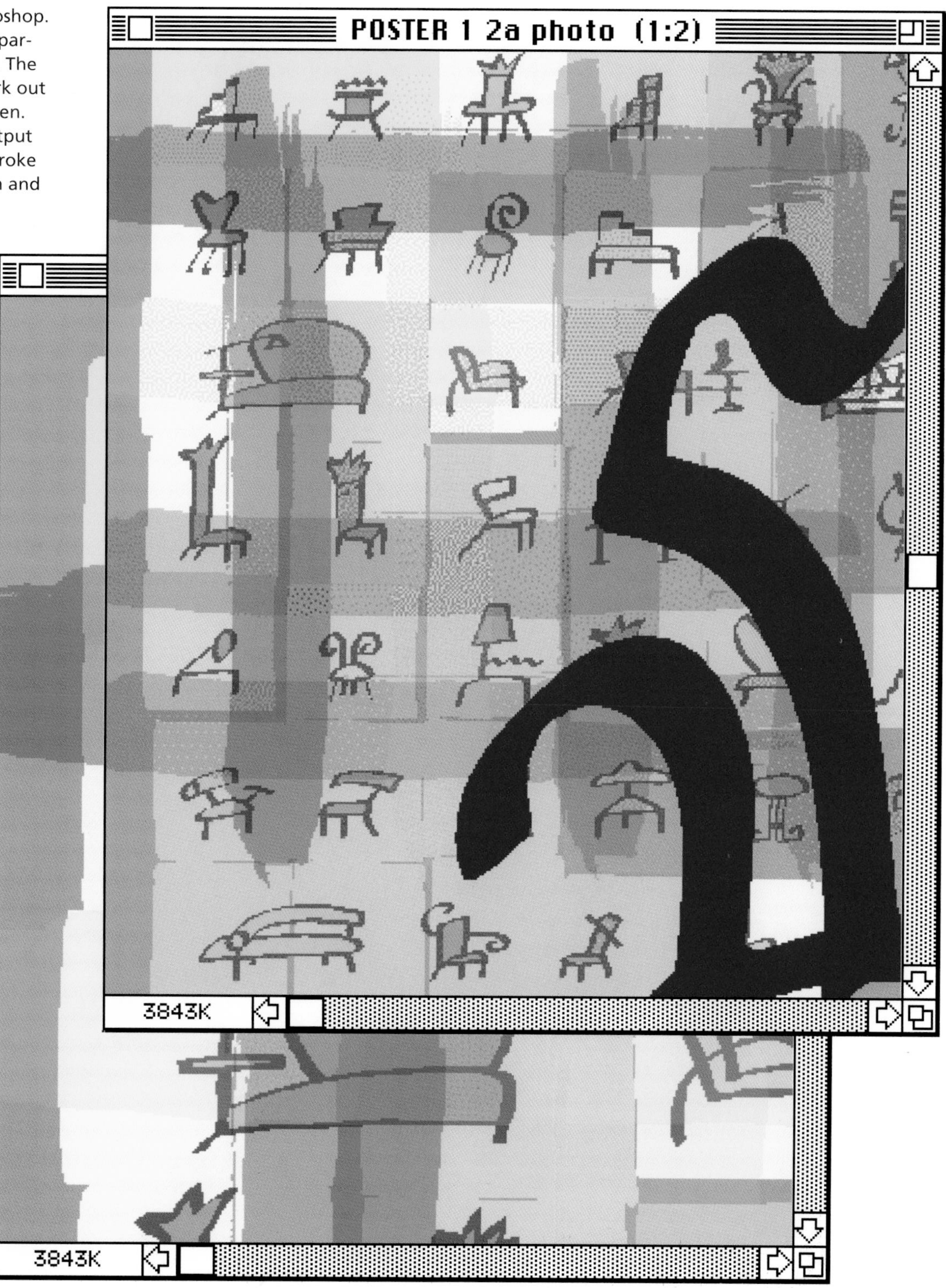

Portfolio

Variations of Corporate Cobi, 1989-90
Cobi Guia Turístic (Patronat de Turisme de Barcelona)
Chinese ink, couche paper,
Adobe Streamline, Adobe Illustrator,
Aldus FreeHand

Calendar, 1990
Damm Brewery
Chinese ink, couche paper,
PixelPaint Professional

Following page:

Shopping bag, 1990
La Pedrera. Olimpiad Cultural S.A.
(for the exhibition on Modernism
"El Quadrat d'Or")
Chinese ink, couche paper,
PixelPaint Professional

MARISCAL

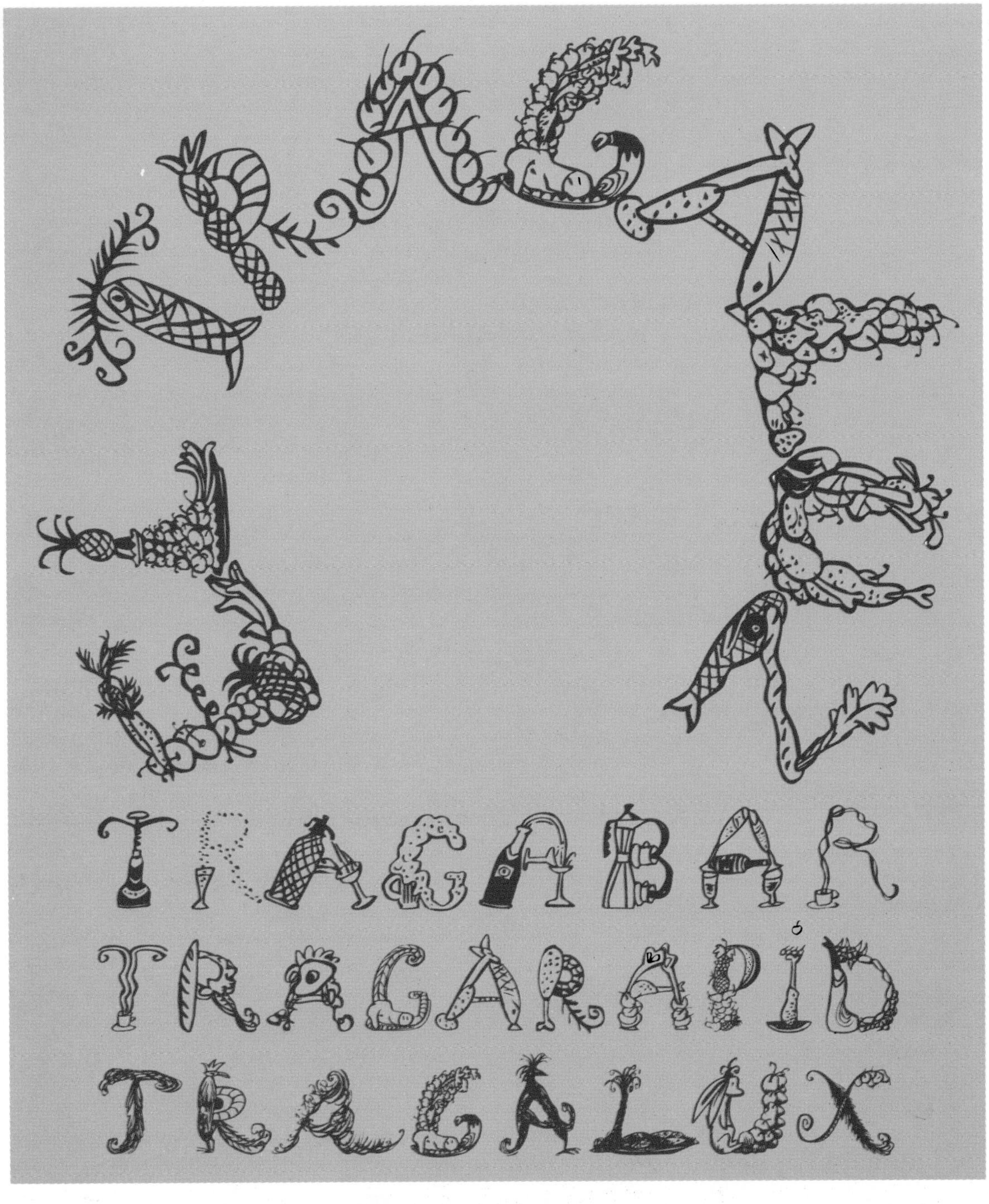

TRAGABAR
TRAGARAPID
TRAGALUX

Logotype, 1990
Tragaluz Restaurant
Chinese ink, couche paper,
Aldus FreeHand

Signage, 1990
Riu de Xiquets, ITVA (children's park)
Chinese ink, couche paper,
Aldus FreeHand

Logptype, 1990
Onda Cero Radio
Chinese ink, couche paper,
Adobe Streamline, Adobe Illustrator,
Aldus FreeHand

Logptype, 1990
Torres de Avila (night bar)
Chinese ink, couche paper,
Aldus FreeHand

Following spread:

Interior design, 1990
Torres de Avila
(left page: first floor central corridor;
right page: "Moon tower")
Chinese ink, couche paper,
Scratchwork, various building
materials

Interior design in collaboration
with Alfredo Arribas

Poster, 1992
The Houston International Festival
Chinese ink, couche paper,
Microtek scanner, Aldus FreeHand

Poster, 1992
Mariscal in London
Chinese ink, couche paper,
Microtek scanner, Aldus FreeHand

Yukimasa Okumura

Yukimasa Okumura's design work is among the most in demand in Japan today. His work is an unusual combination of traditional Japanese painting and computer technology, and may be seen in many places, from cosmetic advertising to music promotions. Okumura's education in traditional Japanese brush painting began when he was four years old. His instructor was his father, who continued the tradition that had been part of their family for generations. ¶ In 1965, however, Okumura decided to turn away from traditional Japanese painting, and to become a designer. He graduated from the Kuwasawa Design Institute in 1969 and spent the next few years in a variety of design projects, including everything from editorial design to stage design. After serving as art director for a popular Japanese rock group, Yellow Magic Orchestra, from 1978 to 1982, he turned back to his roots. Today, his studio is cluttered with paints, brushes and rice paper, along with video and sound systems, and several Macintosh computers.

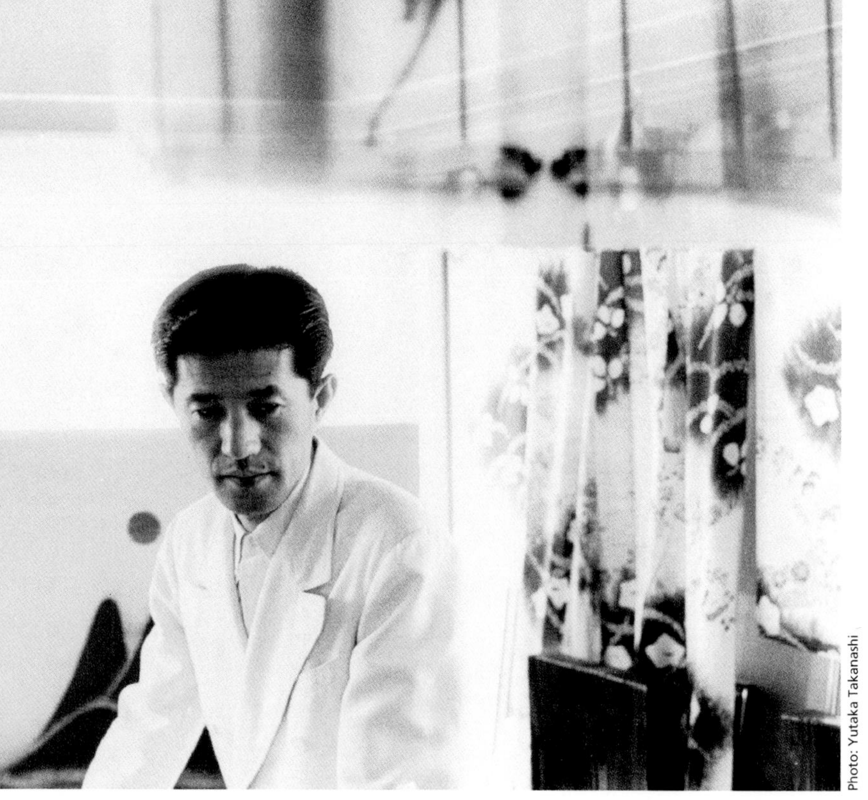

Photo: Yutaka Takanashi

Poster and mark for the popular band, YMO.

It seems your work has an interesting combination of some very old Japanese crafts and the latest computer technology — what were you doing before you started using the Macintosh?

I was born into an artistic family with a long tradition. Both my father and my grandfather were painters, so I was trained in traditional Japanese painting.

But when I discovered the American culture as a teenager, it fascinated me and I tried to break away from the family tradition and change my career from that of painter to graphic designer. My starting point as a designer, then, was when I first encountered American culture about 20 years ago.

Although at that time the information available in Japan on American culture was very limited, I still came across the work of American art directors and movements like the Psychedelic and Pop-Art movements at the end of the 1960s. I spent the next 15 years absorbing many elements of American culture.

During this period, I began to realize that its origin was really in European culture, not only in graphic design, but also in music, and thus I became interested in European culture as well. Through American culture, for example, I learned about the European artists who came to the U.S. before World War II in flight from Nazism. I also found out about Bauhaus and Russian Constructionist and many other styles. My interest in these kinds of things made my family sad, as I was no longer following in the family's painting tradition.

There was a big turning point for me about ten years ago, when I became deeply involved with the band called YMO (Yellow Magic Orchestra). At that time, the music most representative of American music was, of course, rock music. I was very absorbed by the rock music phenomenon, and events like Woodstock. I started working with YMO when I was 30 years old, until age 35. I was their designer and went on a world tour with the band. During that time I did many different things, including video.

Eventually, the band dispersed and each member has since started their own new life. And it's funny that after being so inspired by American culture, each one of us now is trying to find very traditional Japanese elements in their work. Like Ryuichi Sakamoto, one of the main members of Yellow Magic Orchestra, and me, the others, too, are trying to find a universal appeal in very traditional Japanese elements.

Ever since my days with YMO ended, I have felt some doubt about looking towards America all the time. Of course, I still admire many American and British artists, but I have stopped collecting material from outside of Japan and have tried to reflect on my own culture. I found the Japanese elements which I had once tried to escape could be very interesting. After all, there are not many Japanese graphic designers who have received a formal, proper education in traditional Japanese painting.

My view is different from most others. The Japanese design educational system has been strongly influenced by the European Bauhaus style. The older designers especially, 50 years and older, are very fond of that style and were inspired by the Modernism Movement.

These designers may be likely to actually reject any kind of traditional Japanese style or element in their work. They feel uncomfortable when someone like me tries to touch the Japanese essence. Some even feel quite negatively about it. They think designing using Japanese elements is a kind of "backward" step in their design, or they are afraid of being considered too "sentimental." You see, before World War II, they grew up with the philosophy that Japanese culture should be number one in the world. This philosophy was broken into pieces when the war was over. To them, Japanese culture is a lost culture. So they try to avoid the old, traditional

Okumura's studio.

elements in their design because they want to show they have progressed since the war.

Now, in the 1990s, Japanese culture is getting more popular than ever, and we have many exhibits that reflect the beauty of old Japan. However, the concept behind these exhibits, or the thought of the designers or art directors who are putting them on, is that the traditional Japanese culture is too special to touch, like a shrine. I feel a real distance between their ideas and mine.

And in other countries, too, exhibits of Japanese art tend to focus on stereotypes, like a Geisha girl or Mt. Fuji. I don't like that tendency, either.

I want to express the Japanese elements through more universal, worldwide images that everyone can relate to. As you know, the Japanese culture, or tradition, was not really our own, but brought here from other countries on the Silk Road. For example, the city of Kyoto was established by the Emperor Kanmu, who in recent historical study is regarded as a foreigner. Our method of writing came to us from China. So in a way, everything in the Japanese culture has international roots.

Working with YMO helped me to start looking at things with a fresh vision. I really concentrated for five years, dedicating all my energy to very experimental works in video and all kinds of media. During this period, I also received some graphic design awards and began to establish my name in this field.

Often, a designer is satisfied with successful results and tries to keep that same style thereafter. But I changed my style completely after working with YMO. I have always have tried to change my style; after concentrating on one style, I move on to another. This makes my work rather difficult to identify as mine.

For example, there's a great deal of variety in books that I've designed within the last year. In the case of book design, I always try to express the author's style, not my own. Before I start to design, I read the whole book first and then think about the possible solutions. In general, Japanese designers have their own styles and you can very easily tell who designed a given book. But I have many styles, according to the situation and the nature of the book.

How did you first learn about the Macintosh and why did you first start using it?

Before I had a Macintosh, I had an Amiga computer, which I used for creating video and other types of work. However, as you may know, the Amiga cannot prepare files for offset printing very well, and I was not satisfied with the printing quality in general. Then I heard about the color version of the Macintosh that made the output of color separations possible, so I bought a Macintosh II about three years ago.

I like designing printed pieces, so I am always thinking about how I can reproduce my work on a printing press and about which materials and data are needed for printing. Also, about the time I bought the Macintosh II, I decided to investigate what I could do in my work without using any American or European elements. In a way, the Macintosh helped me with this research. I started looking for those Japanese elements with very international motifs, looking at the Japanese elements that I had known so well. I want people to be moved when they see my work. I want my work to have an international appeal.

So the Macintosh came into my studio, and became an important part of my current style. For the first year and a half, we used Illustrator 88. After that, we also used Swivel 3-D. Last year, we used many different programs, and now it seems that we use almost everything available.

How exactly do you use the Macintosh in your studio?

I rarely operate the computer myself. I am commissioned to do so many paintings that I don't have time to sit in front of the computer. At our new studio, however, which will open next year, I want to have my own computer to work on. But right now, if I go into the part of this studio where my staff is, they don't want me in there.

The staff operate the computer and finish the work after I check it. Occasionally, the staff originate the idea and produce the finished work by themselves. But usually they follow my sketches, simulating my paintings or adding surfaces and textures to them after scanning them in.

For example, we recently created a poster for a cosmetics company. I indicated in a very rough sketch that took only a few minutes that the poster should be done by computer, in the shape of many lips forming an overall shape like a flower bursting open. I indicated roughly where the copy should go, and that it should be red, relating to the colors in the lips. My staff took it from there. I checked the piece before we sent it to be output for final film.

I think there are certain effects that can only be achieved by painting, but there are other effects, textures and colors, that can only be created using the computer. I like images created by the computer. My work is a combination of the traditional painting of Japan, in which I was trained so thoroughly, and the computer.

A recent job is a perfect example of this. There is a noh-play called "Dojoji." In this play, the heroine changes herself into a snake, and a fan we designed to be used in the play shows this scene. "Dojoji" is a special noh-play because it's used as a commemorative dance to show the audience that the noh-dancer has finished the first step of formal training. This fan is a present from dancer to the audience. The custom is that the fan is given to the audience from the noh-dancer to celebrate the completed training.

Okumura's fan for the noh-play "Dojoji."

In this fan's design, the background is my painting; a woodblock print, actually. The central motif of the foreground, a cherry blossom, was done on the Macintosh, using Adobe Illustrator.

The fan was then produced by a Kyoto fan manufacturer that dates back to the 12th century. Of course, they wouldn't accept a floppy disk, so the artwork for the fan was provided as hard copy; that is, we gave them my woodblock print, and the Macintosh image was printed out on a 300 dpi color printer. Even the traditional Kyoto manufacturers of Japanese arts and crafts who have rejected this kind of work are now starting to learn to get along with computers.

Since last fall, I have been supplying color separations to the printers, using the Scitex Visionary System in many cases. As you know, the Visionary System is based on QuarkXPress and works with Scitex's Response System. In Japan at this time, there are several printers who have this system including Toppan and Dai Nippon. The cost of Scitex's systems are quite high, but Japanese printers are happy to invest money in them, especially those that can be used with desktop systems like the Macintosh. I imagine many more Japanese printers will install these systems in the future.

In some cases, our client may want to use a specific printer because they have been working with this printer for a long time. If so, I arrange to get the color separations done by those printers who have a Visionary System and then transfer the film to the printer who will actually print the job. In Japan, companies that specialize in color separations or platemaking, and not printing, are gradually increasing.

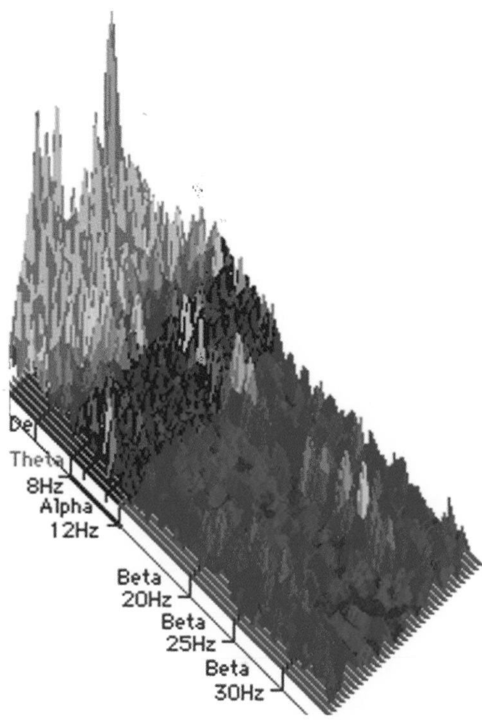

Okumura's brain waves hard at work as represented on IBVA software.

One interesting thing I've found about having computers in the studio is that it makes the young people who work here really enthusiastic about design, and that is very important. In my studio, almost everyone works on the Macintosh, and they are all very enthusiastic about learning as much as they can about operating it. They find a real joy in creating something from nothing. I think this is a healthy situation — that young designers are happy to design using computers — and I welcome it. They enjoy their progress and I believe they find more joy in their work each day. Without joy and enthusiasm, a young designer's life would be very boring. Most of them would otherwise end up working at paste-up and layout for years, or would end up doing odd jobs in the office of some famous, established designer. So in my studio, I give the initial direction, sometimes with a sketch, and sometimes with a verbal instruction, but then I let them create the piece. Of course, they show the work to me as it is in progress, and I indicate changes here and there, but they get to experience creativity of their own.

And there's a rather unique way we're using the Macintosh in our studio. We have a program called IBVA, developed by a friend of mine in New York, which is used for tracking your brain waves. By attaching a sensor to your head, the IBVA software allows you to see a 3-D representation of your alpha and beta brain waves on the Macintosh monitor. Almost every day, my staff and I use this equipment. The purpose of this program is to capture the patterns of your brain waves on a daily basis and help you to harmonize your subconscious activity with your creativity in design. Over time, you are able to change the signal according to your design activity. I often paint with this attachment on my head, and watch my brain waves on the Macintosh. I think this kind of technology will become more and more important in the future, and ultimately very useful to designers and other artists.

How do you work with the fact that color on the Macintosh monitor doesn't exactly match printed color?

Well it's true I have complaints about almost everything related to the computer, like improvements that should be made in the software, the lack of variety of Japanese typefaces available, and the limitations of the hardware. However, I know that all these things are getting better; I don't expect perfection from the computer at this early stage.

Regarding the color problem, in my studio one of my staff, or sometimes I myself go to the printing company and make a press check. The results you get from printers are pretty different if the designer stands in front of the printing presses. Press checks are an important part of the way we work here.

At the proof stage, we check if the data we created is output correctly or not, and try to bring out the best results by working closely with the printer during the proof stage. I've done things like ask that white ink be added to a background, or made indications to add a slight gloss varnish to emphasize a shadow, or a slight matte varnish to achieve another desired effect.

It's unusual, I think, for design studios to get as involved with the final printing process as we do. We watch over the last stage of printing very carefully to ensure that we get the quality I want. This way, we don't have problems with color in our final product. We can't loose sight of the mechanical, physical part of the process, that is, the printing; a great deal still relies on human judgement.

Step by Step

Okumura was asked by National Panasonic Company to design a calendar for 1992. Each page of the calendar depicts a traditional Japanese scene. The page for the month of May, like other pages in the calendar, appears on first glance to be created completely using traditional tools. But, like so much of Okumura's work, the calendar was created using a combination of traditional tools and the Macintosh.

The touch of Okumura's hand can be seen in the painting; sometimes his paintings having been reproduced directly, but other parts of the image are the result of manipulating Okumura's paintings using a Scitex Response system for some, Adobe Photoshop for others. Finally, other parts of the scene were drawn directly on the Macintosh and combined with the other elements on a Scitex system.

The central figure in the calendar page for May, a carp, or *coi* in Japanese, was painted by Okumura, employing the same basic techniques of traditional painting practiced by his family for generations. The white line around the fish that appears in the final image was added using a Scitex Response system.

Thin white lines above the fish are meant to create an effect of the fish falling, reminiscent of a comic strip. The lines were drawn using Adobe Illustrator.

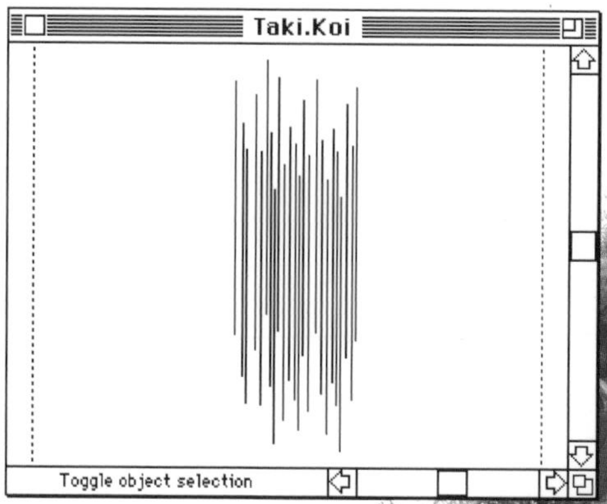

The waterfall was also painted by Okumura, and reproduced directly from his painting.

The flowers that appear throughout were drawn using Adobe Illustrator. The blend tool was used extensively to create the fills of the flower petals and stems.

The rushing water that appears in the lower left and right corners of the calendar image were created on the Macintosh in Shade, a 3D program. The 3D drawing was then opened in Adobe Photoshop, and saved in grayscale. Color was applied on the Scitex Response system, matching the colors in the waterfall.

The gold clouds were painted with black paint on traditional Japanese paper, and specified as a fifth color, gold, on the Scitex Response system.

Okumura's studio sent a photocopy with all the various elements pasted down to indicate position. The entire image was then composed of these parts on the Scitex Response system, and finally output on the Scitex.

Portfolio

Poster, 1989
The Agency for Cultural Affairs
Adobe Illustrator and traditional painting

1

1 Poster, 1990
Ohara School of Ikebana
Adobe Illustrator, Aldus FreeHand, Swivel 3D, Shade and traditional painting

2 Poster, 1989
Ohara School of Ikebana
Adobe Illustrator, Swivel 3D and traditional painting

3 Poster, 1991
Ohara School of Ikebana
Adobe Illustrator, Shade and traditional painting

2

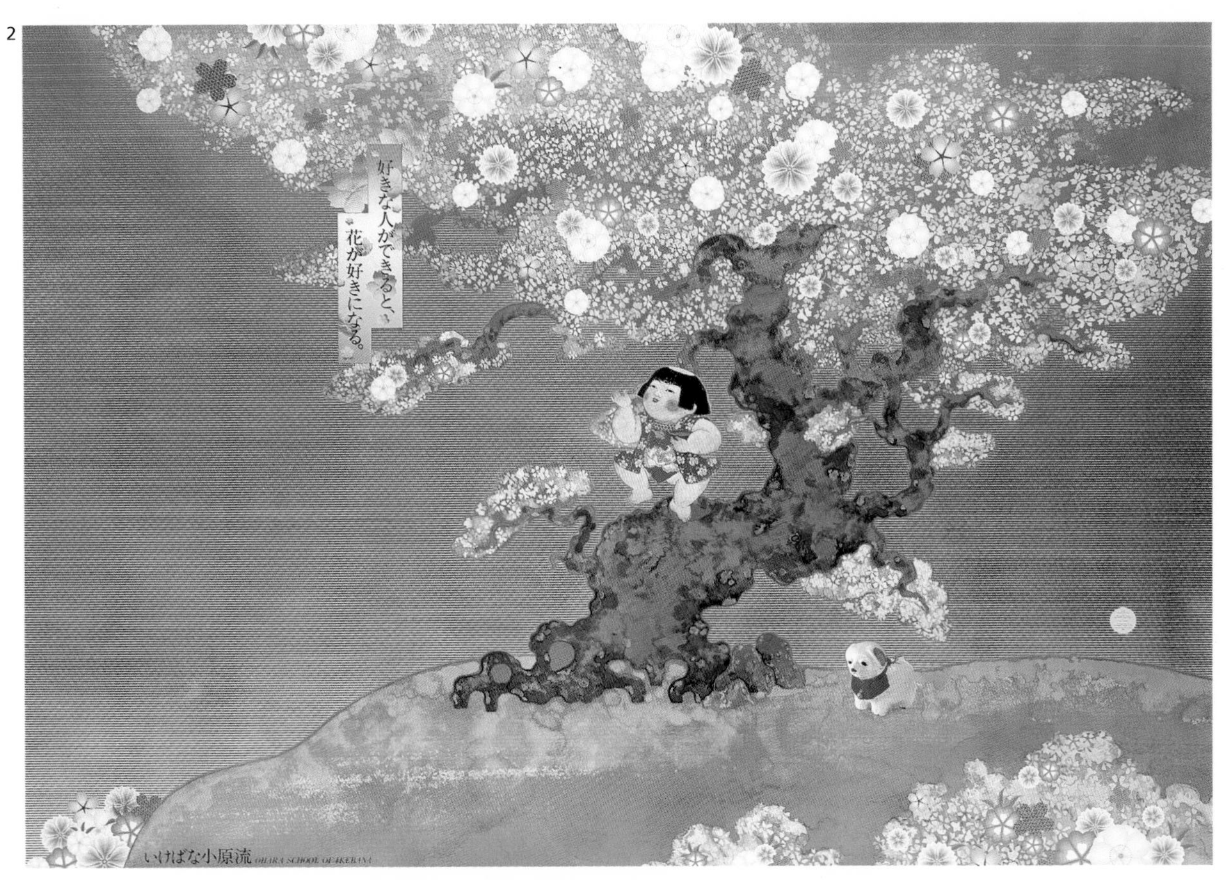

3

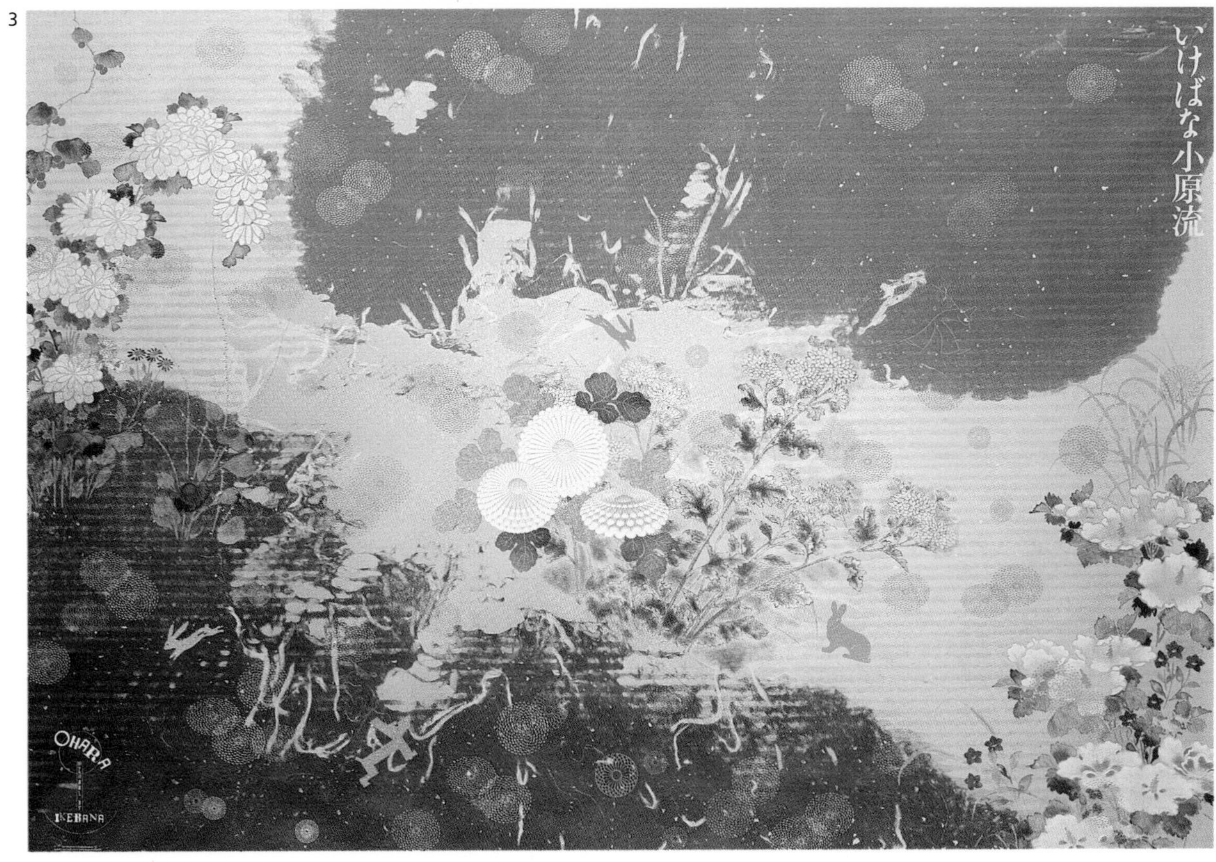

Poster, 1988
Izumiya Co., Ltd.
Adobe Illustrator, Aldus FreeHand

Poster, 1990
Loumar Cosmetics
Shade and conventional photography

菊池武夫大博覧会
'90-91 TAKÉO KIKUCHI FALL&WINTER COLLECTION MAY 16(WED.)1990
MAY 16(WED.)1990
BUNKAMURA THEATRE COCOON
TAKÉO
KIKUCHI
1st OPEN THE DOOR
16:00
RAISE THE CURTAIN
17:00
2nd OPEN THE DOOR
18:00
RAISE THE CURTAIN
19:00
WORLD CO.LTD.

Previous page:

Poster, 1990
World Co., Ltd.
Adobe Illustrator, Adobe Photoshop, Swivel 3D and traditional painting

This Page:

Invitation, 1990
World Co., Ltd.
Adobe Illustrator, Adobe Photoshop, Swivel 3D

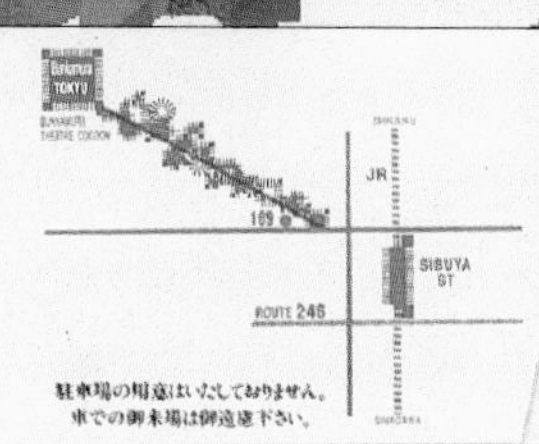

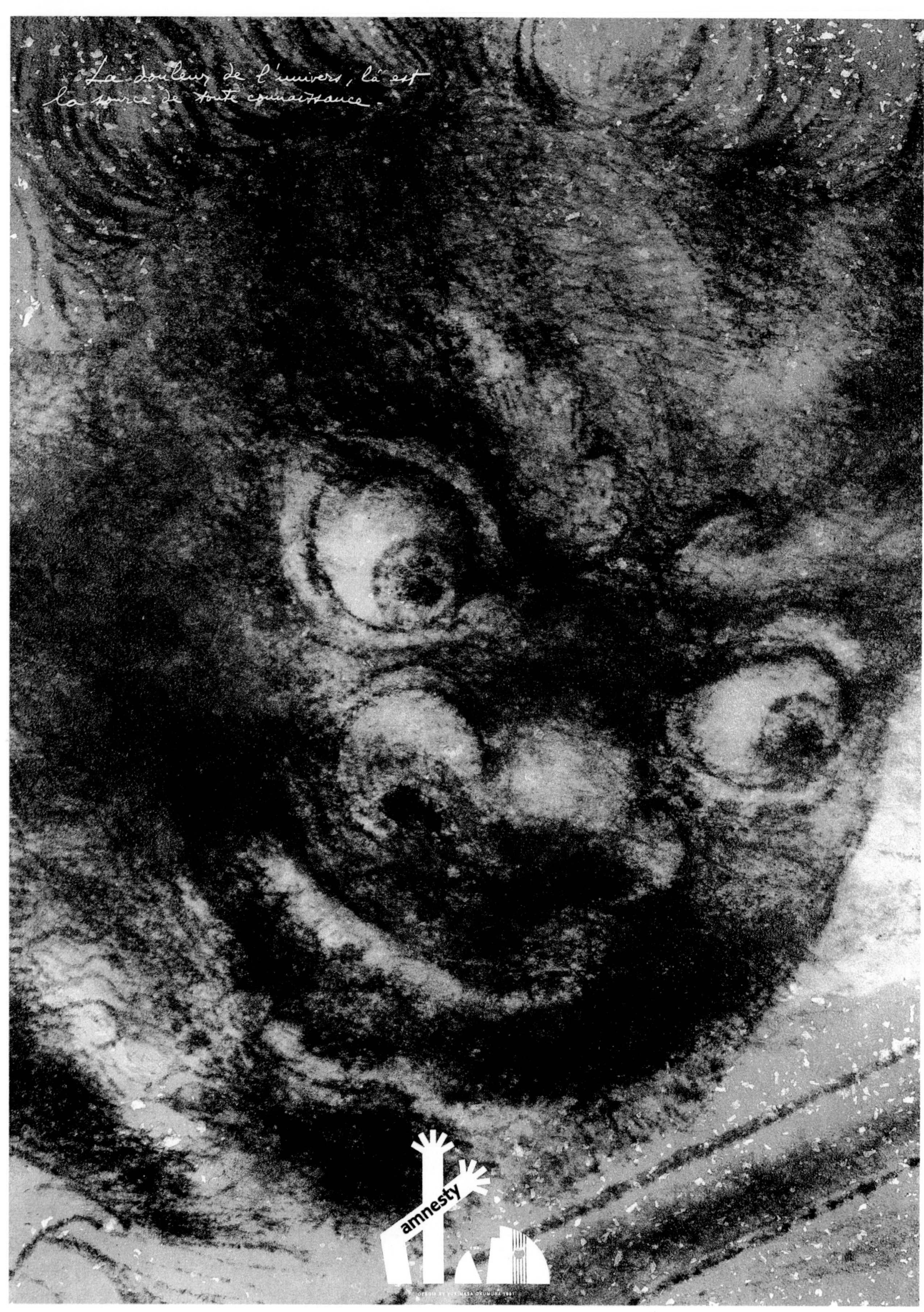
La douleur de l'univers, là est
la source de toute connaissance.
amnesty

Previous page:

Poster, 1991
Amnesty
Adobe Illustrator and
traditional painting

This page:

Album cover (front and back), 1989
Toshiba EMI Ltd.
Adobe Illustrator and
traditional painting

Concert brochure
and illustration, 1991
CO-CóLO Corporation
Shade, Adobe Photoshop

Television commercial, 1992
Matsushita Group
Adobe Illustrator, Adobe Photoshop, Aldus FreeHand, and Shade, for original artwork that was transferred to a high-end computer for video processing

Poster, 1991
Orijin-za
Shade, Photoshop

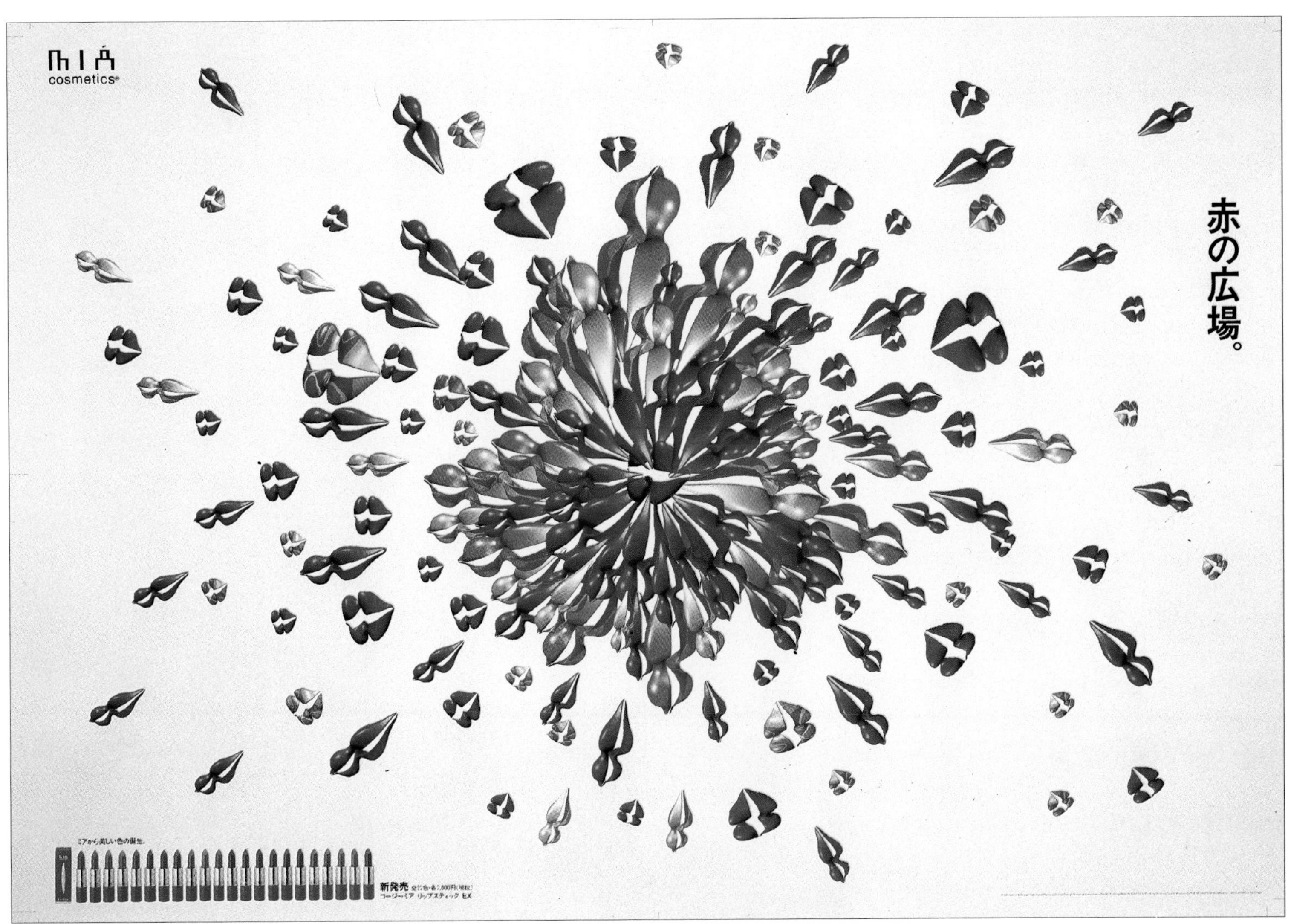

Poster, 1990
Mia Cosmetics
Shade

Erik Spiekermann / MetaDesign

Erik Spiekermann has a fetish for type, which may partly explain why he is a world-renowned typographic authority. After attending Berlin's Free University in the late 1960s, Spiekermann moved to London where he spent several years teaching and working as a typographer. He produced his first type designs for H. Berthold AG in 1979, and then returned to Berlin in 1981. Since that time, he has designed several typefaces and written three books about typography, including *Rhyme & Reason: A Typographic Novel* published in 1987 by H. Berthold AG. ¶ With one foot firmly planted in the traditional and historical roots of typography, Spiekermann has been at the forefront of setting new standards for computer-generated type. His Berlin firm, MetaDesign, has become known internationally for the design of "information" products — forms, schedules and signage. The Macintosh has played a key role in Spiekermann's approach to type and design.

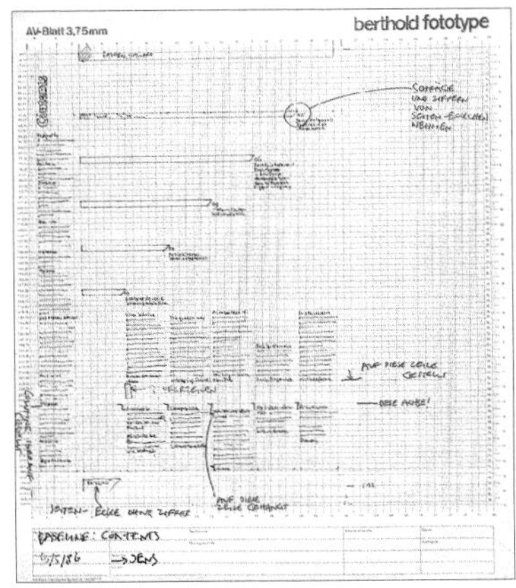

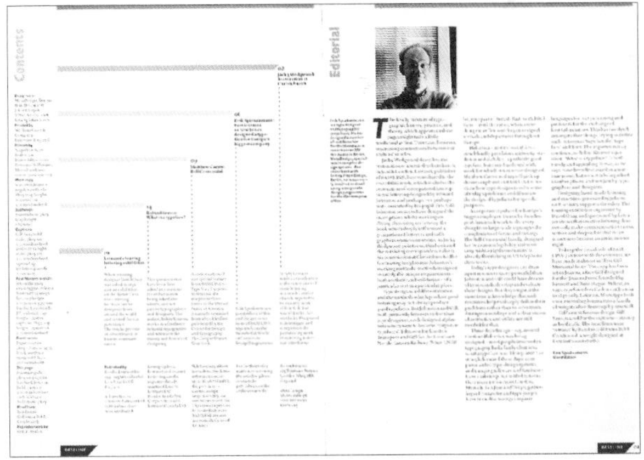

Type specifications on the Berthold grid sheet system developed by Spiekermann, and the finished printed (righthand) page. The typesetter provided films for platemaking – no artwork or camera-work was involved.

What was your life like before the Macintosh?

In some ways, it wasn't all that different because I've always been involved with type, and have been working with computers since the late 1960s. Berthold introduced their first keyboard-operated phototypesetting unit in 1967, called the Diatronic. Since that time, I've rarely used paste-up or artwork, because I've always been marking up copy for typesetting right in position. Since that first machine came out in 1967, we've been able to typeset in position. Berthold's machine could set type on an 11" x 11" piece of film, and you could address any position on that piece of film by using coordinates, which were very precise.

But there was no WYSIWYG; all you could see was one line of type at a time. It was the mid-1970s before typesetting machines had video monitors. To aid in the very careful copy preparation that was required of designers, I developed special grid sheets for Berthold to be used for specifying type. The sheets had different leading grids available, from 1.25 millimeters to 8 millimeters. All the designer had to do was mark the type on the grid sheet, then the typesetter could just key in the coordinates; for example, down 10 units, across 25 units, in hundredths of a millimeter increments. So I've been marking up type this way for over 20 years. And I've been working with computers for that long.

I've always thought about how a design would be done in production. I've always been very production-oriented as a designer, perhaps too much so, because I used to be a typesetter myself, with hot metal type. The computer wasn't alien to me and I was used to keeping in mind how a design would be produced. I used to be quite popular with typesetters because I gave such comprehensive specifications that they did not have to think at all, and they were accurate down to hundredths of a millimeter. You see, typesetters are usually given copy and simply told to make it fit.

I've always had a very structural approach to my work and so, when I saw the first Macintosh, I knew it was what I had always wanted for type.

When did you first see the Macintosh?

Several years ago, we were chosen to do the corporate design and standards manuals for Deutsche Bundespost, which is a huge company, something like AT&T. At that time, they employed over 500,000 people and were the largest company in Europe. Around 1984, as part of this project, I persuaded them to have a typeface designed for them, especially for all the telephone books and the many, many forms that they use. Prior to that, each department in each different area of the country had used different typefaces, anything that didn't have a serif on it, from Futura to Helvetica to Gill. It was a mess and they couldn't control it. I felt that having one typeface would help define a standard for them.

So I designed a typeface for them in two different weights, and by using Ikarus, the standard program used to develop font outlines for most dedicated typesetting systems, it would be available on a number of different manufacturers' typesetting machines, including Berthold, Varityper and Linotype.

During that time I happened to be at Stempel, which was a type foundry owned by Linotype. They had just made a deal, in late 1984, with Adobe, to supply the core fonts for PostScript printers. This was before the LaserWriter was even on the market. While I was there, the head of typography had a little box on the table, a 128K Macintosh; he showed me how it worked and how it printed to an ImageWriter dot matrix printer. I could see that this little machine now made it possible for type to be something I could put on a disk and ship anywhere. I could control it. I had no idea of what it all really implied, but I thought it was perfect for the Deutsche Bundespost to use.

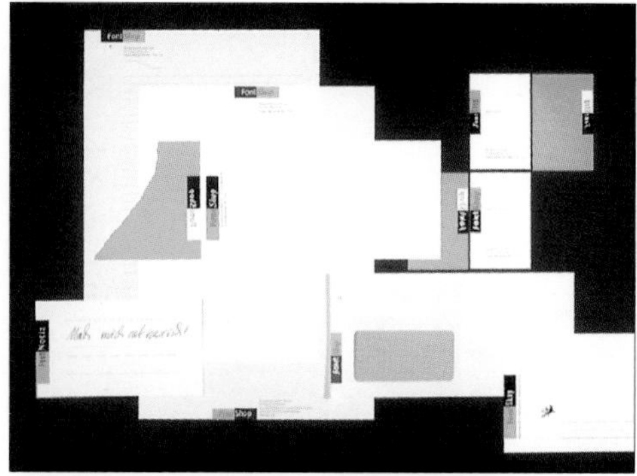

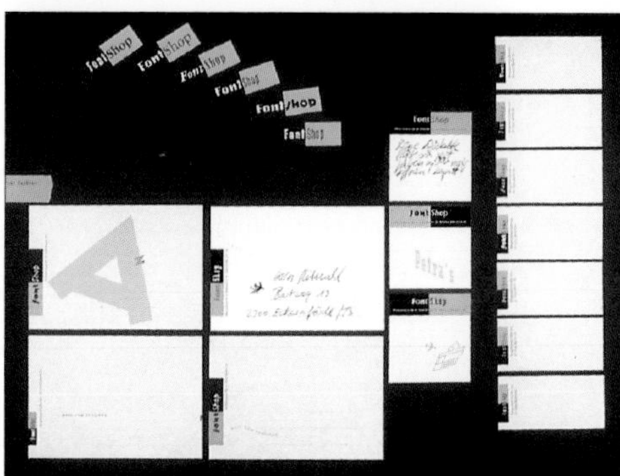

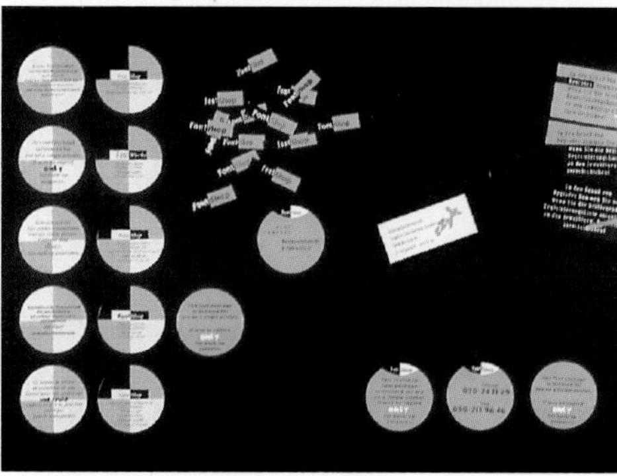

Various applications of the FontShop identity system designed by Alexander Branczyk and Erik Spiekermann.

That very afternoon, I borrowed the Macintosh, took it on a train to Bonn, walked into the Ministry of Telecommunications, and said: "This is your answer." Up until that time, they had thought that having a standard font meant truckloads of hot metal. We already knew that all the phototypesetters would have the standard font available, and on top of that, here was this little box that was the future of what would be happening with type.

I thought that Deutsche Bundespost should put a Macintosh on everyone's desk and send everything from one place to another via modem or disk. And I expected that fonts on the Macintosh were going to be relatively cheap compared to the $2,000-$3,000 paid by conventional phototypesetters for their fonts. So no typesetter would have an excuse not to have the right font available.

Unfortunately, the whole project fell apart and the standard font I designed was never used. But I had seen the Macintosh and I immediately bought one. There was only one wholesaler in Germany and I think I bought the first Macintosh he ever sold. It was a 512K Macintosh, and I got an ImageWriter with it. Then, of course, we bought the LaserWriter as soon as it came out in 1985. We used PageMaker 1.0, MacPaint, and MacDraw, mostly for setting galley type. It took another two to three years before we used the Macintosh properly. Even though it was very limited in those early days, I knew it was the right direction to follow.

From my experience with the traditional type world, I already understood, early-on, outline fonts as a concept. That is, I understood that the font outlines from the Macintosh could be used on any typesetting device, at least in theory. The Macintosh was what I had been waiting for all the time.

How do you use the Macintosh today in your studio?

If we have a simple project, one that just requires a surface design, a brochure, say, then one of our designers sits at the Macintosh right away and does some sort of layout. For larger projects, however, I like to crack the structure first, before anyone sits down at the Macintosh and starts working.

I like to think we are concept-based and not style-based. Unfortunately, with the Macintosh, the one thing it does is offer you immediate physical solutions if you are accomplished and versatile with it. But a concept means something else. A concept means you have some kind of idea behind what you're doing without having to worry about the visual aspect of it at that moment. If we have a complex project, we sit together and talk about it first. I tend to do little thumbnail sketches, like one does as one talks — little squares, with very rough type indications. These sketches tend to be fairly theoretical, trying to solve the problem in my head first. Then, like a reflex, work begins on the Macintosh.

But first, we try to develop a system, not a scheme. In other words, there are elements that are more inherent than spelled out. For example, take the FontShop, our company that sells typefaces for personal computers. FontShop is pretty well known for having a strong, easily recognizable look. Yet we have no logo. The idea, when we first sat down with it, was to come up with certain characteristics. For example, we would always use positive and negative areas, and always use yellow as a second color. The word "FontShop" never appears in the same typeface twice. Since we're selling typefaces, why should we have a fixed logo? What typeface would we use? So it's totally random — every

Spiekermann's studio, MetaDesign, converted from an old factory.

designer who works on FontShop jobs does something different. But there will always be positive and negative areas, and black, white, and yellow. There is no logo, but there is a look. In the beginning, I just did a few sketches, then we did the letterhead and it all evolved from that. So the FontShop look is an idea, a concept. There are no physical restrictions to it.

We don't have house rules, exactly, but there are certain things we just wouldn't do. For example, no one would ever use Helvetica unless there was a good reason. Not because we don't like the typeface, but because it's a ubiquitous typeface that everyone uses by default. Actually, Frutiger is the new Helvetica — everyone now uses this by default. It's a much better typeface than Helvetica, but it's still becoming one of those default things.

Also, we would never use a vertical line on any form; that's "forbidden." I always create vertical lines by white space. Other people use vertical lines, but we do not. We divide space with negative space; a white line, if you will.

We also like to create bleeds, simply because that makes the page more generous. Printers don't like it because they have to go to larger paper, but as soon as you bleed something, you're telling people: "This page doesn't end here, it just happens to be cut off here." Graphic design goes on, beyond the physical edge of the paper.

I try to avoid logomarks. Very often, when a company has a logomark, they think that as long as it appears somewhere, anywhere, they've got a "corporate look." So if I avoid the logomark, I force people to think a bit more about their entire look, about the entire cover, or the page, or form, or whatever it is. I actually have a policy of trying to avoid logos because it means you have to try a little bit harder to make something else, to give the whole thing a look, or a style, or a feel. If you turn a corner and see something that you recognize as company "x" or company "y" without the logo, because it has a unique look to it, then the design is successful, as far as I'm concerned. The whole system makes it work.

It helps that I have confidence in our designers here to get the details right, once the design system has been established. I like different designers to put their hand to a client's work. People have specialties, obviously — some are more publication designers, some are more signage designers — but I like the signage person to work on a book, and I like the book guy to do signage, because it keeps them on their toes. I don't necessarily like everything that everyone does, but I think you have to give everyone that freedom. I like variety, and I don't ever want us to get stuck.

What are some of the problems you run across using the Macintosh?

There are problems that come up because of the shift in who is actually responsible for the typesetting — it's now done by designers, not typesetters. These people are not typesetters, and attention to typographic detail has gone down tremendously.

With the Macintosh, it's so easy to make lots of little mistakes because most designers don't have a person who just proofreads. All this intermediary stuff that the typesetter used to do — we could send a job up to them and then blame them for not being on time — now we have to blame ourselves when the client calls. When the stuff comes off the machine, no one looks at it anymore; they just rush it off to the printer. We've basically lost the two or three day buffer that we used to have in the typesetting process. So we are stuck with the responsibility, and that's one thing I don't like about this Macintosh business.

It's also easy to make style mistakes because the deadlines are getting so silly and everybody's doing stuff under pressure all the time. We get a lot of text from our clients on disk and all these "dtp" errors creep in — like using inch marks rather than quotation marks, foot marks instead of apostrophes, and hyphens instead of em or en dashes.

I find some of the programs on the Macintosh to be somewhat limited, compared to some of the things we could do with traditional typesetting machines. A perfect example of this is the fact that on the Berthold machines, we could exactly address the baseline position of any character. There's no Macintosh software that I know of that tells you exactly where the baseline of a given character is located.

Also, I am not enamored of software that uses the metaphor of an artist's table; that's for creating artwork. That is, you have your board there and you move things around. This is totally alien to my way of working because I've never done that. I've never "moved things around." Maybe it's my Germanic mind — I don't know because I can be very chaotic — but when it comes to design, I like to be precise.

I also get very tired of this kerning discussion that can go on for hours, especially in the United States. Designers are getting caught up in the wrong typographical issues. This concern with kerning is the result of American advertising typography, which completely ignores letter and word spacing. Attention is paid to individual letter pairs without looking at the overall rhythm and color of a line, which is determined by word and letter spacing. We almost always change the default spacing settings in QuarkXPress, the page layout program we use most often, from 100% word spacing to 70% word spacing, and we almost always add units of tracking to the body copy. To complicate matters more, different programs measure tracking in different ways. For example, FreeHand tracks using fractions of points and QuarkXPress tracks in units of an em space of a given font, so one is absolute and the other is relative. It is a nightmare trying to use both these programs for the same job.

Why did you establish the FontShop?

It started about four years ago. When I'd travel to the United States, people used to ask me to bring back fonts for the Macintosh that they couldn't get here in Europe. After this went on for a couple of years, we thought it was ridiculous to keep paying customs, losing money on the exchange rate, and carrying very heavy suitcases back all the time. It was obvious there was demand for fonts.

Since I have been in the type business for my entire professional career, I took advantage of my contacts in the typographic trade — including Berthold, Linotype, and Monotype — and I convinced them that the best way to sell type was for it to be sold by people that really knew type. So the FontShop was born here in Berlin. By now we've established several franchises in Europe and North America.

Our catalog, which we update regularly, lists fonts by the font name, not the manufacturer. Most people don't really care who makes a typeface; they just want the typeface itself to use, and they also need it today, or tomorrow at the latest. We have over 20 different companies supplying type, from Adobe Systems to small outfits in Europe and the United States. We've all these kids who make a typeface that might disappear in a year's time, but who cares?

We make our own fonts now as well and have had a few typefaces designed especially for us by designers like Neville Brody, David Berlow and myself. We're something like an independent label for typefaces.

What do you think about the ease with which programs like Fontographer now make it possible for almost anyone to design a typeface?

Even though I think a lot of the fonts being designed on the Macintosh today are tasteless, I still believe it's a great thing. You wouldn't outlaw tape recorders just because people can record bad songs. I think it's good that the ability to make type has been taken away from an elitist minority. I'm a traditional type designer, but most people would not go through what I have; it's too much trouble. It took almost four years to bring the last face I designed traditionally, ITC Officina, to the market.

Everyone can create a fun font. You can scan in handwriting or make a font that looks like old typewriter print. We've even come up with a random font — it changes each time you open your file. The rules today are that there are no rules.

Step by Step

The reunification of Germany in 1989 was an historical event. One of the many changes that came about as a result of that event was the consolidation of the public transportation system of what had been East and West Berlin. The Berliner Verkehrs-Betriebe (BVB/BVG), the Berlin Regional Transit Authority, asked Spiekermann's MetaDesign to completely redesign everything — from their corporate stationery, to signage, to timetables and maps.

One of the many maps that had to be designed and produced was one showing the routes of buses and trains, which included over 56 different lines. Many of the lines ran in what was formerly East Berlin, and they had never been formally documented. After working out some of the basic design problems, Aldus FreeHand was used to produce the map. FreeHand allowed designers Jens and Kathrin Kreitmeyer, Theres Weishappel, and Marc Mendelson to easily try different color schemes, which had be considered for their informative value, as well as their aesthetic appeal. FreeHand's layering capability proved essential in the massive job of producing a file from which four color process films could be generated directly.

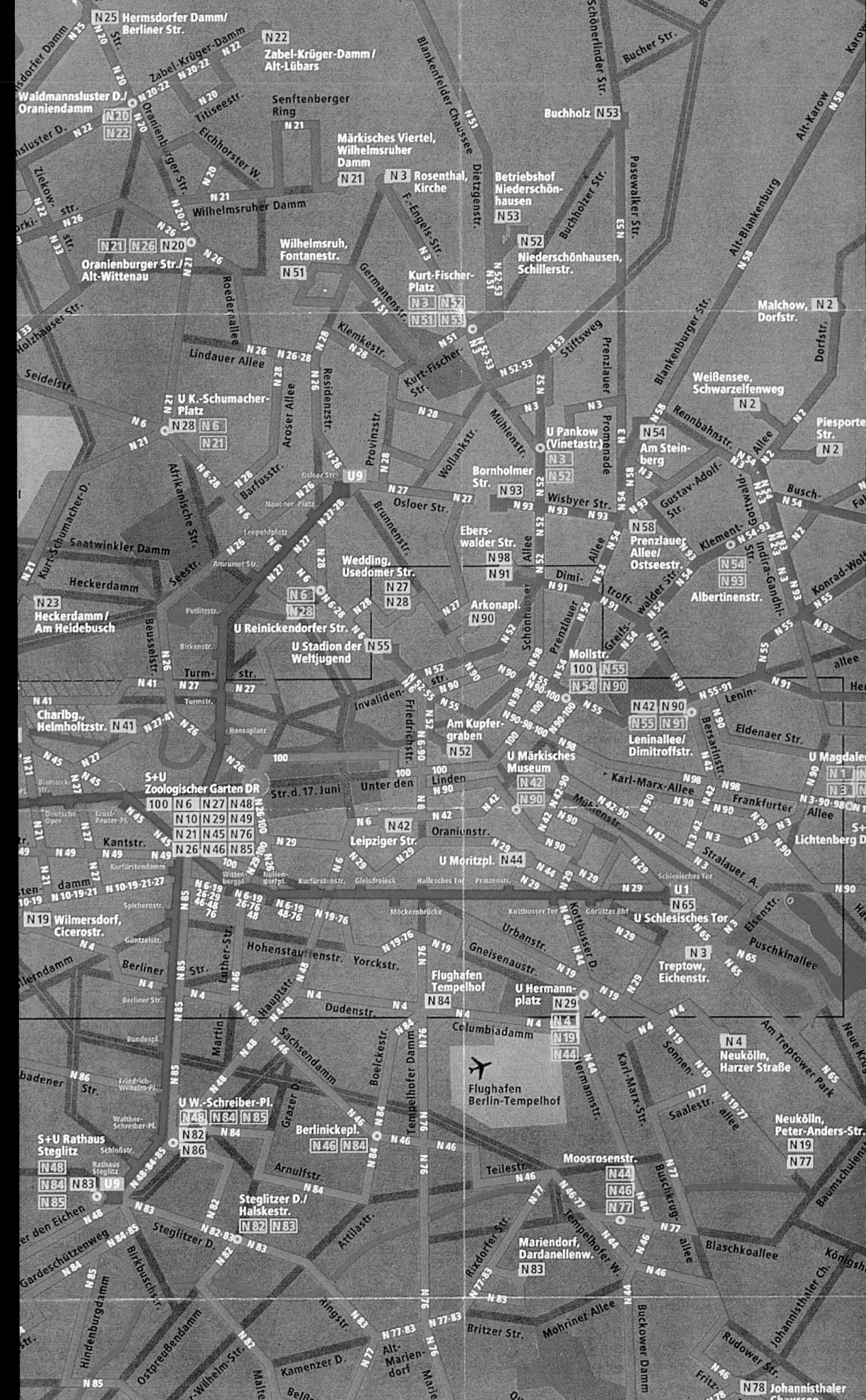

While previous maps existed for West Berlin's night bus routes, there was no such map for East Berlin. A former official from what had been the East Berlin Transit Authority drew the night bus routes on a street map of Berlin.

The first step, then, was to create a simplified map that could be scanned in and traced. Before any work could begin on the computer, decisions had to be made about which streets would be shown. Hand-traced versions of the map were drawn, simplifying the information each time.

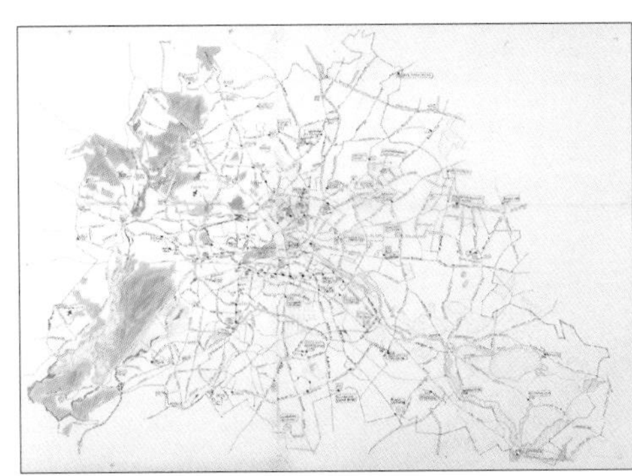

The final ink drawing that was used for scanning and subsequent tracing on the Macintosh was divided into sizes that would fit on a flatbed scanner.

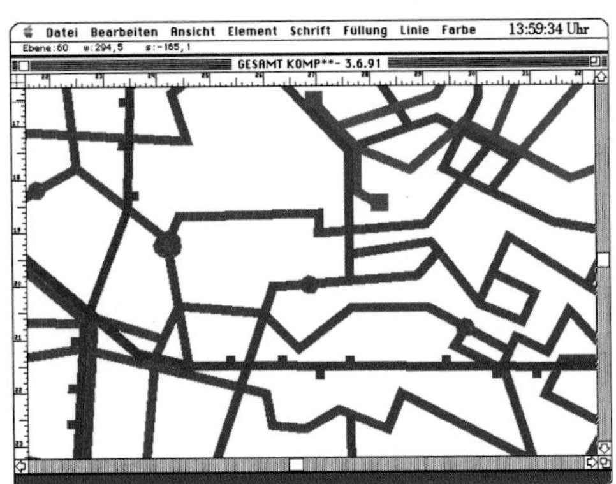

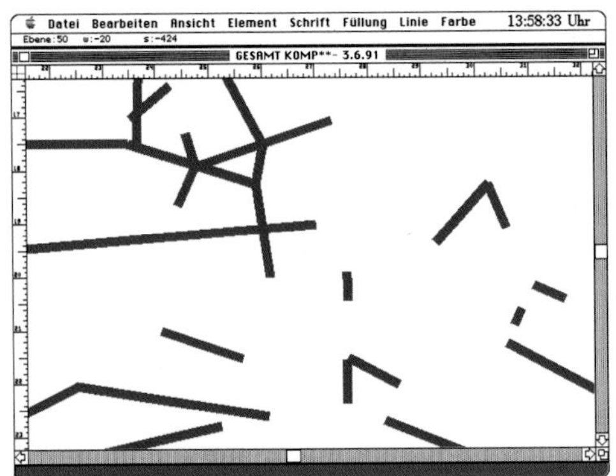

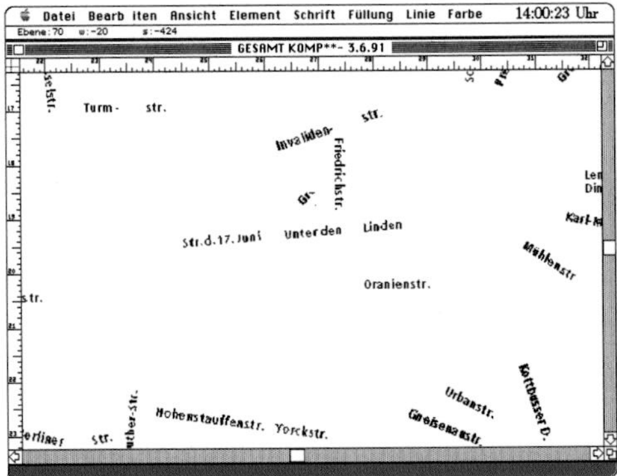

The scanned version of the map was initially traced in Adobe Illustrator because the designers felt that it was easier to trace scanned images in Illustrator than in FreeHand. Once the basic lines of streets, parks, and water were traced, the entire file was opened in FreeHand, where the real work of producing the map began.

One of the key features offered by FreeHand is the ability to put parts of a drawing in different layers. The map was divided logically into different layers, with the streets, the bus lines, various backgrounds, and the text each put on a different layer. This made it easy to work on each component separately.

Decisions about the color for each component of the map were made in FreeHand. Once the basic color scheme was decided, test files were created, four color process films were produced, and proofs were made. These files helped the designers check key issues like trapping, and how a color would look printed against another.

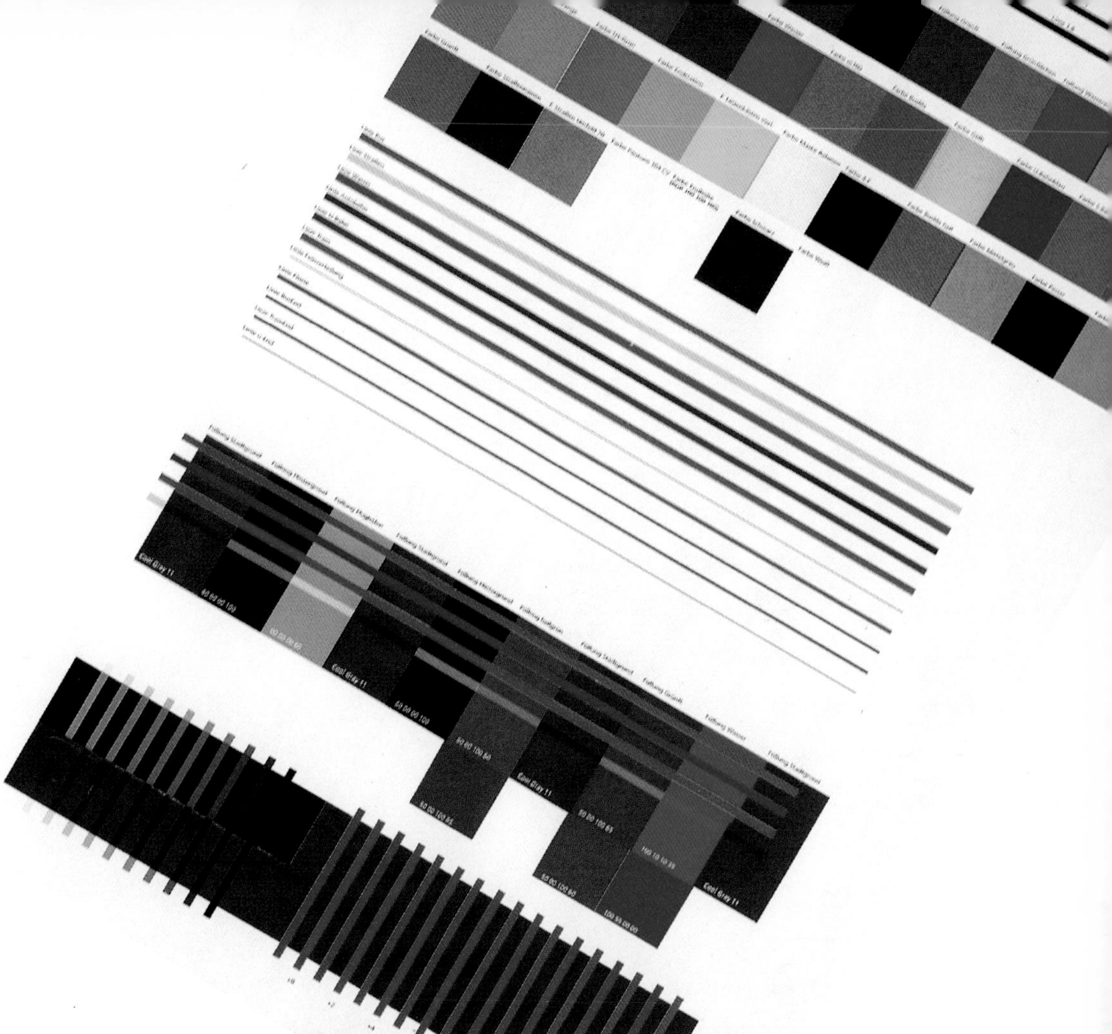

Colors could be easily edited by simply redefining the cyan, magenta, and yellow values for a specific color.

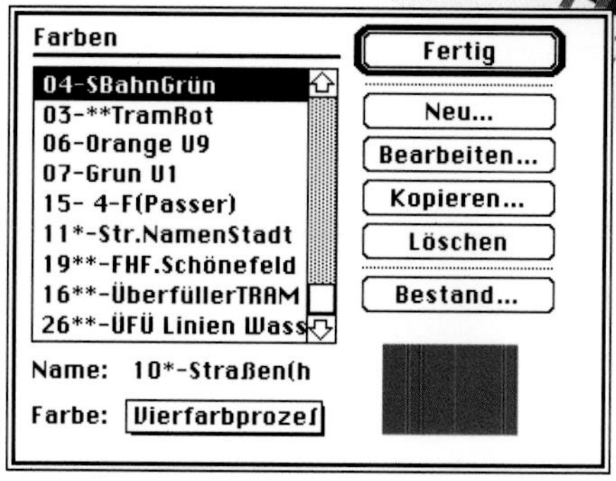

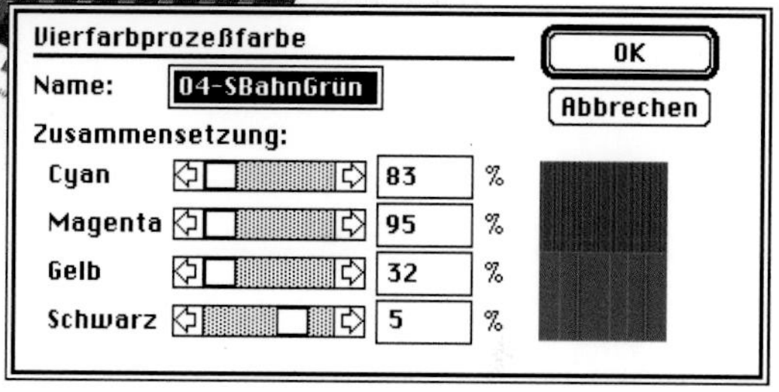

Each bus line was represented by a number. These numbers were created in a separate file, where each was carefully hand-kerned.

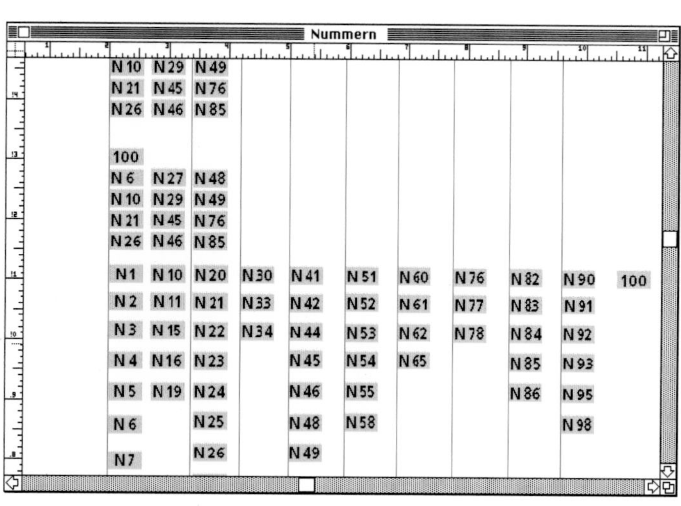

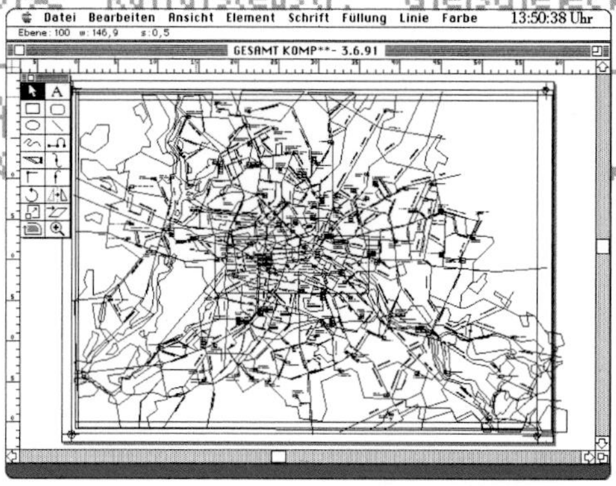

The FreeHand file containing the map became so complex that most work was done in a wireframe mode, without showing the preview of the colors, lines and fills.

Early proofs were printed out in sections on a LaserWriter. As the map neared completion, four color films were output and a color proof was made.

The cover and timetable information for the map were created in two separate files using QuarkXPress.

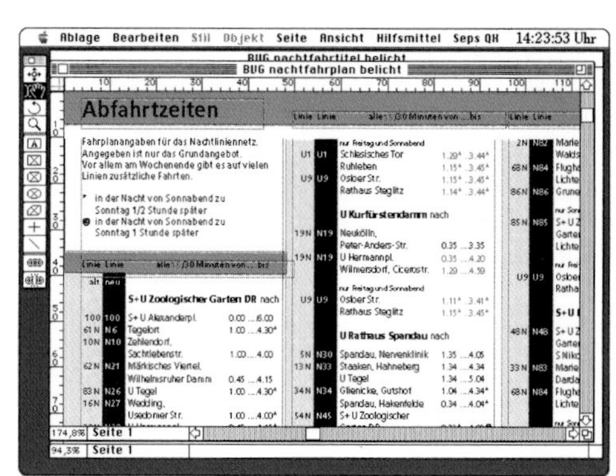

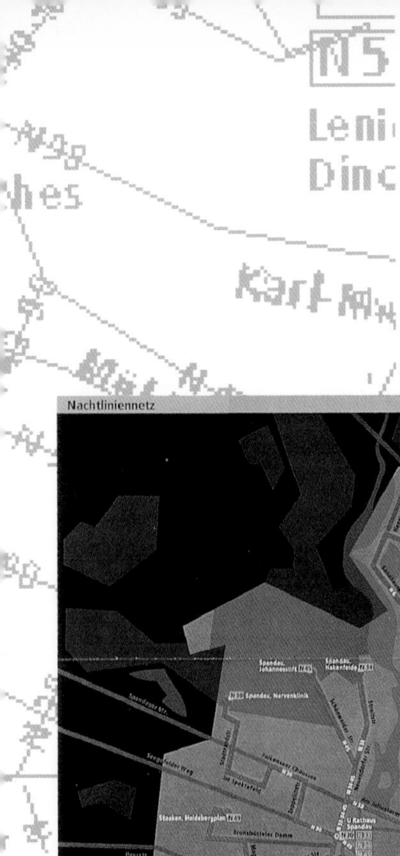

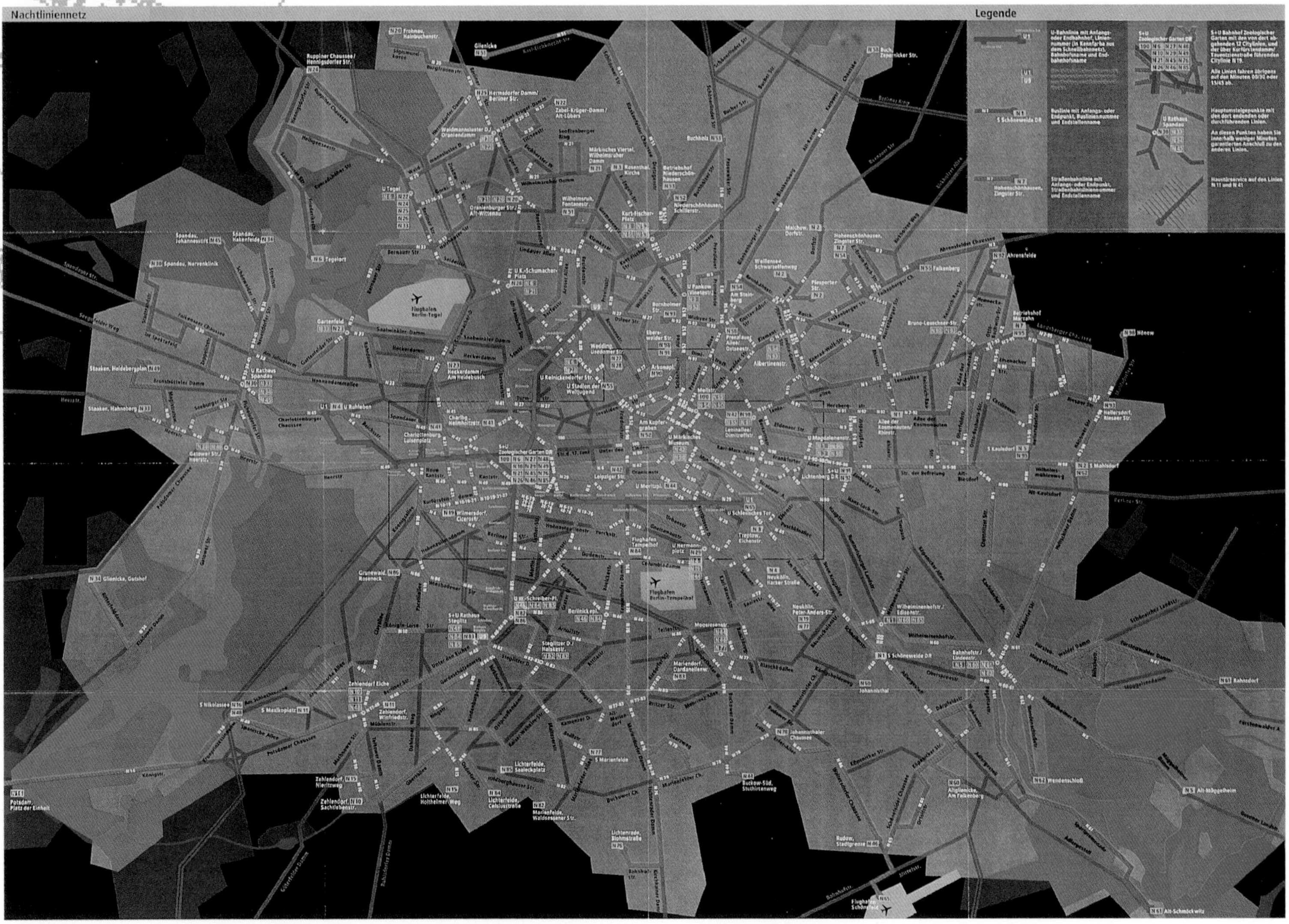

Nachtliniennetz

Legende

When the final map, cover, and timetable were checked, rechecked, proofed and approved, each was saved to disk as a PostScript file for the individual cyan, magenta, yellow and black layers. The files were then imaged at 2540 dpi on a Purup drum recorder to create final films for printing.

Portfolio

1 Maps, 1991
Berlin Regional Transit, bus route maps
Traditional cartography, Aldus FreeHand, QuarkXPress

2 Maps (covers), 1991
Berlin Regional Transit, bus route maps
Aldus FreeHand, QuarkXPress

3 Map detail, 1991
Berlin Regional Transit, bus route maps
Traditional cartography, Aldus FreeHand, QuarkXPress

4-5 Timetable book cover, 1991
Berlin Regional Transit
Aldus FreeHand

6 Timetable book spread, 1991
Berlin Regional Transit
Mainframe computer database, QuarkXPress

7 Timetable book covers, 1991
Berlin Regional Transit, local editions
Aldus FreeHand

Designed with Katja Lanz, Anke Martini, Thomas Nagel, Heike Nehl and Martin Veicht

1

2

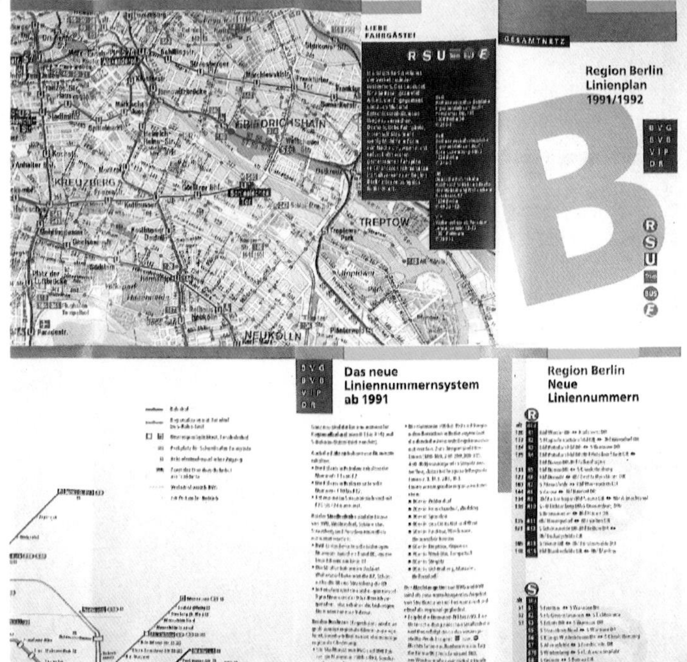

3

KURSBUCH
Region Berlin
Fahrplan
1991/92
BVG
BVB
VIP
DR
KURSBUCH
Berlin
Region Ost
Fahrplan
1991/92
BVG
BVB
VIP
DR
U7
U Rathaus Spandau ▶ U Rudow
U Rudow ▶ U Rathaus Spandau
U7
SONNTAG
KURSBUCH
Berlin Region Süd Fahrplan 1991/92
KURSBUCH
Berlin Region Nord Fahrplan 1991/92
KURSBUCH
Berlin Region West Fahrplan 1991/92
KURSBUCH
Berlin Region Ost Fahrplan 1991/92
KURSBUCH
Region Berlin Fahrplan 1991/92
Region Berlin
Fahrplan
1991/92
4
5
6
7

SÖREN KIERKEGAARD

INSTITUT FÜR SOZIALFORSCHUNG

GILLES DELEUZE

ISAIAH BERLIN

Russische Denker

eva Europäische Bi...

Barenboims RING-Darstellung läßt sich kaum von den szenischen Vorgängen trennen. Die Entfaltungszeiten, die Kupfer für „seine" Menschendarstellung auf der Bühne teilweise benötigt, stellt Barenboim als idealer Theaterkapellmeister selbstlos zur Verfügung.
Gerhard Rohde

Der Abend geriet, weil die wundervolle Partitur zu ihrer Wahrhaftigkeit gesteigert wurde. Kupfer und sein Bühnenbildner Schavernoch haben zur Wahrhaftigkeit beigetragen.
Rudolf Augstein

DER RING

Bayreuth 1988–1992

eva Europäische Verlagsanstalt

Einleitung

	Zur Entstehung dieses Buches
Michael Lewin	Brief an August Röckel, Zürich,
Richard Wagner	25. und 26. Januar 1854
	Richard Wagner und der Ring des Nibelungen
Thomas Mann	Wagners Ring als bürgerliches Parabelspiel
Hans Mayer	Zerstörung und Selbstzerstörung im Ring des Nibelungen
	Der Ring als bürgerlicher Roman
Michael Lewin	Versuch über die Interpretation des Ring des Nibelungen Bayreuth 1988 - 1992
Wolfgang Wagner und Michael Lewin	Ein Gespräch
Herausgegeben von	Michael Lewin
	Leinen mit Schutzumschlag und Schuber
	Alle Bühnenbilder von Hans Schavernoch auf 60 Seiten in Farbe
	Über 300 s/w-Abbildungen
	Portraitphotos aller Mitwirkenden
Format	235 x 297 mm
Umfang	ca. 350 Seiten
Preis	ca. 198,– DM
ISBN	3-434-50005-7
erscheint	Sommer 1991 bei Europäische Verlagsanstalt Parkallee 2 2000 Hamburg 13 Tel 040/44 72 83 Fax 040/44 86 18

Mit Texten von

Richard Wagner
Wolfgang Wagner
Thomas Mann
Hans Mayer
Harry Kupfer
Daniel Barenboim
Reinhard Heinrich
Hans Schavernoch
Siegfried Jerusalem
John Tomlinson
Graham Clark

Parkallee 2
D 2000 Hamburg 13
Telefon 040/44 72 83
Telefax 040/44 86 18

Geschäftsführerin
Dr. Sabine Groenewold

Europäische Verlagsanstalt GmbH
HRB 645 987 Hamburg
Mitglied des Börsenvereins des Deutschen Buchhandels
Verkehrsnr. 10 800

Vereins- & Westbank
BLZ 200 300 00
Konto 46 03932
Deutsche Bank
BLZ 200 700 00
Konto 79 28500

Europäische Verlagsanstalt GmbH
Parkallee 2
D 2000 Hamburg 13

Mit freundlichen Grüßen

Europäische Verlagsans...
Parkallee 2
D 2000 Hamburg 13
Telefon 040/44 72 83
Telefax 040/44 86 18

Book covers, brochures, and stationery, 1990, 1991
European Publishing Corporation (EVA)
Aldus FreeHand, QuarkXPress

Designed with Anke Martini, Uli Mayer and Heike Nehl

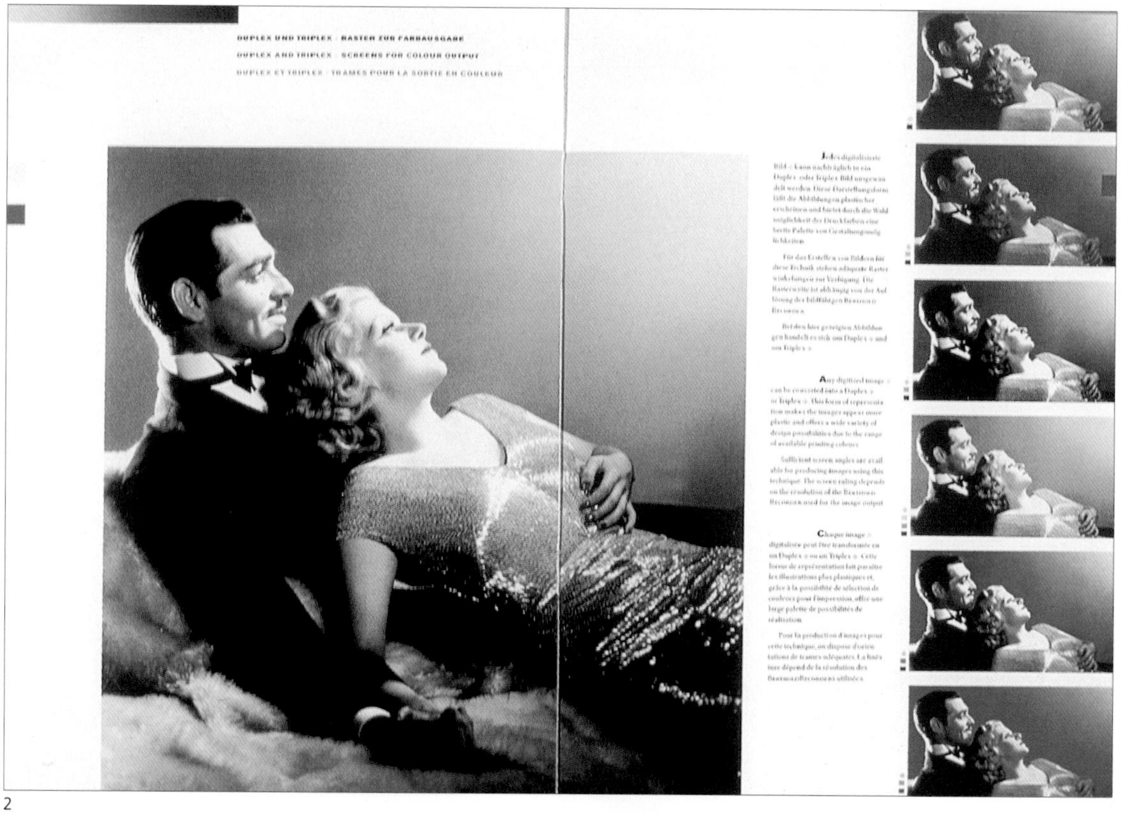

DUPLEX UND TRIPLEX · RASTER ZUR FARBAUSGABE

DUPLEX AND TRIPLEX · SCREENS FOR COLOUR OUTPUT

DUPLEX ET TRIPLEX · TRAMES POUR LA SORTIE EN COULEUR

2

1

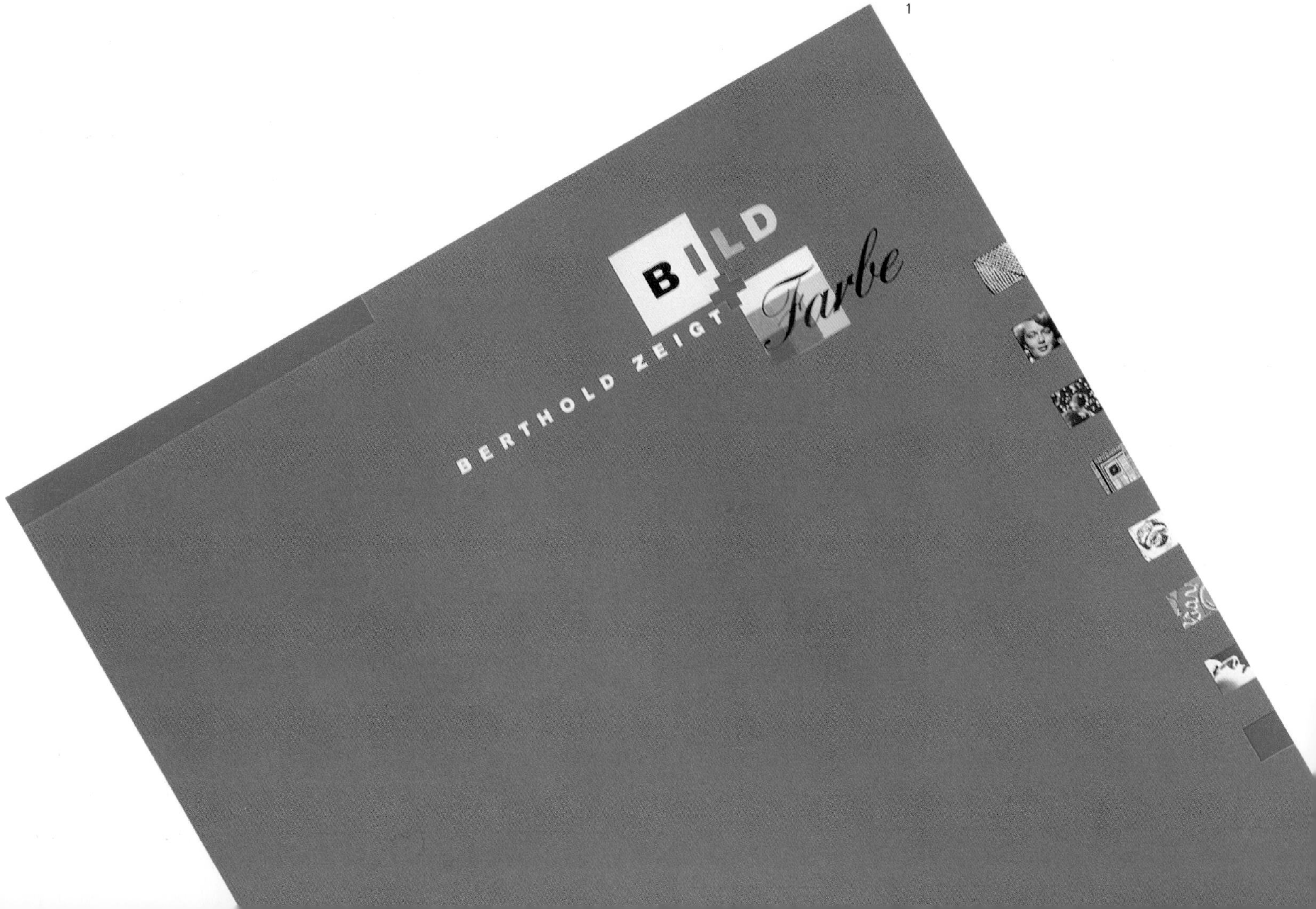

BILD

BERTHOLD ZEIGT

Farbe

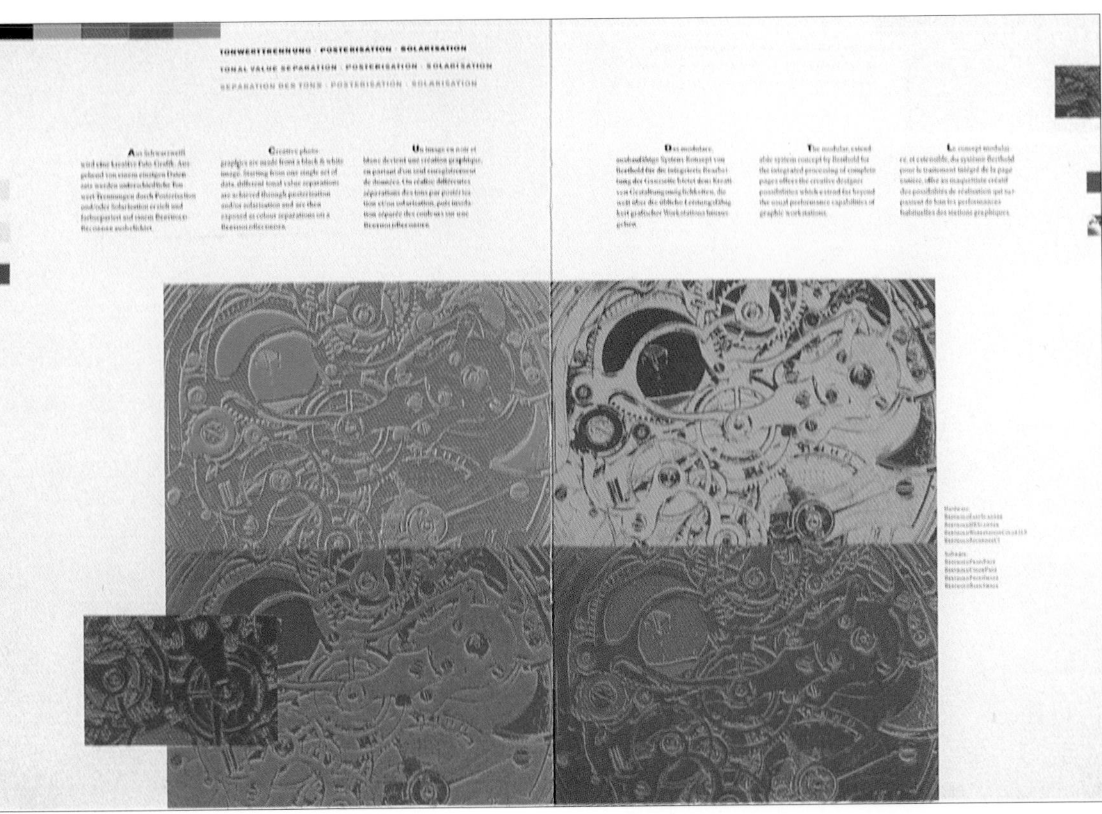

3

4

1 Color system brochure cover, 1990
H. Berthold AG
Berthold M-Series

2-4 Color system brochure spreads, 1990
H. Berthold AG
Berthold M-Series

Designed with Thomas Nagel

Catalogs and stationery, 1990
Marlboro Design Shop
Aldus FreeHand, QuarkXPress

Designed with Alexander Branczyk
and Thomas Nagel

MARLBORO DESIGN SHOP 7
MARLBORO DESIGN
SHOP 7
MARLBORO DESIGN SHOP

This page:

Cover, type specimen booklets, 1988-90
H. Berthold AG
Berthold M-Series and traditional typesetting

Following page:

Type booklet in Miniature (60 x 60 mm), 1986-88
H. Berthold AG
Berthold M-Series and traditional typesetting

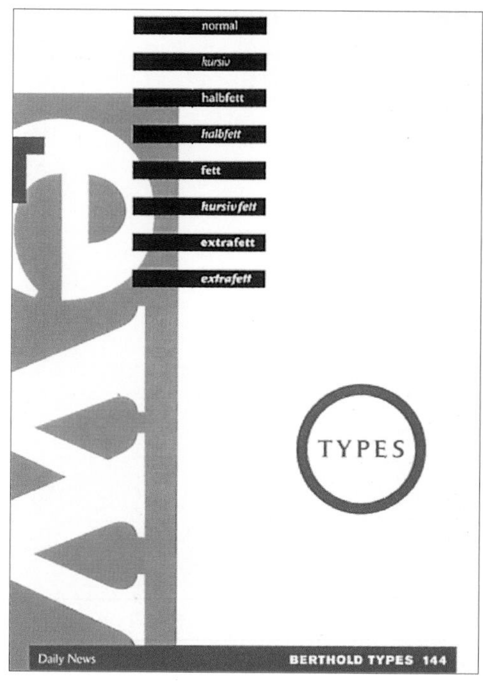

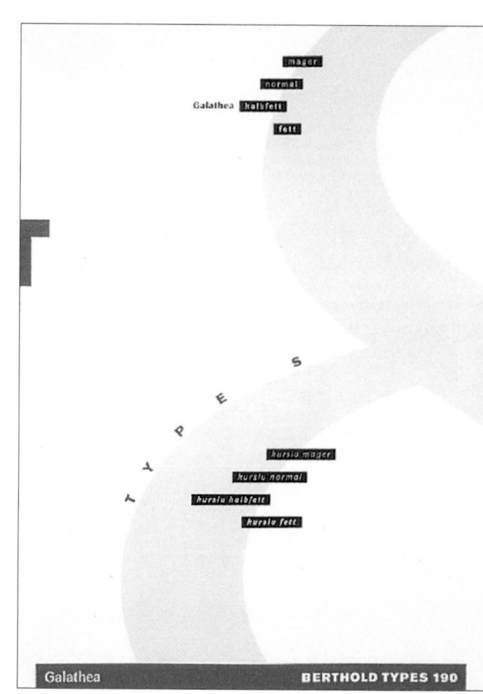

BERTHOLD TYPES

2 6 8
Berthold
Exklusiv
Types

Garamond Berthold
fett · bold · gras
ABCDEFGHIJKL
MNOPQRSTUVWXYZ
abcdefghijkl
mnopqrstuvwxyz
123456789%
(.,-;:!¡?¿–)·[‚'„"»«]
+–=/$£†*&§

Garamond Berthold
schmal · condensed · étroit
ABCDEFGHIJKL
MNOPQRSTUVWXYZ
abcdefghijkl
mnopqrstuvwxyz
123456789%
(.,-;:!¡?¿–)·[‚'„"»«]

BERTHOLD TYPES

Garamond B

abcdefghijkl
mnopqrstuvwxyz
123456789%
(.,-;:!¡?¿–)·[‚'„"»«]
+–=/$£†*&§

TYPES

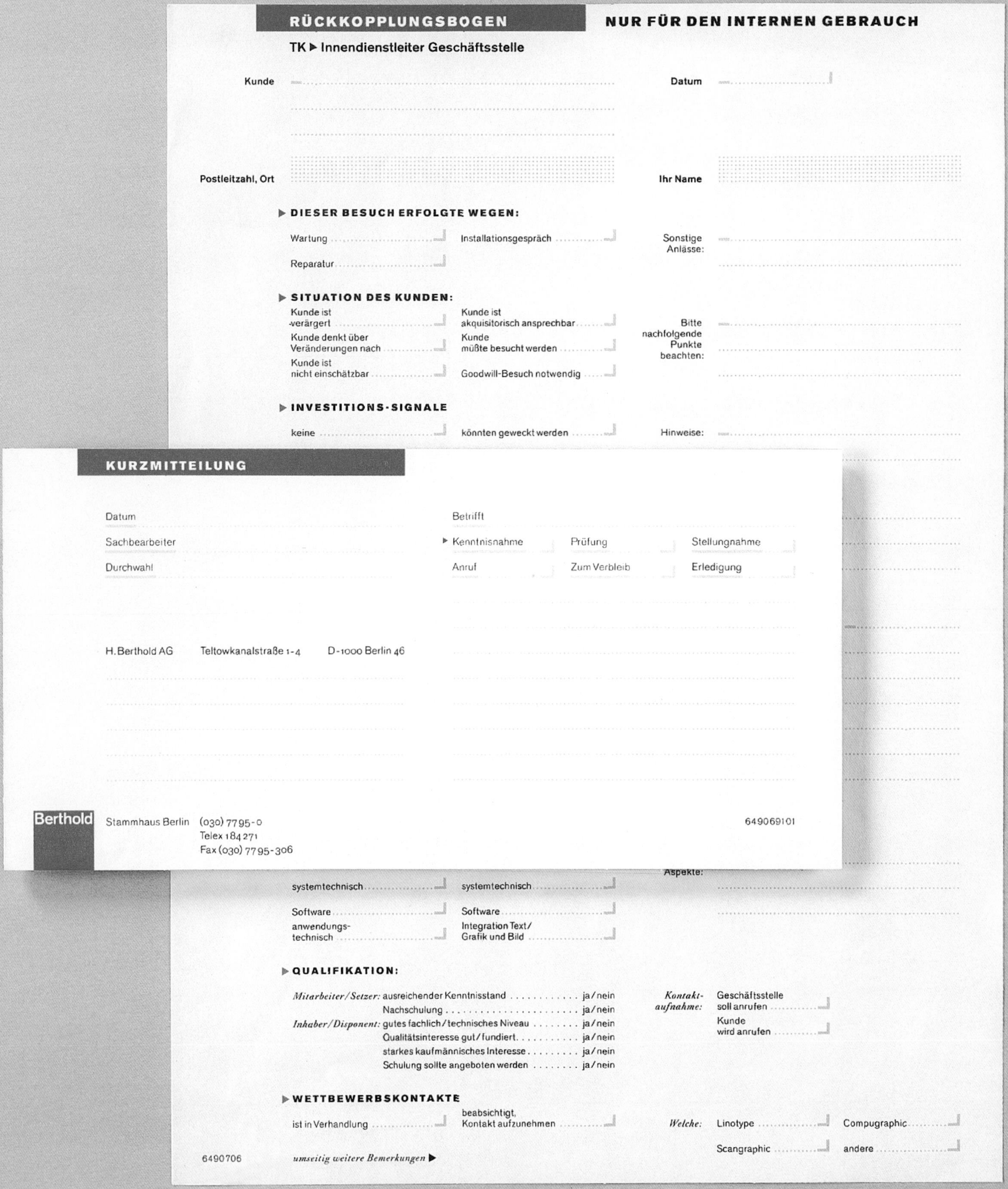

RÜCKKOPPLUNGSBOGEN **NUR FÜR DEN INTERNEN GEBRAUCH**

TK ▶ Innendienstleiter Geschäftsstelle

Kunde .... Datum ....

Postleitzahl, Ort .... Ihr Name ....

▶ **DIESER BESUCH ERFOLGTE WEGEN:**

Wartung .... Installationsgespräch .... Sonstige Anlässe: ....

Reparatur ....

▶ **SITUATION DES KUNDEN:**

Kunde ist verärgert .... Kunde ist akquisitorisch ansprechbar .... Bitte nachfolgende Punkte beachten: ....

Kunde denkt über Veränderungen nach .... Kunde müßte besucht werden ....

Kunde ist nicht einschätzbar .... Goodwill-Besuch notwendig ....

▶ **INVESTITIONS-SIGNALE**

keine .... könnten geweckt werden .... Hinweise: ....

KURZMITTEILUNG

Datum .... Betrifft ....

Sachbearbeiter .... ▶ Kenntnisnahme .... Prüfung .... Stellungnahme ....

Durchwahl .... Anruf .... Zum Verbleib .... Erledigung ....

H. Berthold AG Teltowkanalstraße 1-4 D-1000 Berlin 46

Berthold Stammhaus Berlin (030) 7795-0
Telex 184 271
Fax (030) 7795-306

649069101

Aspekte:

systemtechnisch .... systemtechnisch ....

Software .... Software ....

anwendungs-technisch .... Integration Text/Grafik und Bild ....

▶ **QUALIFIKATION:**

Mitarbeiter/Setzer: ausreichender Kenntnisstand .... ja/nein
Nachschulung .... ja/nein
Inhaber/Disponent: gutes fachlich/technisches Niveau .... ja/nein
Qualitätsinteresse gut/fundiert. .... ja/nein
starkes kaufmännisches Interesse .... ja/nein
Schulung sollte angeboten werden .... ja/nein

Kontakt-aufnahme: Geschäftsstelle soll anrufen .... Kunde wird anrufen ....

▶ **WETTBEWERBSKONTAKTE**

ist in Verhandlung .... beabsichtigt, Kontakt aufzunehmen ....

Welche: Linotype .... Compugraphic .... Scangraphic .... andere ....

6490706 *umseitig weitere Bemerkungen* ▶

Previous page:

Business forms, 1990
H. Berthold AG
Berthold ADS 3000

This page:

1 Layout for postage stamps, 1991
Dutch PTT
Adobe Illustrator

2 Postcard comps, 1991
Dutch PTT
Adobe Illustrator and
conventional paste-up

1

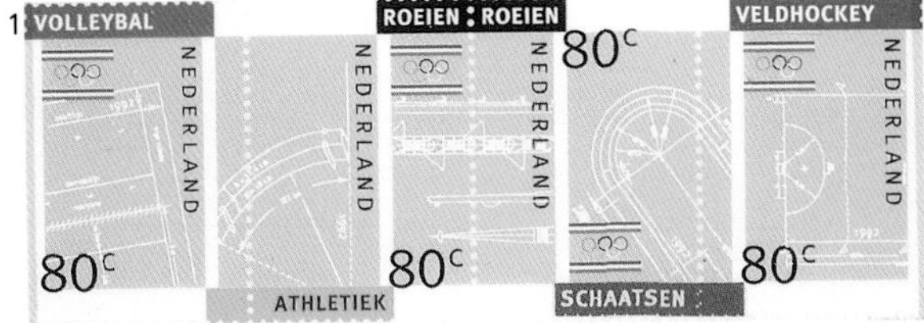

2

GESCHÄFTSBERICHT
GESCHÄFTSBERICHT
DAS GKB PRIVATKONTO
DAS MODERNE LEISTUNGSPAKET, DAS KEINEN WUNSCH OFFEN LÄSST.
DIE GKB LÄDT EIN
DIE GKB LÄDT EIN
DAS GKB FREIE-BERUFE-KONTO
WER FREI ARBEITET UND VIEL BEWEGT, FINDET BEI UNS SPIELRAUM.

Annual reports, 1991
GKB, Bank of Berlin
Aldus FreeHand, QuarkXPress

Designed with Uli Mayer

Why Not Associates

Why Not Associates, founded in 1987 by Andy Altmann, David Ellis and Howard Greenhalgh, is fast becoming one of the most exciting new forces in British design. The three began a formal association upon their graduation from the Royal College of Art in 1987. ¶ Why Not's photographic imagery and special typographic treatment shows a sense of craftsmanship, and at the same time, fun. Their work is as varied as their clientele, and includes billboards for Smirnoff Vodka and identities for trendy shops like Ted Baker and Ing. Howard's pursuit of his interest in video has led to the production of videos for music corporations like CBS, EMI, and Virgin. Their Soho studio reflects their lack of inhibition in experimentation as various toys sit side by side: a video editing deck, a synthesizer, dolls, models and Macintosh computers.

How did you come to form Why Not Associates?

Andy: David and I happened to attend St. Martin's College, and later, all three of us attended the Royal College of Art. Howard has always been more involved with video and David and I with graphic design. Near the end of school, in 1987, Howard was off on a photographic assignment and was asked by his client, an American company, to design and produce a magazine. Howard came to us and asked us to help, and so with that job, from the day we left college, we began to work together. We've never worked for anyone else, so we don't have that many inhibitions about what we're doing.

For the first few months, each of us did a bit of freelance work, and sometimes we'd get work we could do together. After a while, we were working together so much that we realized we needed to give ourselves a name, form a company, and get studio space.

When we were still at college, a friend of ours wrote his thesis about the American designer Bob Gill, who used a lot of visual puns in his work. In the context of talking about what was currently happening in Britain, our friend referred to us three as having a "why not?" attitude. Apparently, when he had asked us why we did something, we said "why not?" Then somebody picked up on that as a joke and called us the "Why Not Boys," and it just kind of stuck with us. When we finally formed the company, we decided on Why Not Associates. "Associates" sounds quite formal, but "why not" doesn't. We rather liked the contrast, and besides, it soon became too late to change it.

When did you encounter the Macintosh and how did you first start using the Macintosh in your work?

Andy: I actually first used a Macintosh at St. Martin's College around 1985. It was a really basic machine, with just one floppy disk drive and a small black and white monitor. One of my teachers asked me to design a poster using the Macintosh. The poster was for a series of computer classes. But no one, including myself, was using computers at the time, and I was reluctant at first. I told my teacher I hated computers, but he encouraged me to have a go at it anyway.

David: At the Royal College of Art there was only one very basic Macintosh at that time, off in the corner in the Graphics Department, along with a Paintbox-type computer called the Image Artist. I used the Image Artist a few times, and the Macintosh once or twice when I specifically wanted to create bitmapped type.

It wasn't until 1988, almost a year after we formed the company, that we began hearing more and more about the Macintosh being used for design. Letraset asked us to design a page for their catalog that showed off LetraStudio, a type-manipulation program on the Macintosh. So I went to the Royal College, where by now they had set up Macintosh II systems with color monitors for typesetting. I worked on the Letraset project in there, and during that time I thought, "This is pretty good." Gradually, it seemed that we had to get one. There just didn't seem to be any reason not to.

Andy: When the Macintosh first arrived, and we'd used it a bit, we almost wept at the number of hours we'd spent previously creating the type on our artwork. It didn't really change

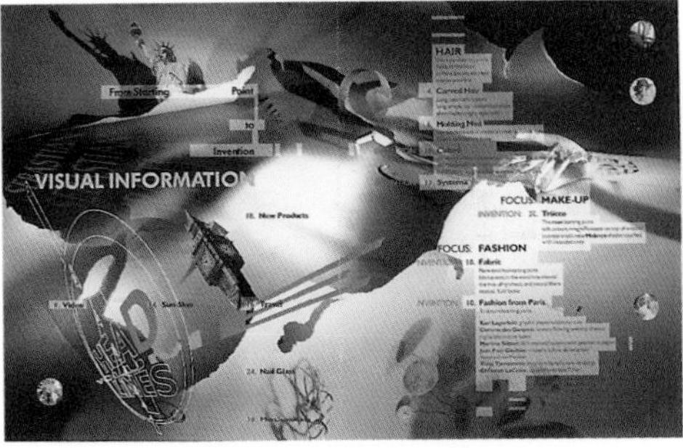

The contents page for *Headlines* magazine – one of Why Not Associates' first projects.

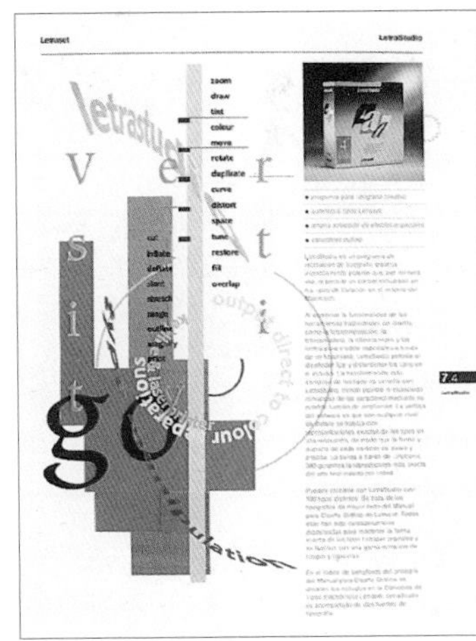

Why Not Associates' first job with the Macintosh was meant to demonstrate Letraset's new software, LetraStudio.

our work, it just made it easier. And it made it easier to meet some of the unreasonable deadlines imposed upon us by our clients.

In the old days, we used to order type in a few different sizes, then we'd get it back, cut it up and start moving it around. Eventually we'd run out of time and we just had to finish the project. In a way, time would kind of decide the thing. With the Macintosh, it seemed like the perfect gift had arrived.

How do you use the Macintosh in your studio?

Andy: In our work, we use absolutely anything that's around us. On our way to the photography studio, for example, we might literally pick up a bit of wire or string, or a piece of metal. Sometimes we draw things by hand and sometimes we use the Macintosh.

David: We use the Macintosh to create only some of the elements we use in our work. We have used it mostly for type, but we've also started creating more images directly on the Macintosh, and recently we've used MacroMind Director to create videos.

Even the way we use the Macintosh for type is not as straightforward as you might think. For example, many times we work out a typographical design on the Macintosh, output it to film, and then taken that film into a darkroom and expose it onto photographic paper. By not exposing it quite correctly, we can get all sorts of interesting effects, like creating shadows and slightly fuzzy looks. We then use that print from the darkroom as one of the photographic images in a piece.

Or another way we might use type created on the Macintosh is to output it in negative on a 35mm slide. We'll then project that slide onto an object, photograph the whole thing, and use that as an image.

Since the newest version of FreeHand makes it easier to paste images inside of type, lately we've been working more with scanning images and using them directly on the Macintosh screen, instead of just looking at them as we worked on the type separately on the Macintosh.

Why Not's animated commercial for the First Direct Bank in the making.

Or as another example, we are currently designing an exhibition in London showing the work of five Japanese architects. To create the signage, we designed it on the Macintosh using MacroMind Director and then had individual Macintosh computers hooked up directly to video cameras that projected onto the exhibits. It made it very easy to have each animation loop play over and over again, something that wouldn't have worked if we had just used video tape.

For print jobs, we're printing directly from the Macintosh to film. At first the printers didn't like it, but by now they're quite used to it. We might give them four or five layers of film, or sometimes we may only print two layers of film and indicate to the printer where color breaks occur. It varies from job to job.

The Why Not Associates studio.

Andy: We also do pop videos for which we generate the type on the Macintosh. Howard does only film work, some for advertising but mostly for pop videos, and we do all the type for it. Gradually, the Macintosh is becoming much more useful for that. Recently, we've done a ten second animated spot commercial for a bank using the Macintosh. It's all type, done on the Macintosh using MacroMind Director, then copied frame for frame onto a Harry. The Harry is a dedicated high-end system that lets you store video and edit it frame for frame with Paint box-type tools.

In the past, we would go into a Harry studio with a storyboard and some artwork. You'd have to tell the operator that this bit should be on the screen for five seconds, then this other bit should be in gray and drop down on the screen after three seconds, and disappear after two seconds. You'd have to try to work out all this stuff in your head and storyboard it.

With the Macintosh, though, you see the results directly, before you go to the Harry. You don't have to try to keep it all in your head. You can see that this bit comes in too fast, or this bit is just right. The Macintosh gives far more control over what you can do, cuts down the time involved, and saves an awful lot of money, because Harry suites can be quite expensive to rent. Compared to traditional animation, using the Macintosh is wonderful. It's quite exciting because it means we have another use for that box in the corner.

Howard has been working with hooking a keyboard up to the Macintosh for music. The possibilities with that little box, and what you can do with it, are just a matter of trying things out. You find a whole new use for it with each piece of new software you try. To me it seems to be the right machine at the right time.

I think it's really important that we keep experimenting all the time. But I think the worst thing is to become completely addicted to something, even the computer. Getting addicted to design is bad for the design. We think of a lot of designers as "train spotters," a name for people here in Britain who, just for a hobby, stand and count trains all day. They're so into trains that just counting them gives them satisfaction. That same kind of mentality can be seen with certain typographers and designers; they're just too involved with their subject, reading only design magazines and talking only to other designers and seeing life as purely in terms of design only. It's very limiting. They don't pay attention to painters, for example, or junk sales, or other kinds of things. I like to spend time in my garden, looking at flowers and not really concentrating on "design" per se. And I think it's important to not treat the Macintosh as the end all and be all; it's just part of what you can use.

Do you use the Macintosh for presentations to your clients?

David: Usually, yes. Exactly what we show our clients, though, depends on the level we're at with a given client. Sometimes if our clients know us well, we may just print rough ideas on the laser printer and fax it to them. They'll reply with a simple yes or no.

Sometimes we print out type and have it made into rub downs. We can then easily apply it to photographs for presentations. Recently we've found one of the best ways to make presentations to our clients is to have 35mm slides imaged directly from our Macintosh files. The colors are pretty good and the definition is much better than printing out to a 300 dot-per-inch color printer. Slides also let you make presentations to larger groups of people easily. We wish all our clients had a Macintosh screen that we could use to present comps, not only for video spots but for our print ideas as well. But until they do, slides are a nice alternative.

Do you think the Macintosh lets you try out new ideas that you might not otherwise explore?

Andy: It definitely gives us different options. For example, we did a poster recently that contained type created by scanning in calligraphy, tracing it in FreeHand, and then manipulating different points on the artwork to create an entirely different piece from the original calligraphy. In the past, we would have probably just used the calligraphy. There's no way we could have achieved the effect we got any other way except by using the computer.

David: Another way in which the Macintosh has given us new options is that it has really changed the way we use color. It's just made it so easy to try out different colors. We end up with color combinations we never would have used if we had just gotten out a paint brush and tried to put a bit of color here and there. It's so quick to try out different colors, and all the colors are available.

If you look at our work before we were using the Macintosh, you'd see there was lots of red and black, blue and black duotones, and maybe gold. Now we use colors that look great together, but which I would have never thought of using individually; for example, crazy, bright greens with purple. We've started using colors that wouldn't work on their own, but because we can try so many colors together so quickly, we can come up with great combinations. One of the greatest features of the Macintosh is that you can try certain things and see the results immediately.

Andy: In college, I used to create sketchbooks. These were not just collections of drawings. I'd stick things I created or things I found into these books, then I'd cut them up and stick them down on another page in combination with other things I found amusing. To me, if every designer had a sketchbook, I'd like to see it because that's where their personality is, and where their graphics should be — getting across their personality, instead of them being faceless designers, and no one being able to tell who has done the work. The Macintosh is like a sketchbook; you can create things and see what they look like. You can use your instinct, just like you can with a sketchbook. The only problem with the Macintosh, I suppose, is knowing when to stop. As has been said: "The paint never dries"; you can always go back in and change something.

What do you think is the proper role of the computer in the education of students who are just now learning about design?

David: We didn't use computers much in college, and I think the problem with a lot of students in college at the moment is that suddenly typography has become something they can do immediately on the Macintosh, without any kind of knowledge of what's gone on before with metal type and all the principles that were set up for it. Sometimes it's good because it can lead to naive approaches, but sometimes, you can see things that are really missing; sometimes students' work becomes too "Mac-like."

The Macintosh lets you do some things quite easily and it will allow you to do certain tricks, things that look good; it can make things look crafted when actually they are not. At a German design college where we recently had an exhibit of our work, students are required to take a course in letterpress before they can take any courses using the Macintosh. I think that's really good. You have to learn the rules before you can start breaking them. You should break the rules to make a point, not just for the sake of doing mad things with type all the time.

Andy: I think there's also a danger when you have a job of going straight to the computer without actually thinking about what you're doing. I still like to draw my ideas, even though very roughly, before I begin. I at least like to start with a sketch of a general layout. Even though I may have no idea about the colors, I know what I want to do with the type and image before I sit down at the computer. Our work is fun, but there's still thought behind it. We like an element of surprise, and surprises can and do occur, even when we start with a plan. But the plan's still the most critical part.

Why Not Associates were invited to have an exhibit of their work at the Hochschule für Gestaltung, an art college in Germany. The exhibit was partly funded by the Type Directors Club of New York and showed Why Not's graphic design work, as well as their work in video.

To create a poster for the exhibit, a variety of "found" objects — a book on ventriloquism, an old bedspring, and some rather unusual calligraphy — were combined using Aldus FreeHand. FreeHand allowed them to combine scanned elements and type, and was used to manipulate the calligraphy, thus to creating an overall "why not?" effect.

VENTRILOQUISM FOR BEGINNERS
Douglas Houlden
A complete set of lessons in the art of voice magic

The poster started with an old book, *Ventriloquism for Beginners*. A page of old dummy heads was scanned in and printed out on a LaserWriter. A favorite head was chosen and the laser print was cut out and attached to old bedsprings to create a kind of doll.

A black and white photograph of the doll was taken, and an 8" x 10" print was made.

The photograph of the doll was scanned in as a grayscale image and saved as a TIFF file. The TIFF file was opened in ImageStudio, where the image was posterized, reduced to only four levels of gray to make it look coarser.

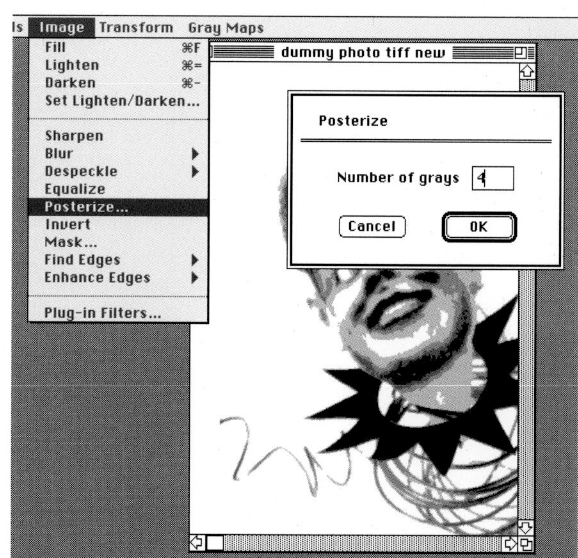

The words "Why Not Associates" were hand drawn by Chris Priest, a member of the Why Not studio. His calligraphy was scanned in.

The scan of the calligraphy was opened in Aldus FreeHand; the outline was traced, then point by point was manipulated to change the overall effect.

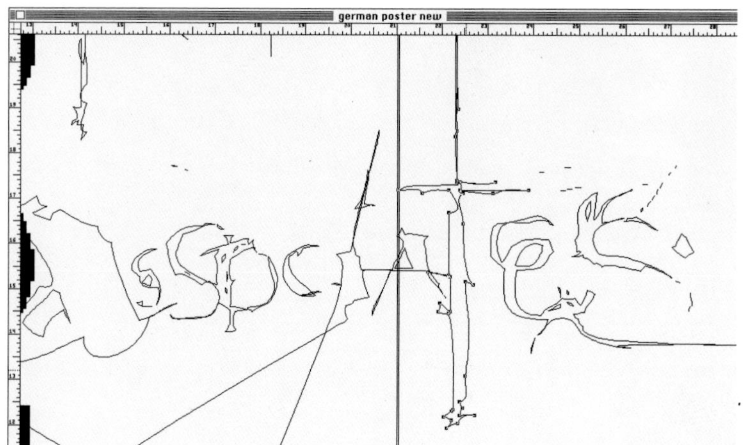

The image of the doll was brought into FreeHand, where it was copied, rotated, and resized.

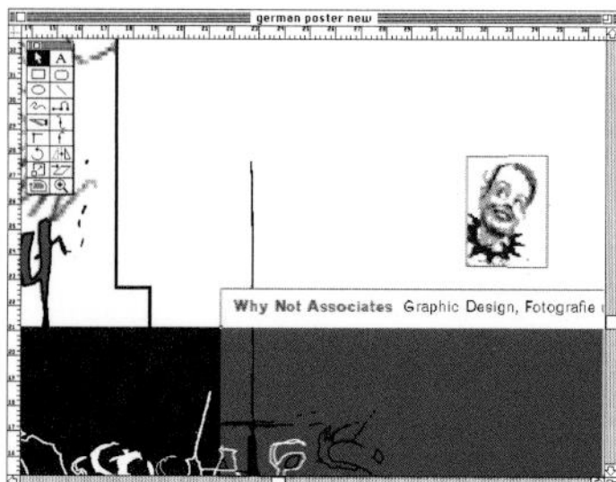

Blocks of color and type were added in FreeHand.

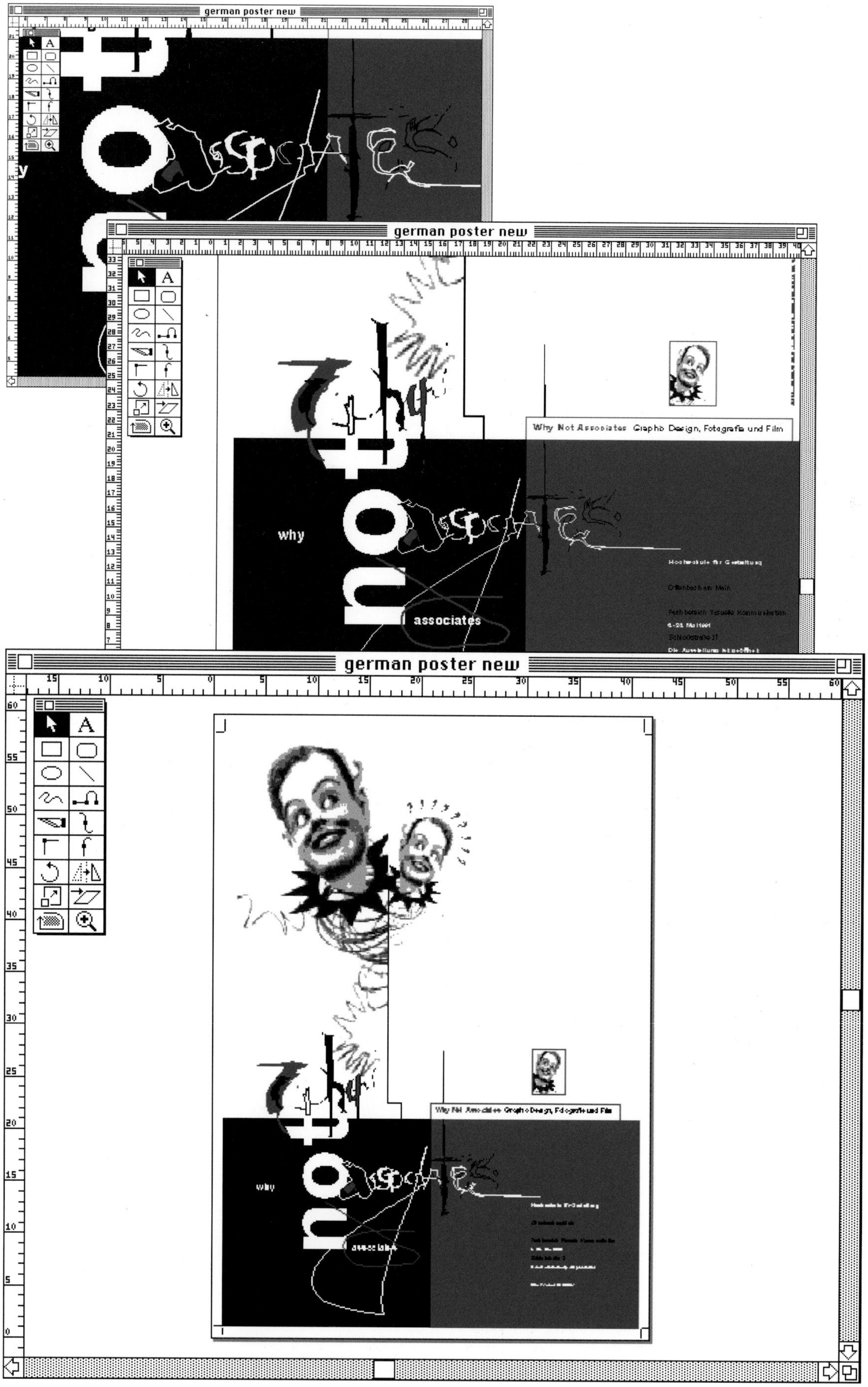

When the poster was completed, two-color film was printed from FreeHand and given to the company that would silkscreen the final posters.

Invitation, 1991
Why Not Associates exhibition
Offenbach School of Design, Germany
Aldus FreeHand, Adobe Photoshop

Television stings, 1991
VH1
MacroMind Director

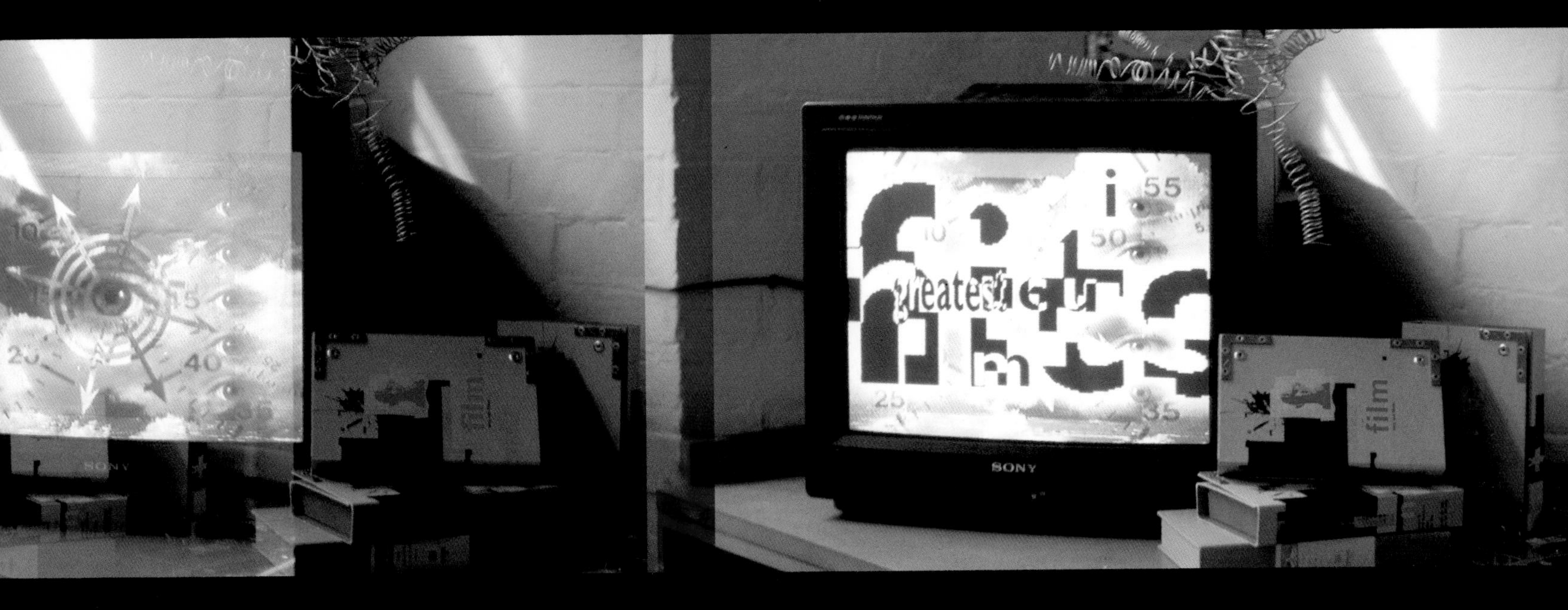
greatest
film
SONY

1

2

This and the following spread:

1-7 Poster for use in London Subway Stations, 1990
Smirnoff
Aldus FreeHand and conventional photography

8-10 Poster three-sided billboard, 1990
Smirnoff
Aldus FreeHand and conventional photography

Photography by Why Not / Rocco Redondo, Models by David Greenwood

8

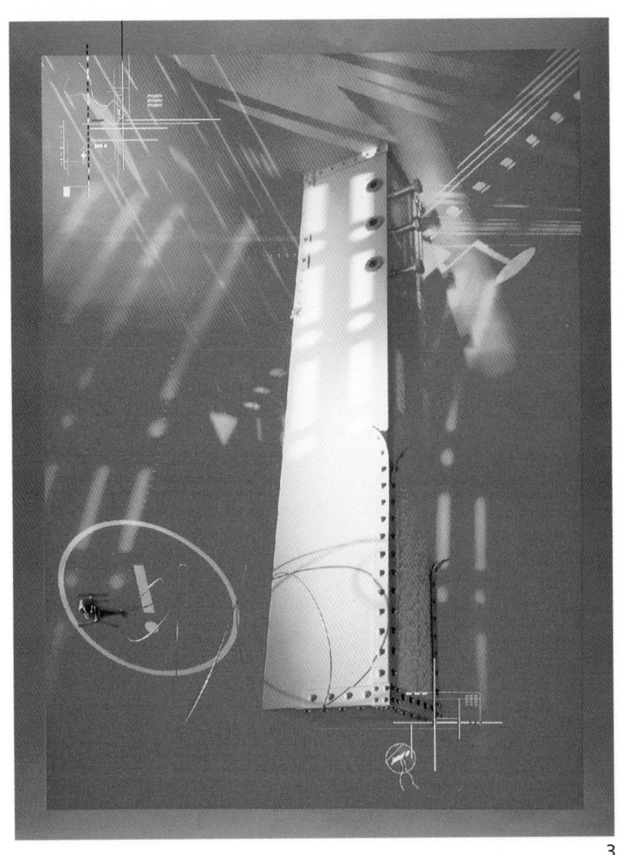
3

4

9

5

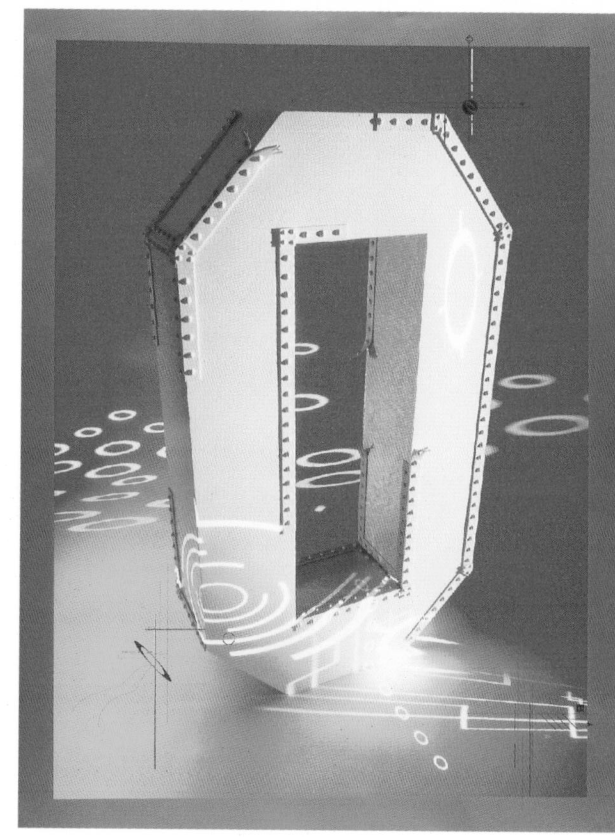

6

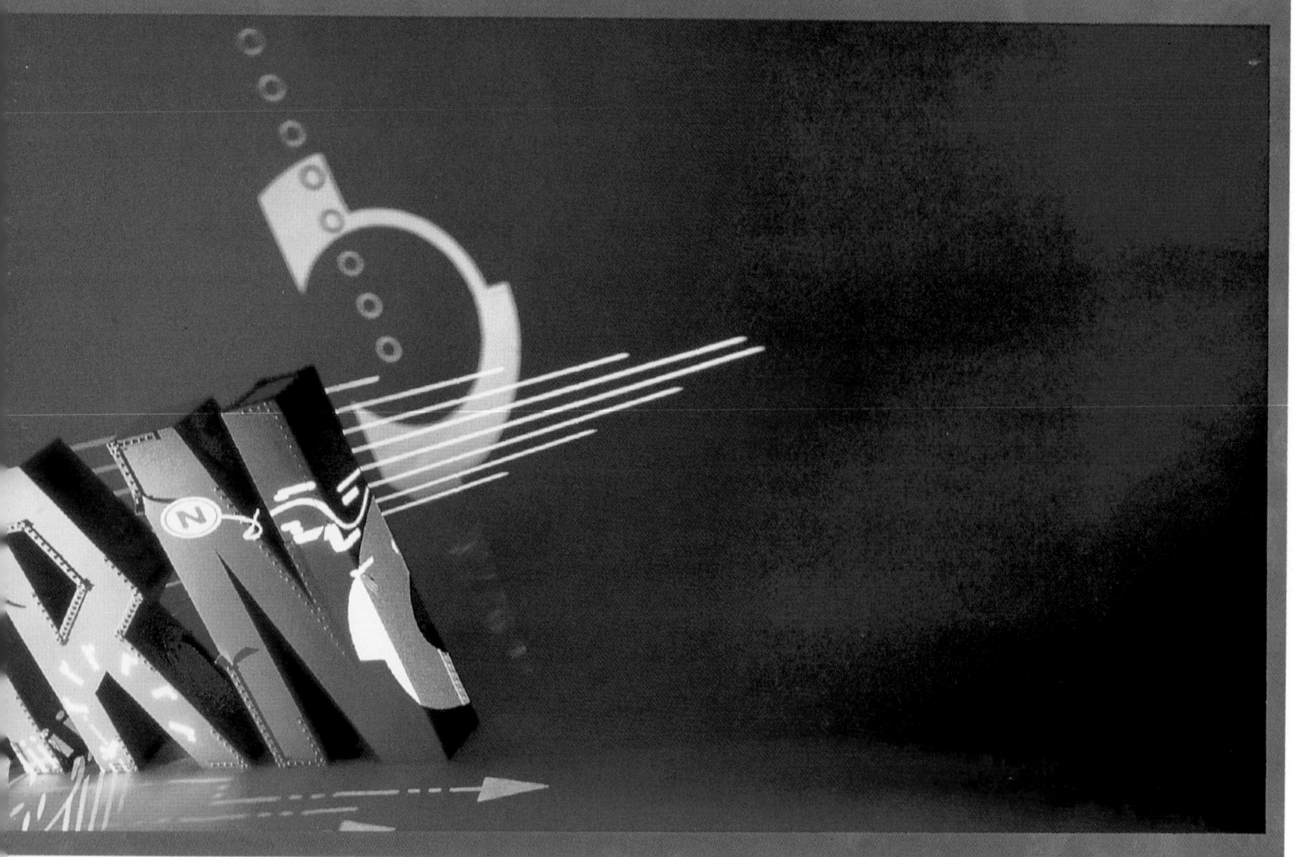

10

7

Poster, 1990
Royal College of Art, Computer Design Course
Crosfield Lightspeed and Apple Scanner

The Royal College of Art
Computer Related Design

Course Leader Gillian Crampton Smith

Developing the role of art and design disciplines in the design of interaction - with electronic tools, products and media.

Multi-disciplinary graduate programmes:
Taught masters course.
Master's degree by project.
PhD programme.

computer related design

Royal College of Art

london

tools for the mind

consumer products

Interface

software tools

Interaction (Interact)

interactcive publications

information design

Design for the Electronic Age

We seek women and men who delight in using their imagination in new and challenging ways and who will develop this new field with rigour and flair. Students are mostly art and design graduates many from graphic, industrial, or a/v design, or from video and animation. We also take graduates from related disciplines such as human factors, media/communications and software, electronics or systems engineering. Some students are sponsored by employers such as IBM, Racal, British Aerospace.

The Taught Course

The two-year course is project-based. Students work on interdisciplinary projects aimed at developing their own discipline's contribution to interaction design, and theirunderstanding of the role of other disciplines. An open mind and willingness to contribute to a team is essential.
The first year is quite structured and opens up a range of possibilities, issues and avenues for exploration. Students decide on their personal direction within this developing discipline and prepare proposals for their second-year projects, often in collaboration with students in other departments or with outside institutions. They can also contribute to research projects within the College.
The staff have backgrounds in graphic design, industrial design, engineering and video, and there is a joint lecture course with Imperial College. There are many visitors from institutions and companies in Britain and abroad.
These contacts allow us to arrange summer placements in Europe, USA and Japan.

Master's degree by project and the PhD programme

Students taking these options have a particular project they wish to undertake. The student and supervisor agree a programme of work which may include elements of the taught course.

Interaction Issues and Projects

Among the College's corporate sponsors are:

Acorn
Aesthedes
Alias
Apple Computer
Canon UK
Coates Viyella
Crosfield Electronics
Gerber
Hewlett Packard
IBM
Letraset UK
Moggridge Associates/ID2
Monotype
Moving Picture Company
MultiMedia Corporation
Psion
Quantel
TDI
Thorn EMI

The Royal College of Art is Europe's only Graduate University of Art and Design. It offers a rich learning environment, with courses in more than thirty disciplines covering design for manufacture, communication design, the fine arts and crafts, and the history, theory and management of design. It draws students from more than twenty countries.
The College is opposite Hyde Park in the centre of London, a block away from its collaborators in the Royal School of Music, the Victoria and Albert and Science Museums, and Imperial College, Britain's leading university institute of science and technology.

TO APPLY

Write, phone or fax for a prospectus and application form to:
The Registry, Royal College of Art, Kensington Gore, London SW7 2EU
phone +44 71 584 5020
fax +44 71 225 1487
Applications should arrive by the end of January

Steelworks cover, 1990
Why Not Publishing
Aldus PageMaker

Following Spread:

Steelworks various spreads, 1990
Why Not Publishing
Aldus PageMaker

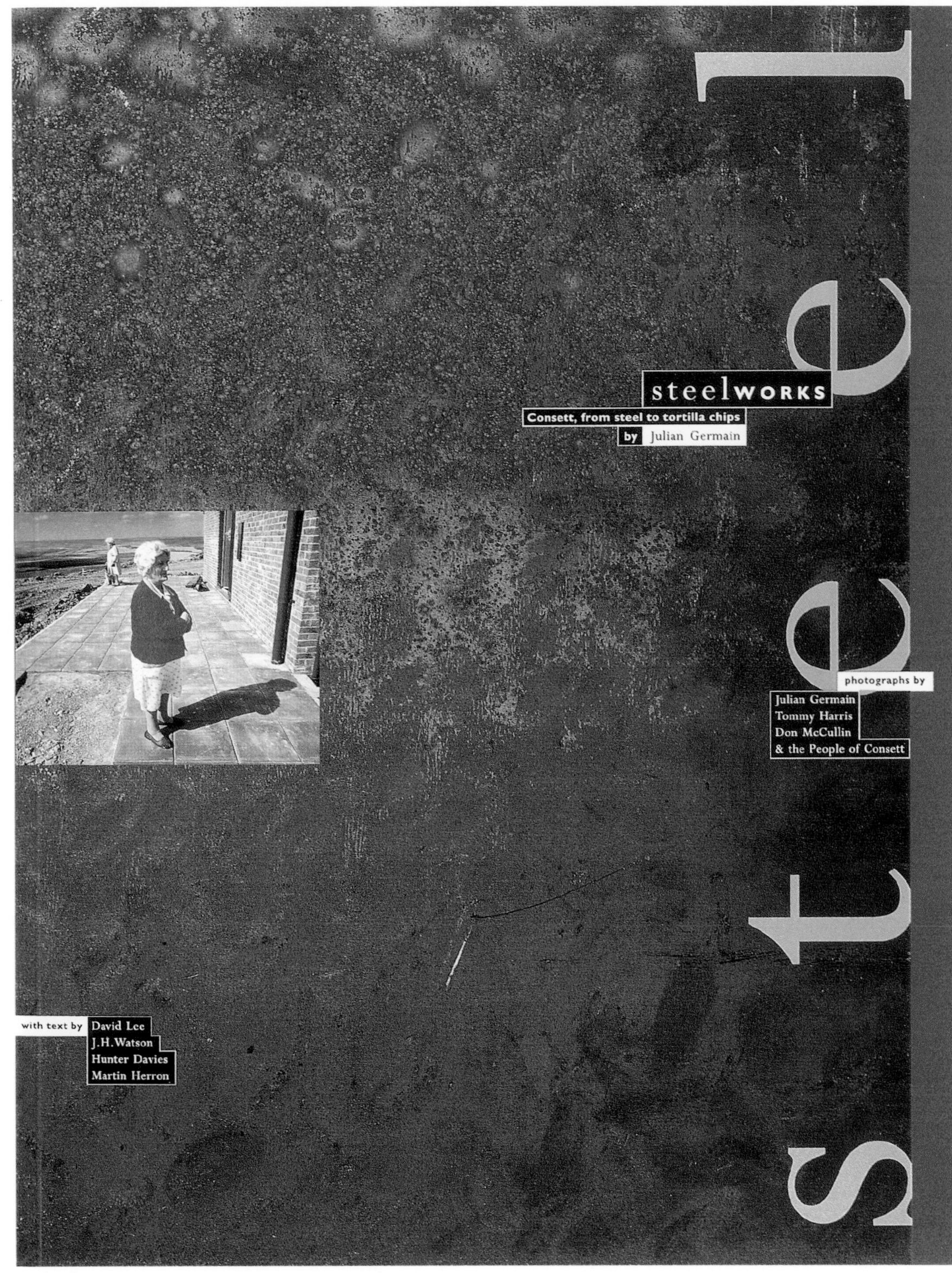

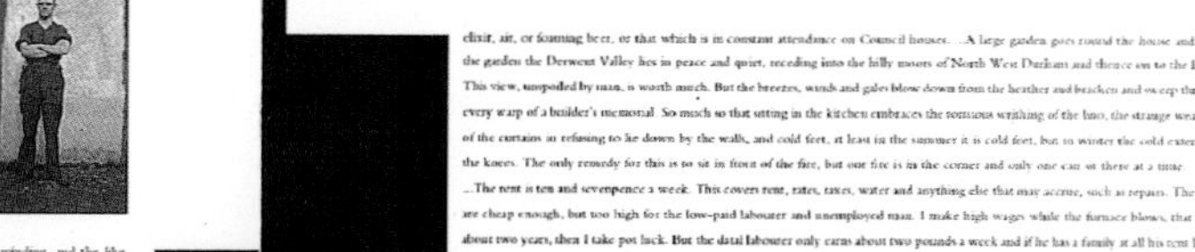

The handling of molten iron is an elemental affair. There is a kinship between it and me. Many times I have known myself to be drawn to it, fascinated, so that I could almost find myself plunging my naked arm into liquid iron to seek a consummation. Yet there is consummation, not final but real, not ultimate but actual. As the big chimney draws into itself the total squalor, the final filth to be spewed out of its mouth with deceptive continuity, so the fundamental metal of modern civilisation is emitted from a furnace in the intensity attending any act of creation and one is drawn towards it. Any young thing is attractive, has a beauty, a quality of emergence, a rose-bud, a newly-born rat, molten iron, but not pen-nibs or shells, they are merely shaped, they are without birth. And with the newly-born, one has the temptation to make contact, even though it spells death for one or the other, so I find myself drifting towards death in the blind reaching out for contact.

...To labour at furnaces is a man's job. There is no problem of sacrificing one's masculinity as there is with clerical work, machine minding, and the like. When the flames from a cast of iron leap up at us like an inferno, when we are weary of the dull grind of incessantly shovelling hot wet sand, I and my mates may curse the day we were born, but the time comes when the iron is safe and at rest and one is free to go home; then it is sweet to have pitted one's strength against the elemental forces. But one must have strength, a ten-mile tramp over the moors is not invigorating to a delicate constitution, so a night in a snowstorm handling molten metal is no job for a weakling.

Bad as my job is, there is a worse, it is the filling of the ore to feed the furnaces. Twelve men do this, two to actually tip the barrows on to the bell, and ten to fill and pull. ...The weight of each barrowful of ore varies according to requirements, but it is never less than seventeen hundredweight and often twenty-one or twenty-two. Thus, with the weight of the barrow added, one man pulls anything up to one and a half tons, a hundred yards, four times an hour, hail, rain, snow or blow... You don't notice the misshapen limbs when the men are actually at work, a man is such an accommodating creature that his bones can bend to any task. But see them in the cabin for bait, giants whose physical perfection should be maintained as an example of balanced beauty, see the crouched stoop of the young men, hidden by a conscious stiffening of the spine, notice the fumbling fingers where the bones and muscles have sacrificed elasticity for efficiency, efficiency for what? To pour coke and ore into the mouth of a devouring monster, not to make necessaries for man, not primarily, but to make dividends, money.

...Housing is a queer affair. I live in a new Council house in a new housing estate over a mile from the town and works. The house has three bedrooms upstairs, a kitchen, scullery and bathroom downstairs. ...The bath has hot and cold water laid on but not the scullery sink. Hot water is heated in a set-pot in a corner of the bathroom, ...and to boil it you must light a fire underneath the pot in the bathroom. With the use of extra good coal, however, the water can be heated from a flue leading from the kitchen fire sufficiently to wash dishes or one's face... This modern system of water-heating is preferred to an automatic water heater with taps into bath, wash-basin and scullery, because it teaches the young housewife to be frugal, industrious and slim and also saves threepence per week on the rent.

We have no wash-basin and I have discovered that the best way to wash is to kneel on the floor with one hip tight against the lavatory bowl, commonly called the "lav" or "seat", one's navel resting on the side of the bath, there in a pagan posture, to be cleansed. The alternative is bathing. ...But there is no luxuriating in soapy water. I can only manage so much of myself at one time. Either the feet, shins, knees head and shoulders are above water, wrestling with icy enamel or ravelled among the taps and plug chain, or the feet are warm but the knees protrude, together with the thighs, head, face, shoulders and hands – hands because people have been drowned in baths according to the papers. To complete the spartan conditions, draughts emanate from round the window-frame, under the window-sill and on all four sides of the door. A draught can either be a prolongation of life in the form of an

elixir, air, or foaming beer, or that which is in constant attendance on Council houses. ...A large garden goes round the house and from the garden the Derwent Valley lies in peace and quiet, receding into the hilly moors of North West Durham and thence on to the Lakes. This view, unspoiled by man, is worth much. But the breezes, winds and gales blow down from the heather and bracken and sweep through every warp of a builder's memorial. So much so that sitting in the kitchen embraces the tortuous writhing of the lino, the strange weakness of the curtains in refusing to lie down by the walls, and cold feet, at least in the summer it is cold feet, but in winter the cold extends to the knees. The only remedy for this is to sit in front of the fire, but our fire is in the corner and only one can sit there at a time.

...The rent is ten and sevenpence a week. This covers rent, rates, taxes, water and anything else that may accrue, such as repairs. The rents are cheap enough, but too high for the low-paid labourer and unemployed man. I make high wages while the furnace blows, that is for about two years, then I take pot luck. But the datal labourer only earns about two pounds a week and if he has a family at all his rent leaves him thirty bob to live on.

It is an amazing thing that nearly every man will offer cigarettes, tobacco or beer to any Tom, Dick or Harry whose company he is thrust into, but when it comes to a discussion on unemployment the same man will deny Tom, Dick or Harry, providing they are abstract figures, with the right to smoke or drink if they cannot afford it. It is quite common to hear a man say of his neighbour, "He shouldn't smoke," if that neighbour is on the dole. As a contrast, an unemployed man puts it this way, "If I go along the street it's 'Hello, Tommy, howay in and hev a pint,' but if I asked the same man for the tanner to buy a loaf he would be insulted."

The way a town is split up for building is another evil aspect of the power of money. Those who can't associate with their fellows because they can't cut a big enough dash (usually because a respectable position is the only thing they've got), have a house built in a cosy little corner where every other little cipher has a house built. This is called suburbia. It invariably adjoins better-class private property or the higher-rented Council house which is also built at a separate end of the town, usually out of sight of the big chimney. Play parks and bowling greens have their place and habitation here so that all the incipient Fascists can prepare to wallop Armadas or retreat into their own little prisons, I mean castles. Of course they are not all without bowels, some have their churches, chapels, Insurance Companies, Freemasonry, dramatic societies, choral societies, all sorts of petty activities which prove an inch behind their navels and a desire to be at one with their fellow-man. The trouble is that they don't acknowledge everybody as their fellow-man. No, they are the folk in power in local affairs, the power which used to be called the Nonconformist conscience. They say where the poor in pocket must live. They set him apart where his presence cannot fret their holy garments, for assuredly they couldn't ignore his simple human needs if he lived in their midst, and they get a kick out of his miseries in their foul system of rent or debt collecting, inquiry agencies for sellers of goods on the hire-purchase system, or the social services committees. They are different from the labourer, they are a class apart, they decree that a Moorside estate should be built, or a Grove, the very names are an insult because they conjure up places of beauty. But Moorside, four hundred houses of which I have one, is built in a field adjoining the sewage disposal system, and it is the old system of flooding the land with sewage, so that the land gets less and less in size and the sewage grows and grows in bulk, until a hot summer day or a still night in winter finds it lying on my doorstep with a stink which would pollute the nostrils of a polecat. The cesspool, which skims the scum off the water from the drains and the mixture from three or four thousand water-closets, lies directly and uninterruptedly opposite my front door at a distance of thirty yards.

16

17

Tommy Harris freelanced for more than once local newspaper. He took his photos in the certain knowledge that all but the centre of the frame, where the subject stood proudly or was posed, would be cropped out. If what appeared in the newspaper was all we know now of Tommy Harris's work it would not be nearly as arresting as seeing the pictures as they occur on the whole negative. It is the oddity of how photography accumulates random, peripheral facts that provides one of the endlessly fascinating aspects of looking at photographs in general and Tommy Harris's in particular. What goes on behind the scenes in his pictures is frequently more engaging than the controlled presentation being acted out under the limelight of flash. Indeed, these accidental interventions and strange correspondences that were deemed untidy and irrelevant, as far as newspaper reproduction was concerned, are now courted by photographers seeking an additional, off-beat depth to their work. It is this idiosyncrasy, this undisciplined, unselective instinct of photography – the way it can't help sucking in matter like a black hole in outer space – which makes it unique.

In Tommy Harris's picture of bodybuilders the bizarre intervention of a chair placed upside down on a high shelf above a girl's head becomes as pictorially significant as the self-conscious poses of the musclemen in trunks and the grinning lasses they hoist aloft. In the presentation of a trophy in a football team's dressing room the stooping, naked player preparing in the half-light for a bath inevitably commands greater attention than the picture's real subject. Likewise, the voyeuristic saxophonist behind a kissing couple. In all Harris's full-frame pictures we viewers become conspirators. We can see secrets invisible to the image's main protagonists.

FEWER ON THE DOLE

DAKS

COLLINSONS

LOWS

see page 25

Tommy Harris's and those of the anonymous snapshooters are happy pictures because, almost universally, they record celebrations. They are taken by proud locals who belonged to what they were photographing and wished to preserve something of its magic. Tommy Harris's are usually pictures of winners and heroes and the snapshots (by definition) celebrate personal kinds of special events. We respond fondly to the innocent optimism of all those unknown, yet strangely familiar, people we see. And, through them, we may gain a glimpse of our own past.

Barbara sings into an audition

see page 27

And then along comes an outsider, from the south, a young man of fervent belief – Julian Germain. Like Tommy and the snapshooters he also uses photography to tell his own story. To have his say. But it isn't necessarily the account a native of Consett would have given. Germain arrives grinding axes and is eager to account for the impact of Mrs Thatcher's supposed "economic miracle" on Consett and places like it. He brings with him a photographic sophistication known only – in this book at least – to McCullin's gaunt descriptions before him. He also brings colour, which is bland to nostalgia and frightens with its blunt effrontery. In colour you can see the effect on faces of the last, bitter cold gust of east wind.

Armed with a developed knowledge and appreciation of snapshot photography, Germain describes a population of individuals forcibly separated, with an ever-widening gulf between them. The literal gulf – those 283 hectares – is formed by the "landscaped" acres of soil on which once stood a world famous steelworks. The spiritual gulf is more telling: it registers as an emptiness of purpose. This area of the collective personality was once colonised by a sense of community, mutual supportiveness and the reliability of employment – those qualities and certainties replaced nowadays by slammed doors and windows, credit ratings and the phoney superficiality of strident, chemical colours and video-culture.

In a picture by Germain what you see is what you get: startling surfaces and dizzying disorientation. Life is 'lived from day to day. And the price paid for modest improvements in material well-being is uncertainty about tomorrow. Unlike in the family snaps and in Tommy Harris's photo-journalism, Germain's subjects rarely look you in the eye. Brassy colours conceal emptiness and would seem to urge temporary gratification. Colour-gloss itself becomes Germain's metaphor for what has been sacrificed in moving socially from a black-and-white world to a full colour one. And the result is that there is nothing left of the naivety and hopeful enthusiasm which shouts from every picture Tommy Harris ever took. Germain's gaudy colours alert us to the *esprit de corps* and deep personal bonds that have vanished and for whose loss the steelworks' closure is only a symbol.

This book describes the process by which the histories and mixed fortunes of some peoples and places have overlapped exactly with a simple story about how photography itself has changed.

8

9

"I did a lot of football matches.

No auto-winds then, you had to follow the ball and time it dead-on.

I remember Consett A.F.C. were playing Wingate in a semi-final. Consett were losing 2-0 when 15 minutes from the end they got a penalty. I dropped a right clanger, I got between the keeper and the kicker and I couldn't see the ball. Then they scored again and it was a draw.
When I went into the darkroom I thought terrific! I've missed the balls. So I took an old shirt button and printed it through onto the netting.

I remember later going up the street and this bloke said to me, 'I'm sure that bloody ball went into the other side of the net.'"

38

39

After all, how can a man be one of the lads when he can't afford any round let alone his round, when the fortnightly cheque has to be scrutinised by the wife before any money, if there's any to spare, can be allowed for a pint!
For many families the 80s - our "perestroika" - were to be years spent in limbo; years of watching the kids grow up, leave school and go on schemes; years of lost identity and purpose.
The Local Authority took the only route it understood. "No work? Keep looking!" The Government pumped in cash, industrial estates sprang up, and incentives for entrepreneurs were unprecedented.
Initially, there was the problem of skill shortage. British steel anticipated this and provided funds for re-training. For a year, ex-steelworkers could attend college on full pay. There they learned how to be Warehouse Operatives (doormen), or took up sociology and articulated their alienation. Some even tried computers. But for most men it was a pain. Steelworkers didn't sit behind desks pissing around with books - they worked. The year passed, and soon there was nothing to do except get on the wife's nerves.
For firms looking for "An Environment for Success" (the District's slogan), Derwentside was too good to be true, rent- and rate-free and grant-aided to the hilt. Some firms came and stayed. Some came, took what was on offer and then relocated. A few such as Integrated Micro Products and Derwent Valley Foods (Phileas Fogg), went on to become national success stories. Many fell by the wayside.

As the years went by there was the occasional suicide. A local photographer told me how he had noticed the increase in demand for certain photos to be copied, innocuous looking snapshots, but with one thing in common: they included a suicide victim who had worked at the Company. A snapshot is a quintessence of ordinariness, and I doubt if the people in these pictures considered themselves to be extraordinary. They didn't want the fantastic and the unattainable with which society confronts and teases. Like most of us they wanted the everyday, the familiar. They wanted work. But it didn't want them and they couldn't cope.

Young people in Consett didn't quite see it like that. If you were young, the fortnightly cheque meant Friday night. I knew people who would blow the lot in a weekend and practically starve until the next signing-on. They weren't trapped. And that's the irony - the people who have survived best are the people who never commanded the respect of the grafters. The grafters have suffered every fortnight of the last ten years.

Throughout the decade sociologists and anthropologists have appeared at regular intervals. They could be seen in the library asking for information about the whereabouts of some ex-steelworker or other. Now and then the occasional TV crew arrives to make yet another penetrating documentary: "Consett: the Town that Came Back from the Dead." or "Consett: the Town that Died But Got Better Again." The townspeople have become bitter over the years, and they see the media attention as exploitation. The local Council is particularly sensitive: "Why can't you show the good side?" "Why do you dwell on the past?" they cry. "Consett's on the up-and-up - and it's healthier!" This is true. Another of the ironies of the last ten years is the inversion of people's attitudes towards the region and its countryside. As the North returns to a semblance of its pre-industrial state, the South gets dirtier and more stressed by the month; London is now 200 square miles of raucous filth.

84

As everybody knows, housing is cheaper up here. Retired couples from the South are selling up and moving up. Derwentside is now a very nice place in which to relocate. And when you have that lump sum or a good job, but you are paying mortgage interest rates verging on usury, then why not! After all, back-to-backs, once the epitome of working-class mentality, are becoming increasingly desirable. In an age where people are looking for the past, but without its authenticity, this is both apt and ironic. (History will judge the 80s to be the point when people in this country stopped noticing irony - and history!)
Since the closure, the Council and the local industrial development agency have done everything asked of them. But as the unemployment figures "went into space" and other communities became "the tragedy of the decade", competition with other districts has become intense. One local council advertised its business incentives with a wad of money being placed firmly on a table. It was a hard sell with no trimmings and a clear message: "Don't go to them, come to us." And as the Government decides that more and more areas have "recovered" and are no longer in need of financial subsidy the 90s will be a critical decade for districts like Derwentside.
Critical to the economic regeneration of many of these districts has been the exploitation of the past. Nothing is so symptomatic of the bankruptcy of Thatcherism as the peddling of industrial decay as an economic solution. Places which once outraged Dickens are now tarted up and sanitised for tourists to come and wile away an afternoon. At the Wigan Heritage Centre an actress is paid to "grieve" over a dummy corpse of her husband who has been killed in a dreadful accident at t'pit. This grotesque parody of something profound and meaningful, the shared experience and memories of a class, is now cosy 'Heritage'.
For Consett there is a problem - it can't sell its past. At a time when industrial hell-holes are all the rage, and the spirit-crushing misery they engendered is conveniently forgotten, there are no Steelworks. There is no industrial heritage. And in the desperate rush to rechristen, the area finds itself a land without a country.

Whereas in the 80s the race was on to attract firms like Nissan, the 90s will be about reinvention - on a massive scale. As you head north, you travel through D.H. Lawrence Country, Last of the Summer Wine Country, Brontë Country, Herriot Country, The Land of the Prince Bishops and Catherine Cookson Country - South Tyneside now uses this title on its rates demands, eviction notices etc. A person can now be evicted from a novelist's fictional world.
At the heart of the matter is the site. The largest reclamation scheme in Europe. Walk to the end of Front Street and there it stands, vast and enigmatic. A hundred and forty years, thousands of lives, and a myriad of experiences, grassed over. Stand in the middle and look back towards the town and you could be in Kansas. Cattle sometimes graze and there is the odd ploughshare, but look closely and the grass grows amongst gravel. For the Council there is the business of trying to attract development. In an attempt to escape the stigma of the past, the pre-industrial name of Berry Edge has been invoked. All schemes have been and will be considered, ambitious and imaginative developers being particularly welcome. At 650 acres, a theme park would be ideal.

85

Party invitation, 1989
Royal Academy
Aldus FreeHand

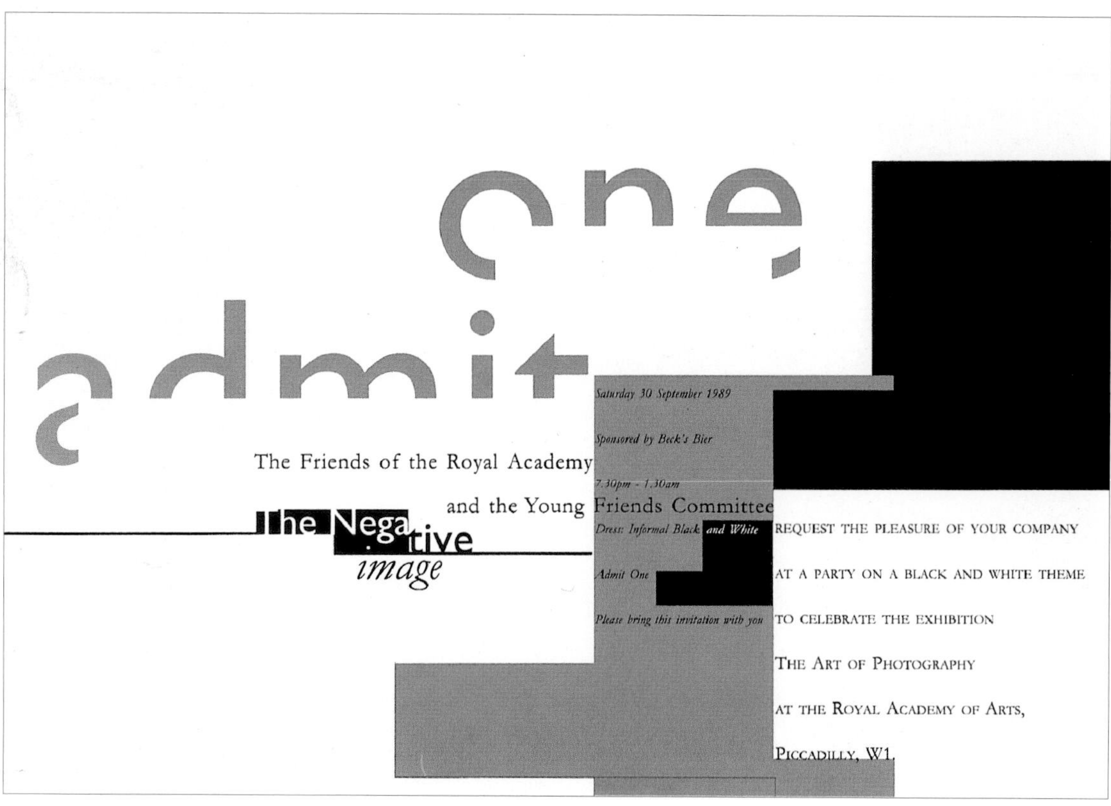

Party ticket, 1989
Royal Academy
Aldus FreeHand

Video cassette packaging, 1990
Why Not Films
Aldus FreeHand

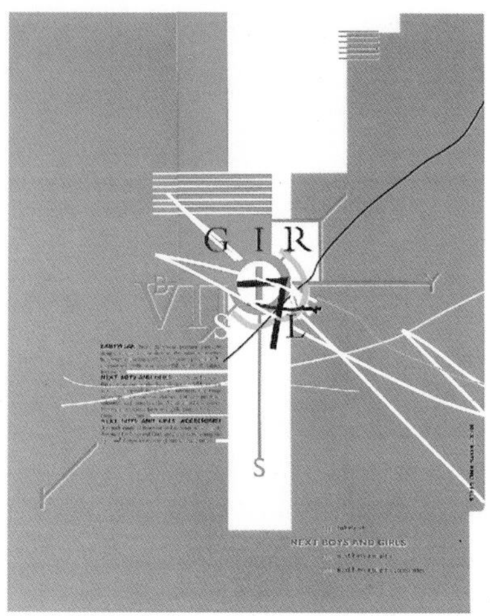

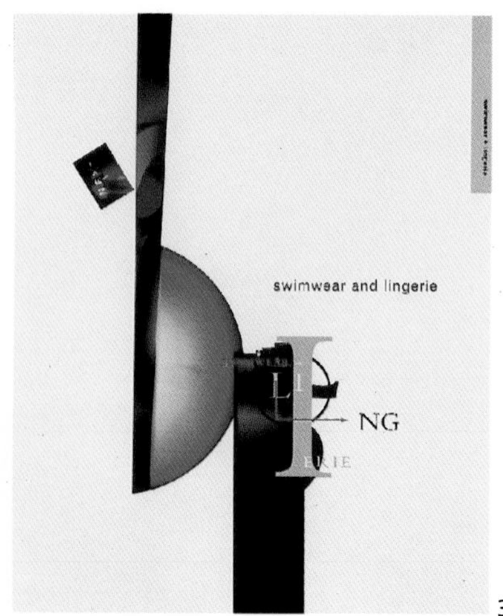

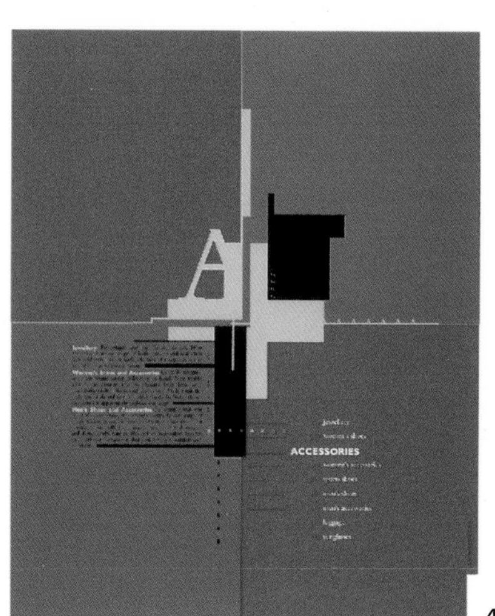

1 Boys and girls section divider, 1990
Next Catalog No. 7
Aldus FreeHand

2 Boys and girls section divider, 1989
Next Catalog No. 5
Aldus FreeHand and
conventional photography

3 Swimwear and lingerie section divider, 1989
Next Catalog No. 5
Aldus FreeHand and
conventional photography

4 Accessories section divider, 1990
Next Catalog No. 7
Aldus FreeHand

5 Directory cover, 1989
Next Catalog No. 5
Aldus FreeHand and
conventional photography

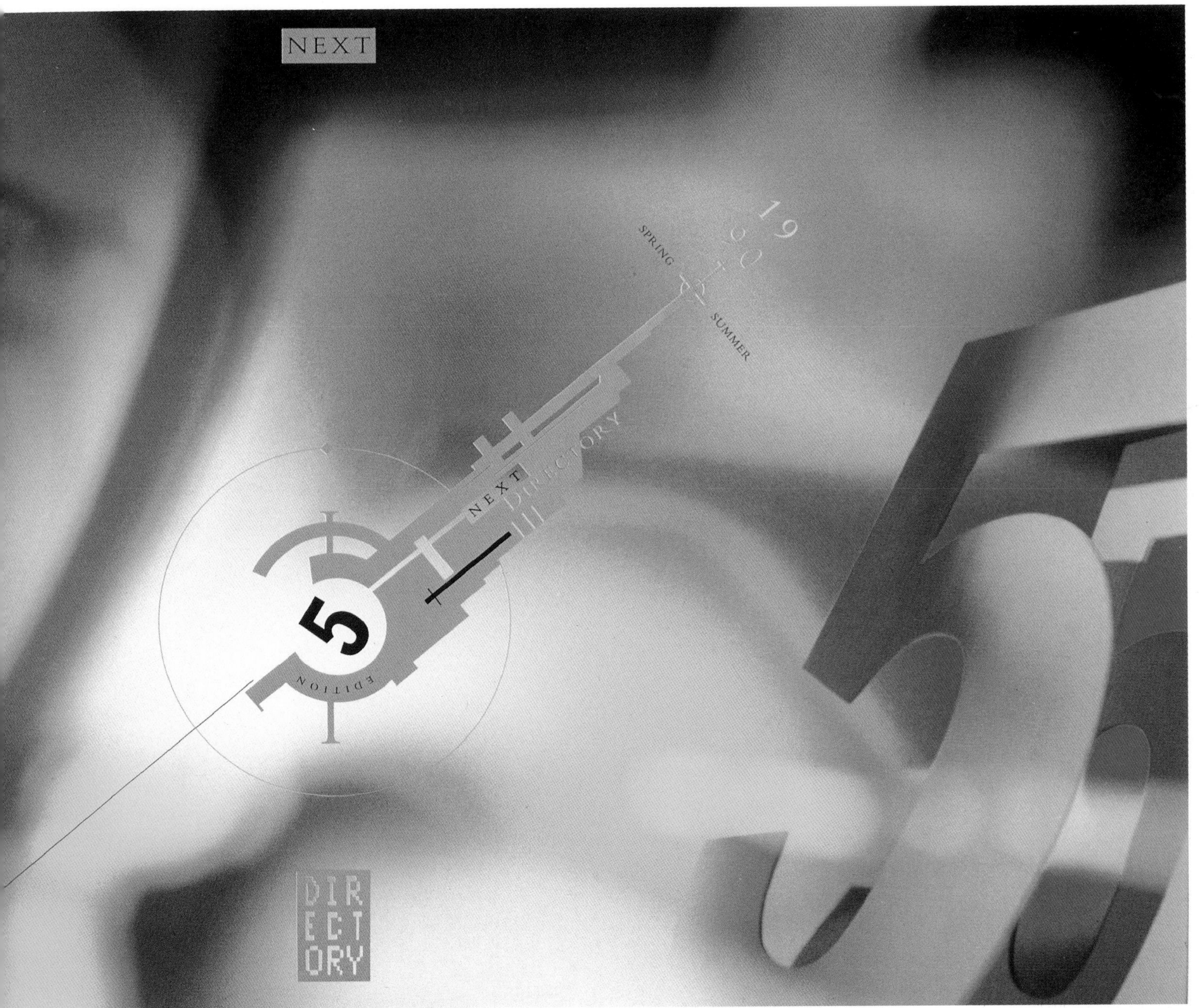
NEXT
19
90
SPRING
SUMMER
NEXT
DIRECTORY
EDITION
5
DIR
ECT
ORY

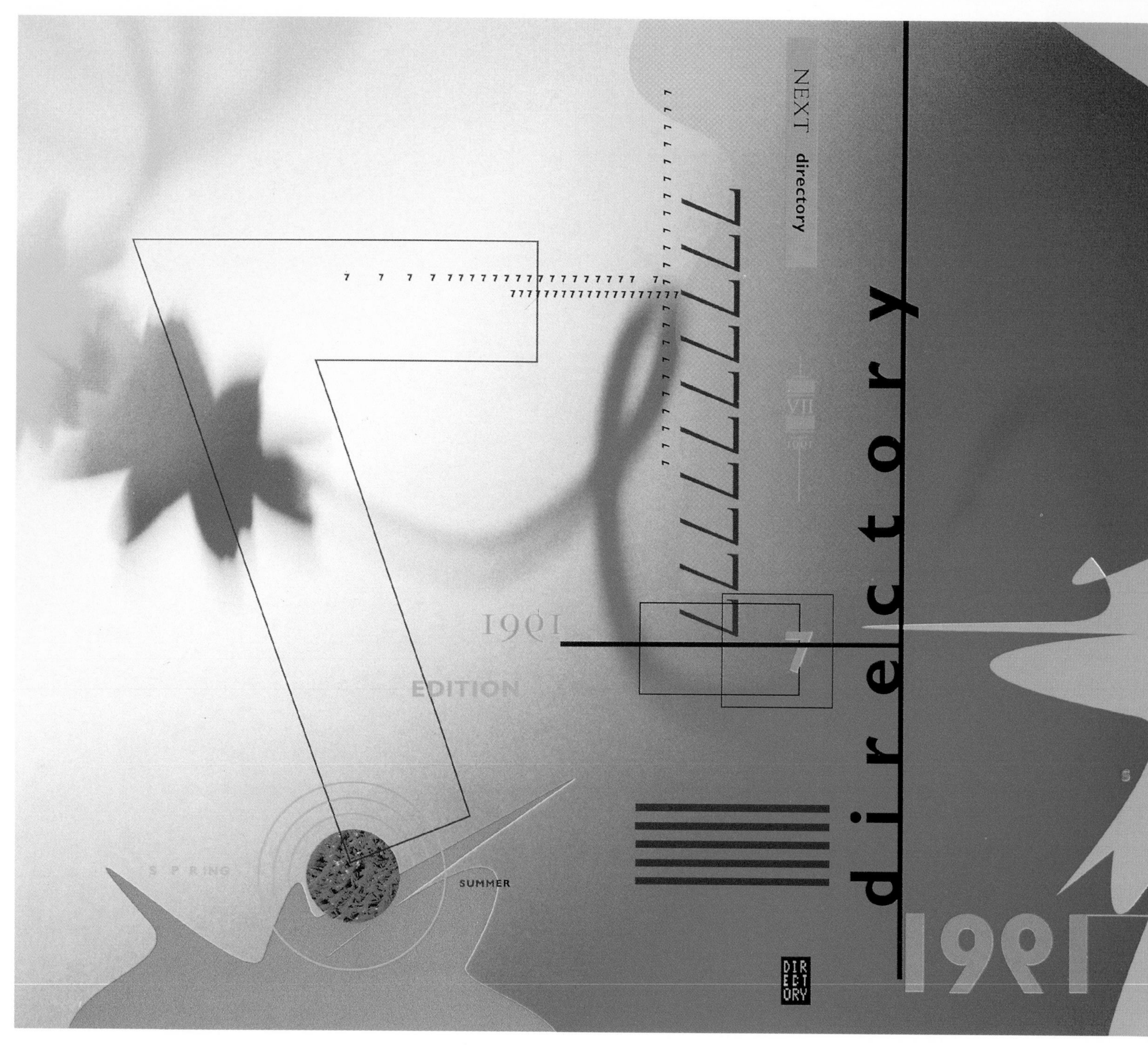

1 Directory cover, U.S. edition, 1990
Next Catalog No. 7
Aldus FreeHand and
conventional photography

2 Title page, 1990
Next Catalog No. 7
Aldus FreeHand

3 Men's sizing guide, 1989
Next Catalog No. 5
Aldus FreeHand and
conventional photography

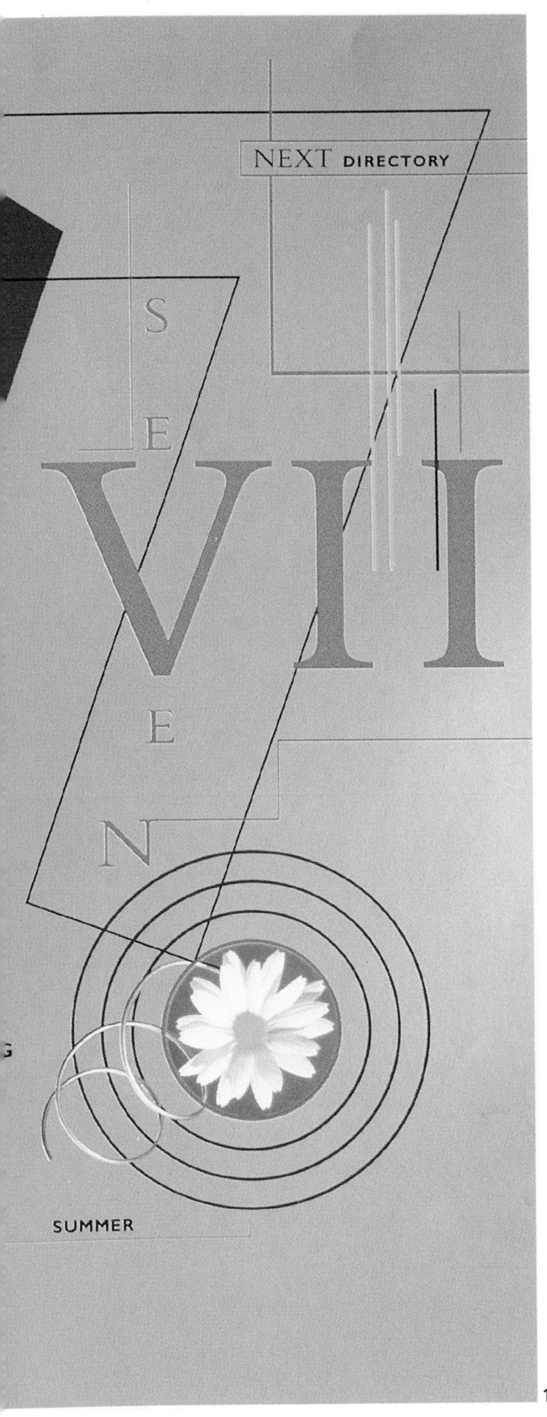
NEXT DIRECTORY
S
E
VII
E
N
SUMMER
1

QUALITY and
DESIGN
2

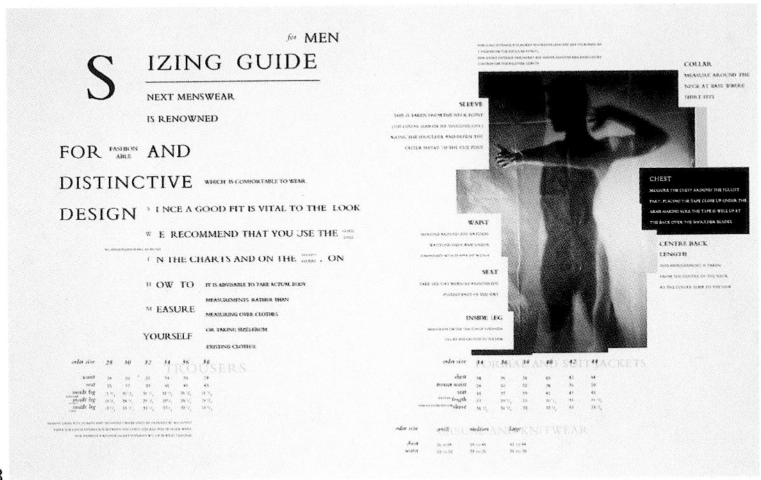
for MEN
S IZING GUIDE
NEXT MENSWEAR
IS RENOWNED
FOR AND
DISTINCTIVE
DESIGN
YOURSELF
TROUSERS
COLLAR
SLEEVE
CHEST
CENTRE BACK LENGTH
WAIST
SEAT
INSIDE LEG
3

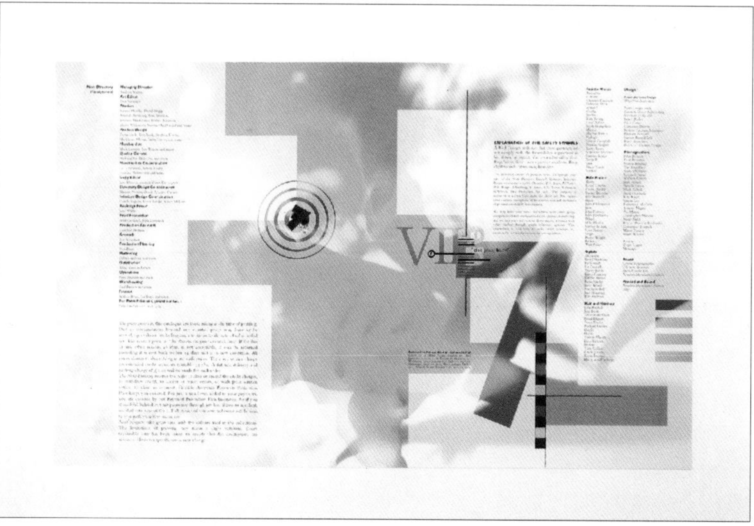

1

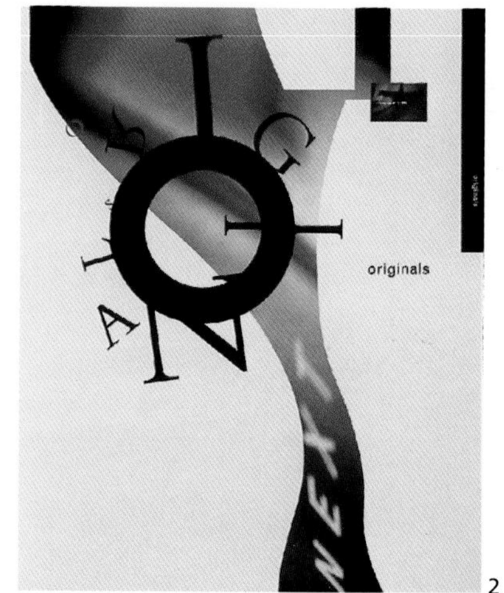

2

NEXT 8
DIREC

3

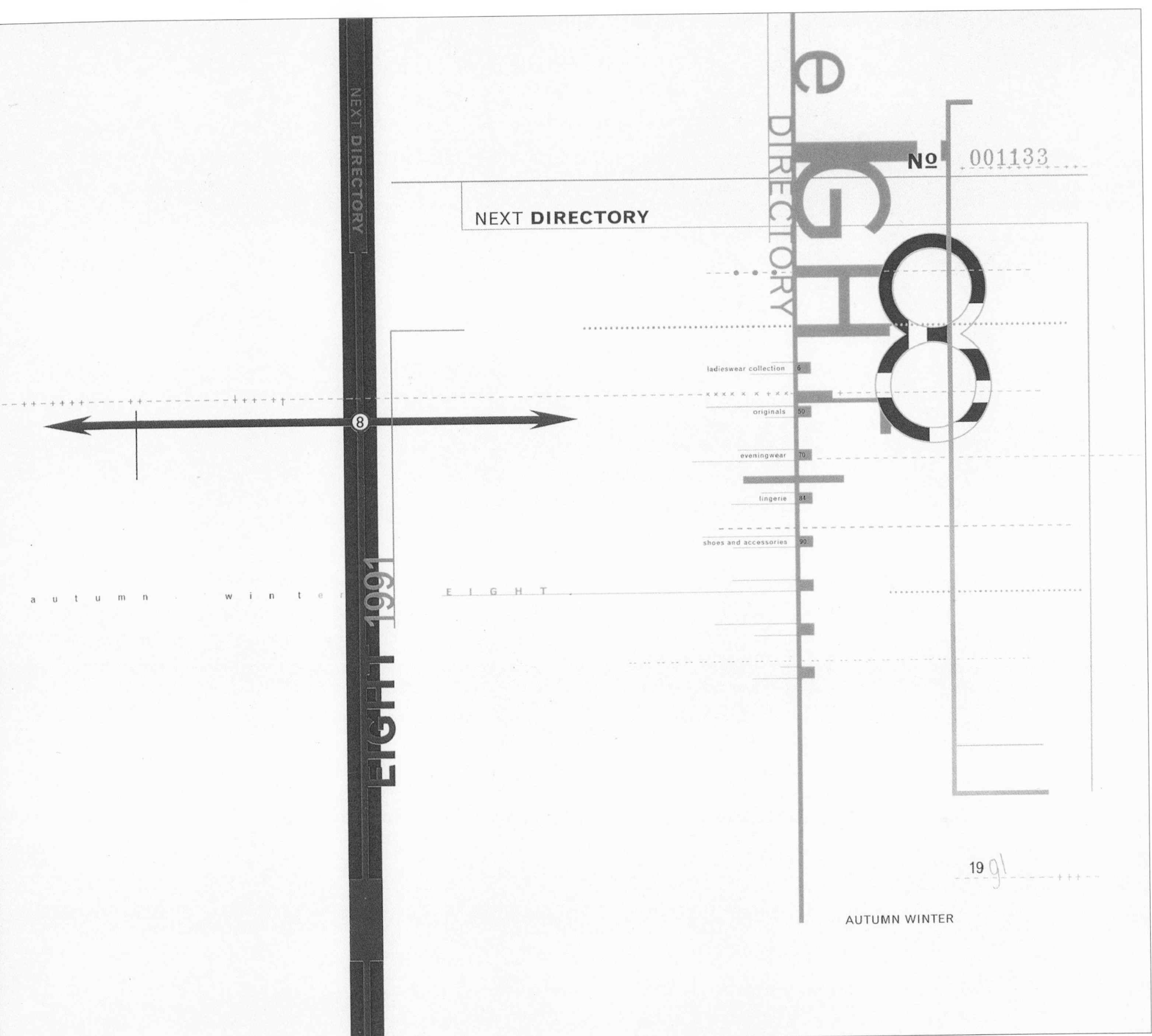

1 Credits page, 1990
Next Catalog No. 7
Aldus FreeHand

2 Originals section divider, 1989
Next Catalog No. 5
Aldus FreeHand and
conventional photography

3 Directory cover, U.S. edition, 1991
Next Catalog No. 8
Aldus FreeHand

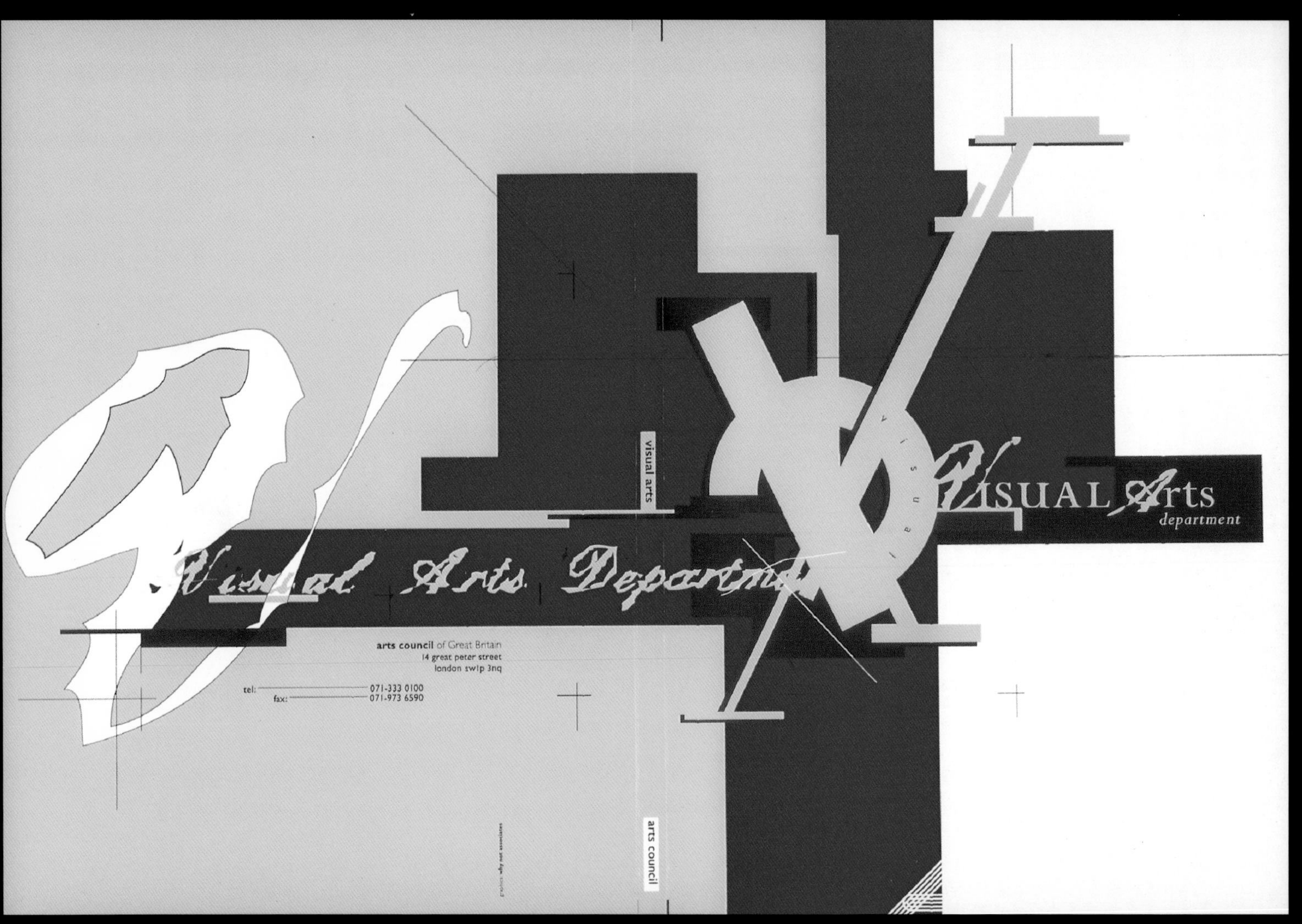

Folder, 1991
Arts Council of Great Britain
Aldus FreeHand and Apple Scanner

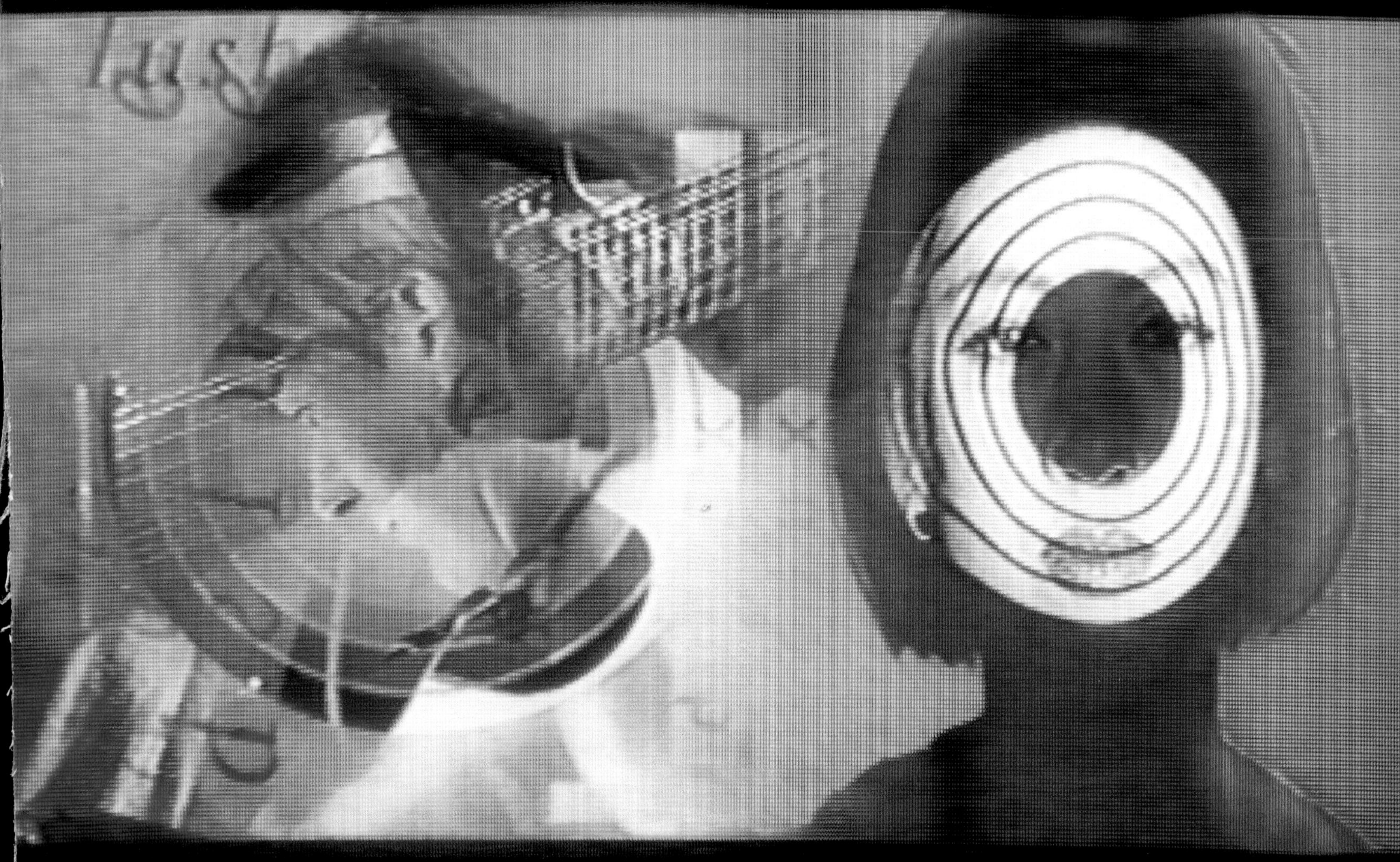

Pop promo, 1990
4AD Records, Lush-Delux
Aldus FreeHand and
conventional photography

Production / Art Direction	Takenobu Igarashi
Text	Diane Burns
Layout / Design	Ross McBride
Cover Design	Takenobu Igarashi, Mary Moegenburg
Prepress / Printing / Binding	Koyosha, Ltd.
Translation	Scott Brause, Rico Komanoya, Subaru International, Inc.
Publishing	Graphic-sha Publishing Co., Ltd.
Coordination	Seiki Okuda

Special thanks to:

Apple Computer, Inc.
Apple Japan, Inc.
Koyosha, Ltd.
Quark, Inc.
Quark, Inc. Tokyo Office
Subaru International, Inc.

Software used:

QuarkXPress
Adobe Illustrator
Adobe Photoshop
PressLink

This book is set in Adobe Frutiger Roman, Frutiger Bold, and Frutiger Black.